SHAKY GROUND

SHAKY GROUND

The '60s
and Its Aftershocks

Alice Echols

COLUMBIA UNIVERSITY PRESS • NEW YORK

Columbia University Press
Publishers Since 1893
New York   Chichester, West Sussex

Library of Congress Cataloging-in-Publication Data
Echols, Alice.
Shaky ground : the sixties and its aftershocks / Alice Echols.
p.   cm.
Includes bibliographical references and index.
ISBN 0–231–10670–X (cloth) — ISBN 0–231–10671–8 (paper)
1. United States — History —1961–1969 2. United States — Social conditions —
1960–1980. 3. United States — Politics and government — 1945–1989
4. Counterculture — United States — History — 20th century 5. Radicalism —
United States — History — 20th century. 6. Political culture — United States —
History — 20th century 7. Popular culture — United States — History —
20th century 8. Nineteen sixties 9. Nineteen seventies I. Title.

E839.4 .E28 2001
973.923 — dc21
2001042141

∞

Columbia University Press books are printed
on permanent and durable acid-free paper.

Printed in the United States of America
Designed by Lisa Hamm
c 10 9 8 7 6 5 4 3 2 1
p 10 9 8 7 6 5 4 3 2 1

Pleasure has no passport, no identification papers.

—*Michel Foucault*

contents

ACKNOWLEDGMENTS

OVER THE MANY YEARS THAT I have worked on these essays, I have had the good fortune of having in my life many wonderful writers and artists. Artist Connie Samaras was my partner and co-conspirator during much of this period. Although our fields were very different, we were grappling with many of the same questions about community, identity, and desire, and she influenced my thinking in ways large and small. It's hard to remember who thought up what, but I do know it was Connie who coined the expression "theory damaged." Her knowledge and enthusiasm about culture—high and low—were an important catalyst for my move into cultural criticism.

When I moved to Los Angeles, I knew I wanted to stay put and that I wanted to orient myself towards writing. Living in L.A., one of the few big cities that remains affordable for artists and writers, has helped make this possible. So have my wonderful friends and colleagues Lois Banner, Ellen DuBois, Tania Modleski, Marla Stone, Devra Weber, Alice Wexler, and sometime Angeleno Wini Breines. Our dinners and hikes together are often ecstasies of discussion. Tania, Ellen, Wini, and Alice also have read more versions of more articles than I'm sure they care to remember. Their influence is all over these essays. Wini, in particular, read and commented on the entire manuscript, and gave me many useful suggestions for revisions.

I also want to thank Ruth Bradley, Charlotte Nekola, Paula Rabinowitz, Sandy Silberstein, Bette Skandalis, and Pat Yeghessian, the maverick Women's Studies crew at the University of Michigan. Searching critics, loyal friends, and (with the exception of Bette and Pat) reluctant disco dancers, they made those years as close to fun as graduate school can be. Particular thanks is owed Paula, who read this manuscript in its entirety and offered trenchant criticisms that proved invaluable. Throughout, my musician friend Bob Currie has not only been a source of terrific music trivia and a knowledgeable critic, he's also been a great support. Thanks as well to Peg Lourie, Laura Downs, and Nora Faires who know hooey—no matter how dressed up—when they see it.

It was historian Lois Banner who in 1995 suggested I put together a collection of my essays. Ann Miller of Columbia University Press got behind the idea, and she has helped shape the book, pestered me to keep at it, and supported me throughout the long process. Series editor, historian Robin Kelley, has been enthusiastic throughout. Thanks as well to editor Peter Dimock, his assistant, Anne Routon, and managing editor Anne McCoy. Bob Hemenway not only caught lots of embarrassing errors and inconsistencies in his final edit, he was also an engaged reader.

I would also like to thank the many fine editors with whom I've worked, especially Sara Bershtel and Riva Hocherman at Metropolitan Books, Scott Malcomson and Stacey D'Erasmo at the *Village Voice Literary Supplement*, Sue Cummings at the *L.A. Weekly*, and Elsa Dixler at *The Nation*. Thanks as well to Carole Vance, David Farber, and the staff at *Socialist Review*. As always my agent, Geri Thoma, has been invaluable.

This book couldn't have been written without the cooperation of those who graciously agreed to be interviewed. I would like to thank everyone who shared with me their memories of the Haight and sixties rock, especially Bob Seidemann, Peggy Caserta, Linda Gravenites, Bob Brown, Jim Haynie, Carl Gottlieb, Milan Melvin, and Joshua White. I would also like to thank John Paul Hammond and Joni Mitchell for agreeing to interviews.

Finally I want to thank Gilda Zwerman for the crucial role she played in this project. A discerning critic, she always let me know when I hadn't yet nailed it. Our talks about the social-change movements of the sixties made me reconsider some of my earlier work. Most of all, her faith in me, love for me, and her full-tilt enthusiasm for life are why I finished this book.

SHAKY GROUND

INTRODUCTION

"**E**AT SHIT! TEN MILLION FLIES CAN'T Be Wrong!" It was the summer of 1969, the year of Woodstock, the Manson murders, and the unraveling of America's leading New Left group, Students for a Democratic Society (SDS). I was eighteen and part of a Quaker-sponsored project to fight racism in the suburbs of Washington, D.C. The Quakers planned and funded our project, chose five teenagers to take part in it, and then, in the self-flagellating style so characteristic of sixties liberals, they handed it over to someone who had nothing but contempt for them and their "squishy politics." Our director was a dour woman with ties to Weatherman, the most outrageously off-the-wall of all the splinter groups to emerge from the meltdown of SDS. Weatherman saw up-against-the-wall revolutionary potential in white working-class kids, so we spent those first weeks dutifully cruising burger stands looking for recruits. Unable to lure them to our coffeehouse where we showed grainy agit-prop films like *In the Year of the Pig*, we took to hanging out at Washington's SDS house, which is where I saw the puzzling graffiti, scrawled on the upstairs hallway wall. I never knew if it was meant as a gross-out or a fake-out, or if it was a send-up of the stupid slogans that passed for analysis in Weatherman. But, then, I was too young to have any idea how this moment fit into the history of the New Left. As a result, almost everything that summer was a bewildering blur, like the time a leading Weatherman, all macho bluster, blew through town and told us it was time to "pick up the gun" in support of the Black Panthers and the North Vietnamese. Anything less was wimpy. By summer's end I had the rhetoric down, but I knew next to nothing about combating racism in suburbia.

I was intrigued by the Movement, even its debased Weatherman version, but I was also relieved to be heading off to a college halfway across the country in rural Minnesota. Carleton offered nothing like the bizarre world of radical politics I had brushed up against in D.C. The closest I came to civil disobedience in those years was poli sci professor Paul Wellstone's course on it. After graduation in 1973, I moved with a group of friends to Santa Fe, New Mexico. I had read *Sisterhood Is Powerful*, *The Female Eunuch* and *Sexual Politics*, but the feminist movement seemed tantalizingly out of reach, a big-city phenomenon. As it turned out, the no-holds-barred, cutting-edge feminism I was searching for was an hour away in Albuquerque at the University of New Mexico's fledgling women's studies program. Women's studies had a beleaguered part-time director, but it was run by a collective that was dominated by a quarrelsome group of lesbian-feminists and socialist-feminists. Those first couple of years, the women's studies program had a deliciously rogue feel to it. The bulk of our courses were taught by graduate students, undergrads, and "community" people like myself who had no connection to the university and whose only qualification was that somewhere along the line they had acquired a B.A. Regular faculty must have taught some of our classes, but the entire university had only a handful of full-time female professors, and, as I recall, they kept their distance from us. Several months after I began attending meetings, I moved to Albuquerque and started working at the university as a groundskeeper, one of several women hired to the all-male grounds crew as a result of affirmative action. Women's studies was located at the women's center, whose grounds were near my bailiwick. I took my breaks at the center where I devoured new and back issues of *off our backs*, *Plexus*, and *Big Mama Rag*, the leading feminist newspapers, which were filled with stories of internecine movement battles that I'd analyze ten years later as a graduate student.

I fell in love with those women's studies meetings, which were all politics, process, and dish. The veteran politicos who ran the show were a mesmerizing bunch—smart, incorrigible, and apparently fearless. They reveled in their ability to out-argue others, and to make the telling political point. I was especially struck by the lesbians, who in so many ways didn't match the cultural stereotype. They weren't the losers of legend. They'd had boyfriends, been married, and were often quite pretty, which for me was a revelation. Being around so many plus-size egos was a wonderful corrective to college where all but one of my professors had been male. However, collective meetings sometimes felt a bit like feminist boot camp. Warm and cozy they weren't. Almost anyone could be cut off, corrected, silenced. Meetings sometimes devolved into parodies of political correctness, most memorably when one woman got up in the middle of a heated discussion to demonstrate how a feminist should walk. She stomped, of course.

My walk passed muster, but in other respects I was found wanting. The ruling clique believed that the collective, which was overwhelmingly white and middle class, should become more working class, more "Third World," and perhaps more lesbian. However, when I first joined the group I was still living in arty Santa Fe, not blue-collar Albuquerque, I had long, hippie-length, blondish hair, and despite considerable effort came across as someone who had attended prep school and a private college. Back then, lesbianism compensated somewhat for class and racial privilege, but I couldn't play that card since I was reluctant at first to declare myself anything. Self-definition didn't always count for very much in those days, anyway. I was quickly tagged bisexual, mostly on the basis of my hair, the telltale sign of my lingering investment in "the patriarchy." This was not a good thing. In those years bisexuality carried the same suggestion of unreliability that liberal did in far left circles.

In women's studies the boundary between good and bad feminism was so rigidly drawn and so vigilantly patrolled that it didn't take brains galore to figure out how to gain acceptance in the group. Over time I learned to be as arrogant and dogmatic as the next person. However, in the end, I could never quite get with the program. I listened to the Rolling Stones and Barry White rather than Holly Near, I socialized with too many heterosexual feminists, and I refused to get the obligatory crewcut. This wasn't all deliberate resistance on my part, mind you, but there was an element of provocation, or at least a bit of a tweak. For better or for worse, my relationship to feminism has been like this ever since.

Taken together, my two movement experiences amounted to less than three years of my life. Yet these were extraordinarily intense years. Although I had no intention of studying the sixties when I entered graduate school in 1976—in fact, in history one couldn't yet study the decade—much of my subsequent work would grow out of my effort to make sense of this period. For eleven years I was a student in the University of Michigan's doctoral program in history. My intellectual home, however, was women's studies. Michigan's program prided itself on its rigorousness and theoretical sophistication. No vulgar Marxism or lesbian-separatism here. And at Michigan some women faculty members, including established scholars like Louise Tilly and Elizabeth Douvan, got involved early on. Feminist scholarship in those years was so dynamic—all dazzling breakthroughs and paradigm shifts—that many of the university's brightest graduate students gravitated toward women's studies. Michigan's program was also unusual in that it encouraged maverick thinking, even when it meant taking on other feminists.

As it turned out, there were plenty of opportunities to do just that in the years ahead. At the very moment that poststructuralists and social historians were taking apart the category of gender and revealing the ways that sexuality was socially and historically constructed, some feminists were beginning to embrace the idea of feminine difference and putting forward essentialist or precultural explanations of gender and sexuality. Poststructuralism hadn't yet acquired the cachet it would have in the mid-to-late eighties, but the new social history exerted quite an influence, especially at Michigan. Social historians emphasized the importance of granting agency to the oppressed and this ran counter to the tendency of some feminists to see women exclusively as victims of patriarchy. These tensions were bound to come to a head, and they did quite dramatically as the feminist antipornography movement took shape. Although the line between activists and scholars was not neatly drawn, the debate about pornography nevertheless revealed a growing rift between academics and activists.

Beginning in the mid-seventies, feminist activists started targeting pornography on the grounds that it promoted violence against women. Within just a few years pornography had supplanted all other issues in the feminist movement. Quite a few of us in Michigan women's studies were dismayed by this campaign, especially its targeting of pornography as the linchpin of women's oppression and its dichotomized view of male and female sexuality. The idea that women seek only reciprocity and intimacy in lovemaking and that men are obsessed with power and domination, as these activists often alleged, not only flew in the face of my own experience, but was a depressing reaffirmation of conventional ideas about men's and women's sexuality. What bothered me most was the ease with which the antiporn crusade defined cuddly sex as feminist and stigmatized as male-identified just about everything else. I couldn't see that the feminist impulse to hold desire accountable to political principle had improved anyone's life, and the movement's ever-narrowing notion of acceptable sex seemed likely to lead to greater repression. I worried that feminism, which had expanded women's sense of sexual possibility (and had facilitated my own coming out), might now be feeding those familiar feelings of sexual shame with which many women, myself included, struggled. After all, whose sexuality could be easily squared with the nice-girl sexuality of the antiporn movement? In the end, I was fairly certain that pornography would survive this new crusade against it, but I wasn't so sure we would.

It's been twenty years since I wrote the polemic that eventually became "The Taming of the Id," an essay that criticized the feminist antipornography movement. I had written it as a seminar paper, but it reached a much wider audience. Friend and fellow grad student Gayle Rubin suggested I submit it for inclusion in *Powers of Desire*, an anthology about feminism and sexuality that Ann Snitow, Christine Stansell, and Sharon Thompson were editing. Ann and Sharon were involved in planning Barnard College's 1982 Scholar and Feminist Conference on sexuality, and when *Village Voice* columnist Ellen Willis decided against giving a keynote talk, I was asked in her stead. I was thrilled to be part of this effort to open up for debate the gnarly question of feminism's relationship to sexual desire. The day of the conference, however, all my bad-girl bravado failed me. I felt only stomach-churning terror as I realized that some of the very feminists I took to task in my talk were bound to be in the audience. Moreover, getting into the auditorium required walking past a vocal group of antiporn protesters. Wearing T-shirts that read "For a Feminist Sexuality" on the front and "Against S/M" on the back, they passed out a leaflet that attacked several women associated with the conference for either having kinky sexual tastes or for supporting those who did. The idea that the conference was a brief for s/m proved a very effective smear. Some people still refer to it as the s/m conference, though Carole Vance and the planning committee carefully framed the conference as an exploration of "the ambiguous and complex relationship between sexual pleasure and danger in women's lives and in feminist theory."

Today most academic feminists view the feminist antipornography movement with smug contempt. Bashing leading antiporn feminists Andrea

Dworkin and Catharine MacKinnon is so routine it's old hat. But criticizing the movement in 1982 was nothing short of heretical in some circles. No one associated with the conference was prepared for the fallout. Barnard College confiscated 1,500 copies of the conference diary, a booklet that included planning committee notes, workshop abstracts, and not-very-racy graphics. More important, Barnard's Scholar and Feminist Conference—an annual event—lost its funding as a result of the controversy. Much of the feminist press was critical both of the conference and *Powers of Desire*, which was published a year later. I didn't live in New York where the sex debates were especially rancorous, but all the bad notices found their way soon enough to Michigan. My essay, a version of which appears in this volume, had a take-no-prisoners quality to it, which guaranteed that it would be judged harshly. Not long after the conference, I broke out in shingles, highly unusual for someone my age. It was about this time that it dawned on me that I'd become notorious in the small world of academic feminism.

Barnard had professional costs for me, but in the long run the conference was spectacularly successful. Our contention that feminism should acknowledge that sexuality is a domain of pleasure as well as danger, which seemed almost scandalous twenty years ago, is now a commonplace, at least among many feminists in the academy. We were, I now joke, prematurely anticensorship. But if the anticensorship forces won the battle within academia, the antiporn movement affected the way feminism was viewed by the public at large. As I argue in "The Dworkinization of Catharine MacKinnon," antiporn feminists, with the help of the media, succeeded in making their views understood as the feminist position on pornography. When the mainstream media featured the porn wars, they chose civil libertarians or women from outside feminism—often the recklessly quotable Camille Paglia—to oppose Dworkin and MacKinnon, et al. The invisibility of anticensorship feminists reinforced the caricature of feminists as dreary, finger-wagging moralists.

Of course, feminists have long been ridiculed as humorless and uptight. None more than the radical feminists of the late sixties and early seventies. Researching "Taming" made me realize that radical feminism was among the most poorly understood parts of the sixties. In fact, most histories of the period marginalized, belittled, or attacked the women's movement, no matter what the tendency or strand of feminism under discussion. Moreover, most accounts of the sixties, whether written by new left-ists or feminists, failed to address the centrality of left-wing thinking to radical feminism. So in 1983 I set out to write a dissertation that analyzed the origins and trajectory of radical feminism through both oral histories and more traditional archival sources. *Daring to Be Bad*, a revised version of my dissertation, was published in 1989, and quickly became a hotly debated book. I've included in this collection two essays—"We Gotta Get Out of This Place" and "Nothing Distant About It"—that draw on and elaborate my work in this book.

What I set out to do in *Daring* was to reveal the vision, vitality, and some-times sheer wackiness of radical feminism, but without ever losing sight of its complicated indebtedness to other sixties movements. *Daring* was also intended to be quite a bit more than an effort to write feminism into the six-ties. I wanted to distinguish radical feminism from cultural feminism, a strand that grew out of radical feminism but contravened much that was fundamental to it. Cultural feminism positioned itself in opposition to the left, traded on conventional ideas about femininity, and viewed feminism as a countercultural activity rather than as a political enterprise. It also brought about feminism's reconciliation with the market, religion, and, most important, the state—the very components of "the system" which the movement had once opposed.

At the time I was working on the book, radical feminism was so misun-derstood, so frequently conflated with what it had turned into, that I felt I had to separate these two strands linguistically. I now think that calling it all radical feminism would have raised fewer hackles. And since I stressed the ways that weaknesses and contradictions within radical feminism helped give rise to cultural feminism, using radical feminism as an umbrella term would have been consistent with my thesis. *Daring* was the first history of second-wave feminism, and some readers, especially movement veterans, wanted a history that accorded a smaller, more discreet role to conflict. But the women's movement, and the radical feminist wing in particular, crack-led with contentiousness and conflict, sometimes destructively so. Howev-er, to me, one of the most compelling aspects of radical feminism was the encouragement it gave women to engage in unladylike disagreement, to dare to be bad. Although I don't regret the book's focus on conflict, I do think that in my effort to chronicle the movement's every ideological twist and turn and the inevitable battles around them, I gave short shrift to the ways—large, small, and contradictory—that radical feminism transformed American culture and society.

One might imagine that my next major undertaking, *Scars of Sweet Paradise: The Life and Times of Janis Joplin,* emerged seamlessly from *Daring.* After all, wasn't Janis Joplin the original bad girl, the woman whose refusal to sound pretty or to behave like a lady anticipated feminism's demolition of good-girl femininity? Although in many ways she was, that's not how I happened to write a book about her. Both my notoriety and the stodginess of my discipline, which usually dismisses as "journalistic" attempts to write about recent history, kept me on the margins of academia. By 1992 I was weary of one-year teaching gigs. I began freelancing and I decided to write a history of rock music that would foreground race, sexuality, and gender in a way that would appeal to a general audience. In the course of reading piles of rock biographies I ran across two about Janis Joplin, which were particularly annoying examples of what Joyce Carol Oates has dubbed pathography, the kind of biography writing that focuses obsessively on dysfunction and disaster. I was complaining about this to fellow historian Robin Kelley when he suggested I write a book about Joplin. Biography was not a genre that especially interested me, and there were already several books out about the singer. However, I had to admit that much about her life—her move from folk to rock (and from North Beach to Haight-Ashbury), her love of black music and culture, her mutable sexuality, and the difficulties she faced as a breakthrough woman in rock—lent itself to my project.

At first, Joplin's story interested me primarily for what it could tell me about the sixties and rock music. But Joplin was too complex, contradictory, and outsized a figure to be reduced to a mere vehicle for my cultural history. As I listened to her music and spoke with her friends and fellow musicians I grew more curious about her, especially the elaborate masquerades that this icon of authenticity, this proselytizer of "being yourself," staged in order to disguise her heroin habit and unconventional sexual desires. However, I never abandoned my aim to embed Joplin in the history of the sixties; in fact, I came to see this as critical to my effort to depathologize her. If readers could see that her recklessness and defiance were not hers alone, but were in many ways generational, I felt I could move them past the familiar portrait of Joplin as a spectacularly screwed-up hippie chick, the poster child of sixties dysfunctionality. Of course, in certain respects Joplin was unique; certainly her openness to same-sex sexual relationships was not typical of most hippies. Very early on in my research I became interested in understanding the ways in which bohemian sexuality changed when Haight-Ashbury superseded North Beach and bohemia became a mass phenomenon, and how this shift affected Joplin. I explore this in " 'Thousands of Men and a Few Hundred Women': Janis Joplin, Sexual Ambiguity, and Bohemia."

Scars of Sweet Paradise also reflected my effort to more fully integrate the counterculture into the history of the sixties. Although more kids passed through the counterculture than SDS, historians, myself included, have focused on the political movements with which they themselves were often involved. *Scars* is, among other things, a meditation on what political activists and hippies shared: a commitment to high-risk living, what Joplin called living "superhypermost." The book also challenges the conventional view that the counterculture was all goofy optimism and that the world of sex, drugs, and rock and roll was one big happy bash—an especially durable myth among baby boomers.

Just as *Daring to Be Bad* is an unflinching look back at the women's movement, so is *Scars of Sweet Paradise* an unsentimental portrait of the sixties counterculture. As I researched the book, I came to believe that the problem with the counterculture wasn't that it went too far—the typical view—but rather that its libertinism and its elevation of the far-out masked the ways that the hippie subculture mirrored the values of the dominant culture, especially in regard to women and gays. Crucial to Joplin's story was the transformation of sixties rock from the bastard child of the entertainment industry to its crown jewel. I wanted to push past the usual tale of co-optation whereby idealistic sixties rockers set out to change the world only to find themselves corrupted and transformed by it instead. My own view, which I flesh out in "Hope and Hype in Sixties Haight-Ashbury," reflects my dissatisfaction with both the gloomy, functionalist understanding of youth culture as a mere invention of hip capitalism and those rhapsodic readings of popular culture as a site of resistance and subversion that are so characteristic of cultural studies today.

At the same time that I am skeptical of work intent on finding the utopian longings and counterhegemonic possibilities in popular culture, my own relationship to rock 'n' roll was profound, even politicizing. When I turned five in 1956 I began listening to rock 'n' roll. I went to sleep at night with a little cream-colored transistor radio beside my pillow quietly playing the same Top 40 songs I watched teenagers dance to on *American Bandstand*. Music was no sideshow in my life. I holed up for hours in the basement listening to rock 'n' roll records. Growing up right outside a black majority city no doubt affected my listening habits. Before long, I graduated from Top 40 to soul-music radio. In my experience, the music and the politics were connected. The Supremes and the Temptations didn't sing "political" songs, but listening to them on WOL, one of D.C.'s two soul stations, made me curious about black culture and politics. I'm not sure I would have been so eager to read books like Black Panther Eldridge Cleaver's bestseller *Soul on Ice* had I not been hooked on soul music. Like so many other white middle-class kids in the sixties who were captivated by "blackness," I invested African Americans with greater authenticity and soulfulness, and an outsider's view of the world. Whites' fascination with blackness—or this particular construction of blackness—is a recurrent theme in postwar America, playing a critical (and sometimes troubling) role in rock 'n' roll and white radical activism of the sixties, and I discuss this in "We Gotta Get Out of This Place," "White Faces, Black Masks," and more glancingly in profiles of musicians Lenny Kravitz and John Paul Hammond.

The notion that blacks are soulful, authentic, and at odds with the dominant culture was widely held in the sixties and was behind hip white kids' love affair with soul music and the black movement. The celebration of soul had roots in the ideology of black power, which promoted this kind of racial typing, but it also echoed the earlier white hipster vision of blacks and was problematic in just the ways that the Jack Kerouac/Norman Mailer view of blacks had been. For African Americans, acceptance was contingent upon matching the racial profile. This only became clear to me ten years later, during the disco years of the mid-to-late seventies, when many whites who had been R&B aficionados turned their backs on popular, contemporary music by black artists. In contrast to the sixties and the nineties when there was intense white interest in the music and culture of African Americans, the disco seventies were years when "blackness" held little or no cachet. Whites' loss of interest, or worse, their hostility to "black" music, made me curious about the process of racial fascination. No doubt, one reason I was attuned to this cultural shift was that starting in 1980 I began working part-time as a disco-funk deejay and saw the racial antagonism up front.

Disco and the backlash against it are among the most curious and paradoxical phenomena of recent cultural history. Although disco developed out of R&B and its leading performers were black, many people thought it was "white" music. The new dance music arose in gay clubs and gays remained a critical audience, but many Americans were clueless about its links to that community. Finally, disco was at once hugely popular and intensely loathed. Indeed, before the emergence of the angry white male, there were the disco wars of the seventies. The backlash against disco had a lot to do with deindustrialization, affirmative action, and the rise of feminism and gay liberation—all of which triggered fears of displacement among white heterosexual males. But discophobia also grew out of the growing divergence of R&B and white rock music in the late sixties. As I discuss in " 'Shaky Ground': Popular Music in the Disco Years," rock and R&B were on a collision course that culminated in the battle over disco.

If African Americans have found themselves on shaky ground in relation to rock 'n' roll—music that it can be argued they invented but has come to be seen as "white"—so have women. All the nineties' hoopla about "Women in Rock,"—the MTV programs and special issues of *Rolling Stone*—only underscores women's precarious position in the male-dominated world of rock 'n' roll. From the beginning, women were at a disadvantage because rock developed at a time when women were expected to be sexy, not sexual. Fifties girls—black or white—could never have achieved stardom by staking out the same sexually transgressive territory that Elvis Presley had so effortlessly claimed. Etta James and Tina Turner tried, but, then, for years their popularity did not extend much beyond the black community. By the early sixties, girl groups like the Chantals and the Shirelles established a beachhead for women in rock 'n' roll, but with the exception of Diana Ross, the singers in these groups remained nameless and faceless, despite the millions of records they sold. Rock 'n' roll was such a boy's game that Wanda Jackson was marketed as the female Gene Vincent and Janis Martin was dubbed the female Elvis. It wasn't until the late sixties when Janis Joplin helped close what one critic called rock's "girl gap" that the situation shifted. Joplin's influence was significant, but she couldn't single-handedly remake the world of rock music. To this day, rock 'n' roll retains a strong masculinist bias. I grapple with women's vexed relationship to rock in a long profile of singer-songwriter Joni Mitchell.

ALTHOUGH THIS BOOK grows out of my ongoing struggle to make sense of the sixties—SDS graffiti and all—it is not narrowly focused on that one decade. Rather it takes as its subject the shaky ground of the post-World War II period through the 1990s—the rumblings of change in the post-war years, the tectonic shifts of the sixties, and the aftershocks that have reverberated ever since. Viewed in this fashion we can see how the conflicts and confusion about race, sexuality, gender and generation have played out over time. I also believe that the sixties is best illuminated when embedded in a discussion of the past fifty-plus years. As I argue in "The Ike Age: Rethinking the 1950s," the fifties helped give rise to the sixties in all kinds of ways. Postwar affluence underwrote the dropout protest culture of sixties youth. Postwar parents' obsession with material comfort and security provoked restlessness and risk-taking in their children. The hyper-domestic fifties provoked a gendered generational revolt among young, middle-class white kids. Even the cold war rhetoric of American democracy and freedom encouraged a critical consciousness about America's support of dictatorships abroad and support of racial apartheid at home. But if the postwar years spurred change, they also cast a long shadow on the culture and movements of the sixties. Sexism and homophobia, for example, were woven into the fabric of these movements. Even sixties rock culture, which certainly favored racial equality, developed an understanding, an ideology even, about the music and blacks' relationship to it, that guaranteed that rock would come to be seen as "white." And though many factors contributed to the emergence of antiporn feminism, part of its appeal was that it echoed older, powerful ideas about sexuality as male and love as female.

Shaky Ground tackles a wide variety of topics—from the counterculture and feminism to disco and the racial politics of culture. It represents my effort to map an alternative history of the postwar years and beyond, one that challenges the usual constructions of that era, especially the idea that the sixties represented a total rupture, a golden moment when the ideas and values of the dominant culture were banished, and that the seventies marked the end of meaningful social and political change. These essays also reflect my ongoing struggle with identity politics. Many of the artists and thinkers whose work I explore in these pages, among them Joni Mitchell, Sly Stone, and Shulamith Firestone, have struggled to blast through the confines of gender, race, genre—the very categories reified by identity politics. While I understand the strategic value of this sort of politics, I long for a politics that doesn't confuse who we are with what we can become, one that can go beyond moralizing and political purity. I offer these essays in the hope that they might help us move a little closer to that goal.

PaRT 1

POSTWar America and THE 1960s:
THE LonG, STranGe TriP

The essays in the following section are focused on the social and cultural movements of the 1960s. Both "Nothing Distant About It" and "We Gotta Get Out of This Place" were written shortly after the publication of *Daring to Be Bad*, and reflect my dissatisfaction with the ways in which most histories of the '60s, with their determined focus on the New Left, marginalize other movements, particularly women's liberation. "Nothing Distant About It," which was written in 1991 and published in David Farber's 1994 collection of essays on the sixties, argues that women's liberation was above all else a sixties movement, even if its greatest impact occurred in the 1970s. "We Gotta Get Out of This Place," which grew out of a 1990 talk and first appeared in a 1992 issue of *Socialist Review*, not only critiques the historiography of the sixties, but also offers some thoughts on how we might remap the field so that sixties historians begin to capture a larger slice of those times.

Working all those years on the 1960s made me more curious about the 1950s. And in 1994, as I was preparing to teach a course on the 1950s, I read a number of recently published books about the period, including some very bold revisionist efforts. I discuss these books and my ambivalent reaction to them in "The Ike Age: Rethinking the 1950s," a 1994 *Village Voice* article that I have lightly reworked for inclusion in this collection. Finally, as I researched my biography of Janis Joplin, *Scars of Sweet Paradise*, I was struck by the absence of good histories of the counterculture. As a result, much of my time interviewing people was spent asking them for their thoughts about and recollections of the counterculture and the new rock music that was so much a part of it. Some of that material was too far flung, too distant from Joplin's story to be included in *Scars*—so I decided to fashion a freestanding essay on the counterculture that would make use of it. "Hope and Hype in 1960s Haight-Ashbury" is largely taken from "The Beautiful People" chapter of the Joplin biography, but this essay contains new material and is differently framed.

1

HOPE AND HYPE IN SIXTIES HAIGHT-ASHBURY

ONE OF THE BIGGEST NEWS STORIES of the sixties was the hippie counterculture. San Francisco's Haight-Ashbury was the counterculture's epicenter and during the summer of 1967 its streets were jammed with middle Americans in cars and on tour buses gaping at long-haired kids, who found themselves competing for sidewalk space with dozens of journalists and TV news crews covering this latest outbreak of rebellion. Hippies remained in the headlines through the early 1970s, yet most histories of the period make only passing mention of the counterculture. When not scornful or mocking, most accounts are clueless, rarely much better than what appeared at the time in glossy magazines like *Time*, which came up with such gems as hippies "scorn money—they call it 'bread.'"[1] If the counterculture appears as a sideshow in most sixties books, it's in large measure because most scholars are interested in the political movements of the day—movements with which they often identified and in which they were sometimes active. Radical activists also left a paper trail of position papers, meeting notes, and newspapers to study, whereas the radicals of the counterculture left little trace of themselves. Most of what exists in the way of a written record was produced by outsiders, and though some of it is brilliant, particularly Tom Wolfe's amped story of Ken Kesey and the Acid Tests and Joan Didion's steely-eyed, no-bullshit account of 1967's Summer of Love, it was not generated from within the ranks.[2]

This essay was previously published in somewhat different form in *Scars of Sweet Paradise: The Life and Times of Janis Joplin* (NEW YORK: METROPOLITAN BOOKS, 1999).

There's another reason sixties scholars give the counterculture short shrift. Bluntly put, hippies aren't hip. In contrast to the Beats, who only acquire more cool and more relevance, hippies (the Grateful Dead excepted) seem sillier and more anachronistic with each passing year.

Make no mistake: the counterculture could be silly. But, then, so could the political movements of that era. And whatever one might think of the hippie phenomenon, it wasn't insignificant. More people passed through "love ghettos" like Haight-Ashbury than took part in Students for a Democratic Society, the leading New Left group of the 1960s. But, of course, the counterculture had musicians as drawing cards. Rock music was key to the Haight's popularity, what made this new bohemia go mass. However, San Francisco's rock scene would not have come together as it did were it not for the city's bohemian subculture, which was the incubator for the eclectic, acid-inspired rock of groups like the Dead and the Jefferson Airplane, and was the audience at the early rock dances. Even *Time* magazine understood that "the sound was also the scene."[3] Although the counterculture and the rock bands fed each other for a time, their relationship shifted in the wake of 1967's Monterey Pop, the festival which put the San Francisco bands on the map and transformed the world of rock 'n' roll.

What follows is a revisionist account of San Francisco's counterculture and the rock bands that were a part of it.[4] This is not the usual gloomy narrative of rock's co-optation by the music business, nor does it confirm the by now familiar portrait of the counterculture, particularly the notion that its reigning sensibility was goofy optimism, that it shared very little with the political movements of the day, and that its undoing lay mostly in its legendary excessiveness. Along the way, I explore the counterculture's beginnings in beatnik North Beach and the factors that came together to create Haight-Ashbury. This is a story of hope and hype, not lost innocence.[5] Everyone knows about the peace, love, grass, and groovy music, but the counterculture was always more complicated—edgier, darker, and more tied to the dominant culture—than most anyone at the time could see.

SPEAKING AT THE 1960 REPUBLICAN NATIONAL CONVENTION, FBI chief J. Edgar Hoover declared "communists, beatniks and eggheads" the most dangerous groups in America.[6] It was an odd, even paranoid, assessment. The CP was shattered, the Beat "rebellion" had fizzled out, and few intellec-

tuals and even fewer college students were challenging the kneejerk anticommunism of the day. College campuses were such "monoliths of conformity" at the decade's start that University of California Chancellor Clark
Kerr confidently predicted that "employers will love this generation" because "they are going to be easy to handle."7 Hoover's rant was paranoid, but
in a way it was also weirdly prescient for over the next few years San Francisco started filling up with young people looking for the Beats they'd read
about and gazed longingly at in mass circulation magazines in the late
fifties.8 Most of the reporting on the Beats was calculated to scare people off,
but it alerted all those kids who felt like mutants growing up in fifties America to an alternative existence, a way out of the awful gray dullness looming
before them. Indeed, Haight-Ashbury would never have happened as it did,
and maybe not at all, without that earlier, and beleaguered, outpost of bohemia—beatnik North Beach.

The pioneers of Haight-Ashbury came to San Francisco looking for the
Beats, but most of their idols had fled North Beach by 1960. The coffeehouses, bars, and Lawrence Ferlinghetti's City Lights Bookstore hung on,
but North Beach was seedy, and had a tourist-trap feel to it. Then in 1965,
just as it was becoming clear that acoustic folk music had run its course and
the Beat scene was completely played out, San Francisco's bohemian world
began to transmogrify in ways no one could have predicted. A year later the
talk was of hippies not beatniks, and Haight-Ashbury had supplanted North
Beach as the epicenter of hipness. There were holdovers from the beatnik
years—a little Zen Buddhism, marijuana, even the term "hippie" itself had
been used by veteran beatniks to put down young wannabes, the junior hipsters. But there was also the new and the shocking—LSD, Day-Glo colors,
and rock music so raw and so doggedly anticommercial that it barely sounded like rock 'n' roll. By the end of 1965, the new bohemia was electric with
possibility. Peggy Caserta, owner of Mnasidika, the Haight's first hip bou-
tique, remembers the moment when the extent of the changes finally hit
her. It was early 1966 and she was minding her store by the corner of Haight
and Ashbury. Photographer Herb Green had just finished shooting pictures
of the scruffy, shaggy Grateful Dead outside her store when her next-door
neighbor, a barber who sensed his shop's coming obsolescence, said,
"Peggy, *what* is going on here?"9 Within a year, the barbershop was gone,
replaced by another of Caserta's stores. By 1966, convention—even history

itself—was on the verge of "coming off the leash," and the unraveling felt inevitable, inexorable, sort of like an acid trip.[10]

News of Haight-Ashbury spread quickly as bicoastal boho kids exchanged tales about this strange new scene. Bob Seidemann, a photographer responsible for some of the most arresting images of the sixties, decided to move there in late 1965 when he ran into a fellow New York hipster who said, "Would you believe that people are taking LSD and dancing to rock and roll music in San Francisco?"[11] The idea was as irresistible as it was implausible and the Haight began filling up with people like Seidemann who were eager to walk away from the straight world. All over America kids who had dropped out of the mainstream were sending their parents what Tom Wolfe dubbed the "Beautiful People letter." After a perfunctory apology for having vanished without a word, the writer would then go on: "I won't bore you with the whole thing, how it happened, but I really tried, because I knew you wanted me to, but it just didn't work out with [school, college, my job, me and Danny] and so I have come here and it really is a beautiful scene. I don't want you to worry about me. I have met some BEAUTIFUL PEOPLE."[12]

It wasn't hard finding them, especially the guys with their Jesus Christ hair and beards. Beautiful people dressed to underscore their freakiness, appropriating the clothes of other times and cultures—Davy Crockett buckskin, military surplus, Buddhist robes, Edwardian suits, Errol Flynn pirate shirts, Native American headbands, capes, cowboy and Beatle boots, hats—bowlers, stove pipe, cowboy, Eskimo, anything—and beads, of course. Being beautiful was more than copping a look, though; it was an attitude, a stance, a vibration. Weirdness mattered, and so did a mellow vibe. Both individualistic ("Do your own thing") and tribal ("Everybody get together"), the hippie scene was philosophically thin: a little Eastern mysticism, eco-consciousness, and the conviction that all things "natural"—with the important exceptions of electric rock 'n' roll and synthetic drugs like LSD ("Better Living through Chemistry" as one poster put it)—were better.

Many factors converged to create the Haight and the hippie counterculture, not the least of them drugs and rock 'n' roll, but the shift couldn't have happened on the scale it did had white America not been at that moment extraordinarily affluent. While white sixties rebels were rejecting America's relentless materialism, what playwright Arthur Miller called "a system pouring its junk over everybody," their revolt was subsidized and underwritten by America's unprecedented prosperity.[13] In the Haight virtually everything, including the space, was surplus. Haight-Ashbury was itself an almost forgotten part of the city, a working-class, interracial area bohemians began moving into when the commercialization of North Beach caused rents to skyrocket. And in this sleepy neighborhood beatnik types didn't have to worry about police harassment, which had become routine in North Beach. San Francisco State College had been located on lower Haight Street until the early 1950s, and a few scattered student or teacher households remained, giving the neighborhood a mildly boho air even before the migration from North Beach began. Because rents were cheap and the area was one quick trolley ride to the new SF State, Haight-Ashbury began filling up with students, graduates, dropouts and even some faculty. Two huge floors of a once-beautiful old Victorian house went for $175 a month, or you could rent a room in such a house, often for as little as $15 a month. Nor were the ballrooms and theaters that were home to the new rock dances in great demand either.

Beautiful people lived on leftovers, the discarded waste of a "post-scarcity society." In 1966, an anarchist group called the Diggers began serving free food in the Panhandle of Golden Gate Park. Named after a group of seventeenth-century English radicals, the Diggers were street-theater "guerrillas" determined to prod society out of its lethargy. The free food wasn't charity, but rather part of their effort to "jog consciousness," according to Peter Coyote, one of several San Francisco Mime Troupe actors who formed the Diggers.[14] "It's free because it's yours," they declared.[15] The food the Diggers handed out was sometimes donated by bakeries, produce markets, and meat markets; other times it was "liberated." Although the Diggers were often praised as "anonymous good guys" or a "hip Salvation Army," some people considered them con artists who used the lingo of liberation to rationalize scamming anyone with even marginally greater resources.[16] The Diggers also ran a free store, filled with used clothes and surplus from local companies like Levi Strauss. The Free Store was so awash with white button-down Oxford shirts—nine-to-five wear that drop-outs no longer needed—that a Digger woman found an ingenious way of reclaiming them: tie dye. Before long, the new fashion was everywhere. Rejected Levi's designs would sometimes make their way into the Digger community, too. At one time almost all the Digger women were wearing super-tight, silver pants made from metallic cloth—designer rejects from Levi Strauss.[17]

San Francisco's two Army-Navy surplus stores were another source for hip clothes, which included sturdy and dirt-cheap Navy bell-bottoms, pea jackets and Army jackets. Truly enterprising hipsters like George Hunter, who formed the Haight's original rock band, the Charlatans, spent hours at thrift stores, the Salvation Army, and Goodwill rummaging through secondhand clothing for cool Victorian and Edwardian styles. They also outfitted their apartments in an "old-timey" look, using unwanted, outdated furniture and appliances. Bob Seidemann remembers, "Everybody's house had the old-timey stove and the old-timey refrigerator even though the fuckin' refrigerator was lousy—the light bulb didn't work and it didn't get the beer cold. They had it because it was old timey."[18] Even the overhead projectors that light artists used during rock concerts were World War II vintage, available at military surplus stores. Many kids lived on welfare. Richard Hundgen, a future roadie for San Francisco bands, claims that groups of hippies began calling themselves "families" because of their dealings with the San Francisco Welfare Department. All of a sudden lots of unrelated people were living under the same roof, and welfare workers began designating them families, he says, so they'd be eligible for food stamps.[19] However, according to Peter Coyote, whose communal household survived on three welfare checks, the Welfare Department workers were sticklers for the rules. The department made periodic inspections of recipients' households, and he remembers that on those occasions everyone "extraneous to the legal definition of 'single family' would disappear so that the welfare workers would always discover . . . three indigent women."[20] On the whole, these middle-class white kids worried not about whether they'd find jobs, but rather about how they could best avoid them.

The people of the Haight were partly driven to drop out by the "junk"— but also by a vast sense of spiritual and emotional emptiness. Jim Haynie of the San Francisco Mime Troupe was "tired of the gray life."[21] Like others, he hungered for connection and an experience of intensity. Peter Coyote came to the Haight after "twenty years of marshmallow, plastic, and hopscotch," determined to "lay life." "I want to taste it, beat it, feel it, kill it, fuck it," he said, "and I want to have all those things done to me."[22] To the Diggers, the way out of the gray life—"civilian living," as one of them put it—was what they called "life acting," or playing for keeps, not compensating for "the meagerness of one's own existence" by living vicariously through others' achievements and adventures.[23] Living large and taking risks seemed the solution. After Janis Joplin became famous, journalist Nat Hentoff once asked if she was concerned her voice could withstand the abuse she put it through when she sang. For her the question assumed generational significance. She believed you could "destroy your now by worrying about tomorrow. We look back at our parents and see how they gave up and compromised and wound up with very little. So the kids want a lot of something now rather than a little of hardly anything spread over seventy years."[24]

And by May 1965, a UC Berkeley drop-out, Augustus Owsley Stanley III, or "Owsley," was providing an instant cure for the lack of emotional, intellectual, and artistic stimulus that so many felt growing up in postwar America—lysergic acid diethylamide. LSD was legal but not widely available until Owsley, whose grandfather had been a U.S. Senator from Kentucky, began manufacturing it with help from his girlfriend, a former chemistry graduate student from Berkeley. When Owsley's acid began making its presence felt in the Haight, people were eager to get psychedelicized and experience that "orgasm behind the eyeballs."[25] Acid was the antidote to the "adventure shortage."[26] Unlike most other drugs, it wasn't about feeling good. LSD trips were sometimes a "bummer"—originally a Hell's Angels' expression for a bad motorcycle trip—but mostly spiritually cathartic, even transcendent.[27] Nor was LSD addictive, because, as one aficionado puts it, getting hooked on it would be "like being addicted to having the shit beat out of you."[28] Psychedelics (originally called psychodelics) opened up the mind to that flood of stimuli that the brain under normal functioning reduces to a manageable trickle, as Aldous Huxley, an earlier advocate, had explained.[29]

Jerry Garcia claimed that psychedelics allowed him to enter a reality he had "always thought existed but had never been able to find." For the most part, acid revelations were strictly of the moment, not easily translatable. Bob Seidemann remembers some "derelict" guy telling him during an acid trip: "The floor is neutral and the ceiling is positive." According to Seidemann, "That was a major revelation. My mind was blown, though I could never begin to reconstruct what truth was revealed to me then." Psychedelics also affected the music people listened to and played. Folkies began to pick up electric guitars to make noise, to combat the adventure shortage, and to match in some way the monumental stimulus—the high-voltage charge—provided by psychedelics. The first time Phil Lesch of the Grateful Dead plugged in, he played for seven hours straight. When the music is amplified, Lesch explained, "you can hear it all. That's what the electronics do—they amplify the overtones to a degree never thought possible in an acoustic instrument." Acid and electricity were a perfect match.

San Francisco's 1965 transformation from the home of folk to the home of acid rock happened just as dramatically. Acid hit, Bob Dylan went electric at the Newport Folk Festival, and British rockers kept pushing the envelope with songs like the Rolling Stones' "(I Can't Get No) Satisfaction," 1965's number one single. Until the British Invasion there was little room in commercial music for anything that wasn't squeaky clean. Even the Shirelles' "Will You Still Love Me Tomorrow?" with its hint of premarital sex, was too suggestive for some. When the Kingmen's great garage-rock song "Louie, Louie" became a huge hit in 1963, the FBI launched an investigation into the meaning behind its slurred and garbled lyrics. While the Beatles proved the commercial viability of cheeky pop, the Rolling Stones demonstrated there was a market for something darker, more forbidding. Ironically, the British Invasion conquered America with her very own music—early rock 'n' roll, hard-driving R&B, and the blues—black music that had been shut out of American Top 40 radio. Hits like the Beatles' "Twist and Shout" and the Rolling Stones' "It's All Over Now" had already been recorded by black musicians in the States, but most white Americans were unaware of that. What made England's near-stranglehold of the American charts ironic was that mod young Brits had grown up worshipping America. "The most exciting thing about being alive was looking at Americans," recalls one British writer. "America was where we all wanted to be," not drab Britain where rationing lingered on and the economic recovery from World War II took more than a decade.[30] "The first books I ever bought were about America," Eric Clapton recalls. "The first records were American. I was just devoted to the American way of life without ever having been there."[31] Just a few short years later Americans were looking longingly at Britain, especially London's hip Carnaby Street, as the source of everything cool.

Like everyone else, Bob Dylan was mesmerized by the Brits. By 1966 he was claiming folk had just been a "substitute" for rock during the late fifties and early sixties, those years when many observers felt rock 'n' roll had lost its edge and devolved into teenybopper dreck.[32] The English had changed all that, he said, by revitalizing rock music. Dylan had loved the Animals' 1964 rock version of "The House of the Rising Sun," a folk song he'd sung on his first album. When he toured England in 1965, he had hung out with the Animals and the Beatles, and had fooled around in the studio with Britain's premier blues band, John Mayall's Bluesbreakers. Other U.S. folk musicians, including the Cambridge purists, were also smitten by the Beatles. Dylan's sidekick, the painter and guitarist Bob Neuwirth, was "taken" with the way they had moved "European harmonies into an Everly Brothers sack, shaking them up with rock 'n' roll, rockabilly beat and throwing them back across the Atlantic."[33] Even in notoriously snooty Greenwich Village, folk music veterans were intrigued, recalls John Sebastian, who would form the Lovin' Spoonful. In California, folkies David Crosby, Gene Clark, and Roger (Jim) McGuinn were "Beatle struck" after seeing "*A Hard Day's Night*." Crosby remembers "coming out of that movie so jazzed that I was swinging around stop sign poles at arm's length. I knew right then what my life was going to be. I wanted to do that. I loved the attitude and the fun of it; there was sex, there was joy, there was everything I wanted out of life."[34] The three musicians formed the Byrds with Chris Hillman and Michael Clarke and quickly had a smash hit in the spring of 1965 with their folk-rock cover of Dylan's "Mr. Tambourine Man." Neuwirth recalls hearing the Byrd's electric version as he sat with Dylan and Albert Grossman, Dylan's manager. "It was great because no one could figure out how anyone except Peter, Paul, and Mary could ever cover any of Bob's songs."[35] According to Roger McGuinn, when Dylan first heard the Byrds' version of his song he said, "Wow, man, you can dance to it."[36]

Much is made of Dylan's plugging in at the Newport Folk Festival in 1965, but as Cambridge folkies Eric Von Schmidt and Jim Rooney point out, Dylan had already made his intentions known earlier that year on his fifth album, the half-acoustic half-electric *Bringing It All Back Home*. So mercurial his friend Richard Fariña once dubbed him the "plastic man," Dylan was reinventing himself, just the first of many reincarnations.[37] The album cover shows Dylan "in the lap of outrageous luxury. Albert Grossman's wife, Sally, desirable, elegant, aloof, in flame-red, reclines behind Bob . . . Dylan's attire is early English mod: French cuffs, button collar, no tie. . . . It was an optical celebration of opulence and disdain. A visual open letter to the Old Folk

Guard: Kiss off."[38] Dylan summoned the Paul Butterfield Blues Band, an interracial Chicago blues group, to back him at Newport because it was the only
American band that came close to sounding like England's Bluesbreakers.
Dylan's electric set, like the Butterfield Band's earlier set, antagonized the
acoustic ideologues. Dylan's performance was especially jarring coming on
the heels of traditional folksinger Cousin Emmie's set, which included the
hopelessly hokey "Turkey in the Straw." Under-rehearsed and ragged-
sounding, Dylan's makeshift electric ensemble sped through three songs at
ear-splitting volume. Musicologist Alan Lomax and folksinger Pete Seeger,
both festival board members, were furious with Dylan and the sound mixers
who refused to turn down the volume. A distraught Seeger yelled, "If I had an
axe, I'd cut the cable right now!" Peter Yarrow of Peter, Paul, and Mary supported Dylan's right to go electric but says it felt like a "capitulation to the
enemy—as if all a sudden you saw Martin Luther King, Jr. doing a cigarette
ad."[39] However, Dylan wasn't making music to please the old or young fogeys
of folk; he was looking to beat the English at their own game. Producer Paul
Rothchild, who would work with the Doors and Janis Joplin, recalls listening
to a rough mix of "Like a Rolling Stone" with Dylan and Neuwirth. They'd already played it about twenty-five times when Rothchild showed up, and were
"grinning like a couple of cats who'd swallowed canaries." Rothchild soon
understood why. "What I realized while I was sitting there was that one of
US—one of the so-called Village folksingers—was making music that would
compete with all of THEM—the Beatles and the Stones and the Dave Clark
Five—without sacrificing any of the integrity of folk music or the power of
rock 'n' roll."[40]

Dylan could count among his greatest supporters the poet Allen Ginsberg. According to music critic Ralph Gleason of the *San Francisco Chronicle*,
Ginsberg, Lawrence Ferlinghetti, Ken Kesey and two Hell's Angels sat together in the front row at Dylan's Berkeley concert in December 1965. To
those who argued Dylan had sold out, Ginsberg replied, "Dylan has sold out
to God. That is to say, his command was to spread his beauty as wide as possible. It was an artistic challenge to see if great art can be done on a jukebox.
And he proved that it can."[41] With Ginsberg weighing in on his side, Dylan
seemed to have pulled off the impossible—reconciling the artistic with the
commercial. For San Francisco folkies the ramifications were felt immediately. "When Dylan went electric," recalls Bill Belmont, then a San Francis-

co State student, "everybody went out and bought an electric guitar. Literally! That was the end of the beatnik movement and the beginning of electric rock 'n' roll as we know it."[42]

American prosperity, acid, the British Invasion, and Dylan's plugging in were the catalysts that sparked the hippie revolution, and San Francisco was uniquely poised to respond to the shift. Just south of the city in La Honda lived Ken Kesey, author of the much-acclaimed *One Flew Over the Cuckoo's Nest*. Kesey had been psychedelicized in 1960 when he'd signed up as a $75-a-day guinea pig in an experiment at a local Veteran's Administration hospital. Kesey and his friends—the self-proclaimed Merry Pranksters—were acid proselytizers who began turning on San Franciscans in 1965. In contrast to the other major acid outlet, Timothy Leary's operation in Millbrook, New York, which appealed to an elite group of writers, artists and jazz musicians, the Pranksters turned on anyone and everyone at their public happenings, or "Acid Tests." And while Timothy Leary devised a cautious protocol for tripping, which emphasized the creation of a controlled environment ("set and setting"), the Pranksters would urge the people they dosed to "freak freely," their solution to the unpredictability of an acid trip. Unlike Millbrook, which was all cool and meditative—"one big piece of uptight constipation" to the Pranksters—Acid Tests featured rock music, weird electronic noodling, and spoken-word experiments.[43]"Lumpenbeatnik" Jerry Garcia and the Warlocks (soon to be the Grateful Dead) became the Pranksters' house band, and would play loud rock 'n' roll on a sound system purchased by their biggest supporter, acid king Owsley.[44]

San Francisco quickly became the scene of wild parties, of which the Pranksters' were the most off-the-wall. The Bay Area boasted a "huge party circuit" in the mid-sixties because there were so few venues for live music.[45] Many of the party-goers were students at San Francisco State and the San Francisco Art Institute—people who later formed the core audience at Bill Graham's Fillmore Auditorium and Chet Helms's Avalon ballroom. The parties evolved not only from the music and acid scenes, but also from political protest. The Free Speech Movement at UC-Berkeley in 1964 had given rise to more protests as activists looked beyond the campus to end racial discrimination in San Francisco's restaurants, hotels, and auto dealerships and, of course, to rally against the escalating war in Vietnam. Berkeley politicos stayed clear of the Haight, but the same wasn't true of the activists at San Francisco State. In fact, political demonstrations were often followed by big bashes, and dissenters of all persuasions—the political and cultural radicals—seemed to gravitate to each other. Boho kids like George Hunter of the Charlatans would mix with activists like Tracy Simms, the black woman who helped lead the successful protest against racial discrimination at the Sheraton Palace Hotel.[46] One of the most visible left-wing San Francisco groups, The Du Bois Club—dominated by red diaper babies, children of Communists, and fellow travelers—was famous for its post-demo parties. Terence Hallinan, a cofounder of the local Du Bois Club, was well-known to the Haight's musicians and artists. Other members included Bill Resner, who with his brother, Hillel, would open the Haight's electric ballroom, the Straight Theater, and Luria Castell, who claimed to have met Che Guevara in Cuba, but who now resided at 2111 Pine Street, a notorious hippie house where life was "one giant party."[47] There was no effort to bring together these two groups until Yippie was formed later in the decade, but San Francisco's freaks and politicos clearly felt some affinity with one another. Even rock musicians—probably the least activist element within the Haight—played benefits for political groups.[48]

San Francisco's artistic ferment was a multimedia happening, involving not only politicos, Pranksters and musicians, but artists, dancers, poets, and actors. Although it was the "San Francisco Sound" that grabbed journalists, the first rock 'n' roll dances featured poets, dancers, theater troupes, and light show artists. One of Big Brother and the Holding Company's first gigs was "The Blast," a multimedia event that drummer Dave Getz says was "way ahead of its time. There was a rock 'n' roll band on one side of the stage, a free jazz ensemble on the other side of the stage, with dancers in the middle, light projections and this black operatic singer, Crystal Mazur, who was like what Diamanda Galas is now. Years ahead of her time. They projected comics on the screen and she sang the words. Sometimes both bands would be playing. It was totally spontaneous. It was so avant-garde, no one's ever heard of it."[49]

In fact, the Bay Area had a thriving avant-garde. The San Francisco poetry renaissance, spearheaded by Kenneth Rexroth in the late forties, had put the city on the literary map. The experimental Anna Halprin Dance Company created quite a stir with its nude dancing; the Tape Music Center was home to experimental electronic musicians Pauline Oliveras, Ramon

Sender, Morton Subotnik, Zack Stewart, and Steve Reich. This small but vital community of avant-garde artists also included Berkeley's Open Theater; an improvisational troupe, The Committee; and the American Conservatory Theater (ACT) from which Ronny Davis split to form the lefty San Francisco Mime Troupe, which performed hard-hitting political satire, not pantomime. Painters Joan Brown, Wally Hedrick, and Jay DeFeo were part of the mix as well. The Pacifica radio station, KPFA, brought artists and intellectuals together; KPFA regulars included Kenneth Rexroth on books, Pauline Kael on film, Alan Watts on philosophy, and Ralph Gleason on jazz. Despite all the activity, outsiders treated the Bay Area's art scene as if it were a mere echo of New York's—an idea that made local writers and artists bristle. When Tom Wolfe asked Ken Kesey if an Acid Test was like "what Andy Warhol is doing in New York?" Kesey's chilly reply was, "No offense. But New York is about two years behind."[50]

The light show, for instance, was a San Francisco innovation, invented by Seymour Locks, an art professor, in the early fifties. Unlike the light shows associated with Timothy Leary or Andy Warhol, in which static images were projected, Locks projected light through glass dishes filled with paint, which he would swirl and stir to trippy effect. He taught the technique to student Elias Romero who in the early sixties became the "real Johnny Appleseed of light shows" in the Bay Area.[51] Romero began collaborating with painter Bill Ham, and by the spring of 1965 Ham was presenting light shows in his Pine Street basement, sometimes to classical music and sometimes with a group of jazz musicians from an after-hours club around the corner. Alton Kelley, the future poster artist, recalls someone inviting him to Ham's place for a light show. "What the fuck's a light show?" he asked. He went along, wondering, "What's he gonna do, turn on little light bulbs?" Instead "the windows were blacked out, the lights went off and the music started. Then little dots started to move and swirl and change colors." The image was like a "moving abstract painting," projected against the wall.[52]

Light shows, rock 'n' roll, psychedelics—by late 1965 the hallmarks of the hippie era were all in place. Today, however, hardly anyone at the forefront of the "sixties" will admit to having been a hippie. Dave Getz, the drummer in Big Brother and the Holding Company, claims, "I never called myself a hippie, ever. I hated it." Peter Berg of the Mime Troupe and the Diggers says he never thought of himself as a hippie.[53] "White kids who weren't that hip," was the Digger view, and that of many other Haight pioneers who were older than the kids who later flooded into the Haight.[54] Photographer Bob Seidemann maintains, "We called ourselves freaks, never hippies." Carl Gottlieb, a writer, says, "hippies were the people who borrowed your truck and didn't return it." Pat "Sunshine" Nichols, who made pot brownies for the Avalon Ballroom and whose name alone seems incontrovertible proof she was a hippie, insists she was a beatnik instead. Hippies, she explains, were "people who just kind of showed up and didn't seem to have any sense. They didn't know how to take care of themselves. They didn't know how to wash their clothes, hold down a job, or make sure they were going to live through it."

At the time, the Diggers actually denounced the whole hippie image as a "Love Hoax" and claimed the hip Haight merchants who perpetrated it were trying to mask "the overall grime of the Haight-Ashbury reality."[55] Many longtime habitués of the neighborhood blamed the notion of hippies on the media. Milan Melvin, who worked at San Francisco's first underground radio station, still snarls at the word. To him, hippies were the wannabes who flooded Haight-Ashbury when Scott McKenzie's insipid ode to the Emerald City, "San Francisco (Be Sure to Wear Some Flowers in Your Hair)" hit the charts just before June 1967's Monterey International Pop Festival. That song, he argues, "was the real last nail in the coffin. The squares were on the march, kicking down little old ladies' picket fences to get flowers in their hair so they could arrive dressed to the code described in the papers."[56]

The flower child wasn't invented out of whole cloth by the media, however. Reporters could always find young people who fit the profile easily enough. Chet Helms was among those willing to oblige reporters. Bob Simmons, who worked at Helms's Avalon Ballroom, recalls the press thinking Chet "looked 'just perfect.' Him in that Afghani leather jacket . . . preaching love, enlightenment, renaissance, etc. Mostly everyone just said, 'Go Chet, talk to the press, say what you want, just help keep the party going.'"[57] Meanwhile, journalists intent on hyping the hippie codified and popularized a caricature that kids then came looking to become. Before long, the myth was set in stone: hippies and beatniks were polar opposites. Whereas the beatniks were all doom and gloom, the hippies were all dopey optimism.

It was never that simple, though. Before the media descended on the Haight like an invading army, hippie and beatnik coexisted, one shading into the other. Both the underground and mainstream press used *hippie* and *beatnik* interchangeably until the spring of 1967. In fact, when *hippie* first appeared in the press in a September 1965 *San Francisco Examiner* article trumpeting Haight-Ashbury as "a sort of 'West Beach,'" the headline read, "A New Paradise For Beatniks."[58] In 1963 when David Crosby met Michael Clarke, with whom he later played in the Byrds, Clarke was driving around in an old mail van and carried a conga drum. This was "standard hippie gear, only this was before anybody was calling them hippies," Crosby recalls. "They were still beatniks."[59]

In a long essay on hippies in the *New York Times Magazine*, journalist Hunter S. Thompson acknowledged the nuanced connection between the two groups. Hippies, he reported, "reject any kinship with the Beat Generation on the ground that 'those cats were negative, but our thing is positive.' They also reject politics, which is 'just another game.' They don't like money, either, or any kind of aggressiveness." However, Thompson did note that if love was the "password" in the Haight, paranoia was the "style," and that the ex-beatniks in the love crowd saw hippies as "second-generation beatniks" rather than a "whole new breed."[60] Years later Jerry Garcia claimed greater affinity with the Beats: "the media portrait of the innocent hippie flower child was a joke. Hey, everybody knew what was happening. It wasn't *that* innocent. Our own background was sort of that deeply cynical beatnik space which evolved into something nicer with the advent of psychedelics."[61] Bob Seidemann puts it more starkly, "Fuck the Love Generation! That was bullshit, man. That was a scam. It was always a dark, eraserhead world."[62] Hippies might blather on to the press about peace and love—and, as Garcia and Seidemann suggest, this was sometimes a strategic deflection from what was actually happening—but it was the desire to "lay life," to live recklessly, that defined the Haight-Ashbury experience.[63]

Garcia and Seidemann saw the darkness, but the media was slow to see the "apocalyptic edge" of "what looked like a huge party in perpetual progress."[64] In fact, the media sometimes treated hippies like comic relief, a diversion from race riots, assassinations, and the horror of the ever-escalating war in Vietnam. But despite the talk of dropping out of straight America, there was no escaping the larger culture. For young unmarried men not enrolled in school, which was most of the Haight's male population, the draft and the nightmare of serving (and possibly dying) in the jungles of

Vietnam hung over their heads. And as the war heated up it became harder to avoid being drafted. Claiming you were gay or showing up at an induction center toothpick-thin, zonked out from drugs and lack of sleep—common strategies—didn't always work anymore.

Listening to the "hippie" music of the time, one hears almost as much dread and foreboding as flower-power goofiness. For every "Get Together," or "Wooden Ships" there's a song like the Buffalo Springfield's "For What It's Worth," with its memorable line: "Paranoia strikes deep/Into your heart it will creep."[65] Darby Slick's "Somebody to Love," which opens with the line "When the truth is found to be lies/and all the joy within you dies" doesn't sound much like a Love Generation tune. Nor does Country Joe and the Fish's antiwar anthem "Feel-Like-I'm-Fixing-to-Die Rag." When Grace Slick of the Jefferson Airplane sings "White Rabbit" it's not bubbly acid enthusiasm you hear in her voice, but something closer to menace. The musicians themselves were not always emissaries of peace and love either. Light show artist Joshua White remembers the first time he encountered the new bands at Toronto's O'Keefe Center in late 1967. "For us this show *was* the San Francisco Scene—the good vibes, the love—coming to Toronto. What came to Toronto, however, was an extremely unpleasant group of people known as the Jefferson Airplane and a very strange bunch of kinda hostile guys known as the Grateful Dead. And then there was the Headlights Light Show which was two guys who were fighting with each other."[66] It should have been obvious that, as Darby Slick puts it, there was a "darker side" to all this.[67]

Which is not to say that hippies were no different from beatniks. Even though Allen Ginsberg palled it up with the Pranksters and Neal Cassady actually drove their bus, not all the Beats were so enthralled. Kerouac, for one, walked out of the Prankster party Ginsberg and Cassady had taken him to. Kerouac didn't like the ear-splitting rock 'n' roll and he was offended that the young hipsters had draped an American flag across the back of a sofa. Kerouac walked away from the party, but not before rescuing the flag.[68] Poet Diane Di Prima moved easily in both bohemian worlds and wouldn't have been rattled by the Prankster party. But she maintains that these "were two different lineages. Those kids were raised softer than we were," not having "witnessed the blacklisting, the Rosenbergs, and the insanity of World War II. That's a different world."[69] To Kerouac, whose iconic status as America's best-known Beat brought him both painful opprobrium and debilitating celebrity, it wasn't just that the Pranksters' rebellion seemed superficial, rooted only in the pursuit of the outrageous, but that Kesey and company pulled it all off with such cocky confidence, as though they knew they'd get away with it.

Indeed, the Pranksters took chances the Beats never dared to take. Although both Beats and hippies were nomadic, on vacation from work and the consumption it subsidized, the Beats traveled unobtrusively, while the Pranksters advertised their weirdness as only those who feel untouchable can, crossing the country in a 1939 school bus, painted in a rainbow of Day-Glo colors. The Pranksters represented, in the words of Tom Wolfe, "something wilder and weirder out on the road."[70] If the Day-Glo paint didn't attract the cops, the words emblazoned on the bus—"Furthur" in front and "Caution: Weird Load" in back—did. Compared to the Beats, hippies seemed positively adolescent, or even younger. After all, it wasn't a car the Pranksters were driving but a school bus, the traditional site of childhood pranks. What better place for their public put-ons or "pranks"? The Beats had never felt the sense of immunity or limitless possibility that characterized the mid-sixties, however fleetingly. The Dead may have come out of a "cynical beatnik space," but they were drawn to the Beatles by their movies which Garcia described as "very high and very up." That, he said, "looked better than down and out."[71]

Race, sexuality, and gender played themselves out differently, too. For Beats, blacks had signified hipness; the new bohemians, whether out of choice or necessity (by the mid-sixties, black power was beginning to eclipse fantasies of integration), insisted on their own hipness—Kesey claimed to have "outniggered" blacks, as he put it.[72] Contrary to Tom Wolfe's claim, African Americans weren't completely irrelevant to the new bohemia, but neither did they occupy the central position they once had. The Diggers did stop by the Oakland headquarters of the Black Panther Party with a box of fish—sole, to be specific—and reportedly suggested that the party begin a breakfast program for kids.[73] However, there was virtually no connection between San Francisco's black community and white counterculture. And whereas the Beat scene had been, if anything, queer-inflected, the hippie counterculture was relentlessly straight, even homophobic. All the talk of free love brought lots of gay people to San Francisco, but the

Haight was "overwhelmingly heterosexual."[74] Timothy Leary even proclaimed LSD "a specific cure for homosexuality."[75] Even the more politically-minded Diggers harbored the same clichéd ideas about gay men as the larger culture. When Digger Emmett Grogan broke up a 1967 SDS meeting, he shouted at the startled group, "Faggots! Fags! . . . You haven't got the balls to go mad. You gonna make a revolution?—you'll piss in your pants when the violence erupts."[76]

Nor were relations between women and men quite the same as what had prevailed in the beatnik world. The Beat vision was explicitly masculine. Kerouac even claimed the "core" of the "Beat Generation" was "a swinging group of American men intent on joy."[77] By contrast, Kesey and company were sexist for sure, but coed. In fact, if the Beats were about escaping the family, hippies were about reconstituting it, in all its inequality. "Hippies treat their women like squaws," was reportedly the blunt assessment of the mother of the Grateful Dead's co-manager, Danny Rifkin.[78] Certainly, for women, the so-called sexual revolution was a mixed blessing. Women were having more sex (and with less guilt), but they were also more sexually vulnerable. Instead of undoing the deeply rooted sexual double standard, free love only masked it in countercultural pieties. Nor did hippie households pioneer an alternative to the traditional division of labor. Although many hippie guys managed to avoid nine-to-five jobs, few hippie girls avoided housework. Baking, cooking, sewing, tending the children were a "women's thing." As Bob Seidemann points out, relations between men and women in the Haight were "old timey," like the furniture. "The hippie ethos was a cartoon image of a woman making an apple pie and setting it on the windowsill while Dad, having toiled in the marijuana fields for the noble quest of selling pot, carefully folds it in plastic Baggies."[79] The Diggers were no better. The men talked ideas, wrote broadsides, and worked on cars while the women used their feminine wiles to wangle food out of the guys manning the produce stands and meat markets they cruised. Reflecting on those years, Peter Coyote admits that the gendered division of labor in the Diggers now "seems archaic, particularly for a visionary community."[80]

To Joan Didion, all the talk in the Haight about "the woman's trip"—her supposedly unique talent as housekeeper, mother, and all-purpose caretaker—seemed like nothing so much as Betty Friedan's "feminine mystique"; the sense of emancipation hippie women professed demonstrated, she argued, people's ability "to be the unconscious instruments of values they would strenuously reject on a conscious level."[81] In truth, most people in the Haight—women included—wouldn't have rejected sexism even had they been aware of its presence in their lives. When Travis Rivers, manager of Haight-Ashbury's psychedelic newspaper, the *Oracle*, proposed to his staff that the paper organize a roundtable discussion on women's issues with hip sex worker Margo St. James, poet Lenore Kandel, and Janis Joplin, "there ensued a huge fight and virtually the entire staff quit."[82] Writer and actor Carl Gottlieb believes the rigid gender roles clearly reflected "patriarchal" attitudes.[83] "The vast majority of women in that scene were subordinate to men," Seidemann admits, but they seemed more than happy to be that way. "The women all wanted children real bad. Get pregnant, have the kid, and hit the welfare office."[84] The women of the Haight were having sex with lots of different men and living in alternative families, but they were still expected, and many of them still wanted to be, pregnant and dependent. In this way, the counterculture was even less hospitable to ambitious, creative women than the older beatnik subculture where women could at least occasionally gain entry by acting like one of the guys.

ACID AND ROCK were transforming San Francisco's bohemia, but the elements came together hundreds of miles away at the Red Dog Saloon, a hip bar and restaurant that opened the summer of 1965 in Virginia City, Nevada.[85] The Red Dog was originally conceived as a folk nightclub that would book musicians traveling between coasts, but with San Francisco's first hippie rock band, the Charlatans, handling the music and Pine Streeters Bill Ham and Bob Cohen doing the light show, it became the first hippie rock saloon instead.[86] For baby boomers raised on a steady diet of Westerns, the Red Dog, which was modeled on the saloon in *Gunsmoke*, was a dream come true. The men outfitted themselves with guns and quick-draw outfits. For Cohen, who spent the whole summer there, it was "vanishing America. . . . This was the Wild West, a big fantasy world where you could be whoever you wanted to be." Mostly, people copped an old-timey look. "That's where all the fringe and the leather came from, which became such a big part of that whole hippie image," explains Cohen.[87]

When the summer ended, the Pine Street group (now calling themselves the Family Dog) returned to San Francisco. Inspired by the Red Dog, they decided to put on rock 'n' roll dances. No one wanted to give up dancing, which is one sign that the sixties were truly on—having fun and showing it were a clear break with the cool coffeehouse culture. Luria Castell suggested the Family Dog hold its dances in the meeting hall of the International Longshoremen's and Warehousemen's Union. Jim Haynie of the Mime Troupe says the choice "was kind of poetic in a way because of what [red-baited] Harry Bridges and the West Coast Longshoremen's Union represented—lefty philosophy and the working man, the working person. . . . We felt some poetry in being aligned with the most maligned people."[88] The Family Dog named its first dance "A Tribute to Dr. Strange" after the Marvel Comics character.[89] Alton Kelley designed the poster, which was plastered all over town. Bill Ham did the lights and the Great Society, the Charlatans, and the Jefferson Airplane all played. General admission was $2.50 and $2 for students.

Somewhere between four hundred and twelve hundred people showed up at the Longshoremen's Hall the night of October 16, 1965. That weekend fourteen thousand protestors from across the western states gathered to march on the Oakland induction center in the Bay Area's first big antiwar demonstration. Turned back by the police on the first day, and by the Hell's Angels on the second day, some of the protesters found their way to the Family Dog dance. Allen Ginsberg, who'd spoken at the march, was, like others, "astonished" by the "energy in the air and the number of strange people."[90] Alton Kelley remembers being "stunned by all the freaks who showed up. I didn't know there were that many freaks in town because we thought *we* were the cool guys."[91] The shock of recognition hit everyone. As he surveyed the crowd Chet Helms marveled, "They can't bust us all."[92] Darby Slick maintains everyone was overwhelmed with the "certainty of the birth of a scene."[93] Music critic Ralph Gleason wrote about the dance in his *San Francisco Chronicle* column, alerting more people to the emerging scene.[94]

The Family Dog envisioned its dances transforming San Francisco into "the American Liverpool," but despite its role in launching the scene, its members weren't around long enough to preside over the transformation.[95] The person who presided over San Francisco's transformation was Bill Graham, the business manager of the San Francisco Mime Troupe, and someone who knew nothing about rock or folk music. Graham was in charge of organizing a benefit for the troupe, which had just been busted for per-

forming in the park without a permit after the Parks Commission had can-
celed its permit for alleged obscenity. Graham's November 6th benefit happened right on the heels of the first Family Dog dance, and featured poet
Lawrence Ferlinghetti, The Committee, jazz saxophonist John Handy,
folksinger Sandy Bull, and two rock groups—the Jefferson Airplane and the
Fugs from New York. Almost four thousand people showed up at the Mime
Troupe's loft, which held only six hundred. Many people were turned away
at the door, but the troupe still took in $4,200 that night. The next benefit
was held at the much larger Fillmore in the heart of the black Fillmore district. The three benefits staged by Graham were the "towering cultural
events leading to Haight-Ashbury," according to Peter Berg of the Mime
Troupe. A real "cultural revolution." Robert Scheer, editor of the radical
magazine *Ramparts*, recalls driving up to the benefit on the back of Graham's motor scooter and finding "this fucking line going around the building. It was *incredible*. People were all around . . . We were saying things like,
'Wow! Wow!' Then Bill turned around on the motor scooter and said to me,
'*This* is the business of the future.'"[96]

Chet Helms, manager of the rock group Big Brother and the Holding
Company, saw the dollar signs, too, and soon opened up a smaller, funkier
dance hall, the Avalon Ballroom.[97] Helms's style was mellow hippie, whereas Graham, who was first and foremost a businessman, had a surfeit of what
some would call "negative energy." Despite their considerable differences,
Graham and Helms represented a new breed of rock promoters. Unlike
Dick Clark and Murray the K, whose teen cavalcade shows treated rock musicians like "pop plebes," they treated musicians like artists. Both Helms
and Graham put on eclectic shows, mixing popular hippie bands with R&B,
blues, or jazz acts little known to their young white audiences.

The way that Graham and Helms stumbled into rock promotion was typical of the San Francisco rock world of the mid-sixties. Just about everything in this scene was makeshift. Bands were often managed by friends
whose sole business experience, if they had any at all, was as smalltime
marijuana dealers. At first there was none of the extravagance that came to
characterize big-time rock 'n' roll—no limos, fancy hotels, or contract rid-
ers stipulating what brands of liquor, or kinds of food, or color of M&Ms
were required backstage. Of course, the performers were not in a position
to ask for much because they were amateurs themselves, folkies who had

little experience playing electric rock 'n' roll. Indeed, the bands were often accidental, the result of chance meetings and shared moments of stoned-out bliss. For better or for worse, they were committed to eclecticism and experimentation, drawing on everything from free-form jazz and jug band music to Indian ragas. To the extent there was a "San Francisco sound" it consisted of extended jamming and soloing. Even if the bands had wanted to perform tight, concise songs, they lacked the chops to do so. Blues and R&B aficionados were often offended by the sloppiness of their playing.[98] "The Dead could barely play 'In the Midnight Hour,'" griped blues player Steve Miller, "and they played it for 45 minutes."[99] But for San Francisco bands professionalism was viewed as an impediment to innovation.[100] "It was very hard to show anyone anything then," concedes Sam Andrew of Big Brother, Janis Joplin's band. "Everyone wanted to arrive at whatever it was by experimentation."[101]

Musicians like Andrew were a part of the Haight and it took a while before the audience deified them. "The music was the thing, not the musicians," says Jim Haynie, who managed the Fillmore for Bill Graham. "You knew the band and you dug the sound and you might even know some guys' names and stuff. But it wasn't like everybody was dying to meet them. You were going to hear the music." In fact, at this point, the audience could barely see the musicians. "There were no stage lights on the performers," according to Haynie. "We had one 750-watt ellipsoidal on the balcony that never moved and was one hundred feet away or something. It was *very* dim. All the light was from the light show spilling onto the stage."[102] Most musicians preferred to be shrouded in darkness. "You didn't want spotlights," says Bill Belmont, who later road managed Country Joe and the Fish.[103] San Francisco bands preferred light shows to bright lights because they were unwilling or unable to provide any visual stimulation. "The musicians barely did anything," according to New York light show artist Joshua White. "They just played, and often with their backs to the audience. They would tune and tune and tune between songs. No one wanted to do a slick show. Anyone who did a really tight show in that very modest period of time— about two years—was considered slick and not authentic."[104] Musicians counted themselves part of the community, not entertainers. In fact, pulling the musicians off the dance floor and getting them on stage could be tough.

The scene was primitive and funky, with none of the big money and glitz that would soon come to characterize rock music. Which is not to say that the San Francisco rock world was an Edenic community of equals beyond the reach of commerce. The musicians might have mixed with the audience, but they were set off by an aura of superior hipness. Nor were they indifferent to money. Paul Kantner of the Jefferson Airplane got into rock 'n' roll because, he says, "some of my friends were making five thousand a night as the Byrds."[105] None of the bands—not even the Dead, whose scraggly, scowling keyboardist, Pigpen, was always scaring off record companies—was opposed to making money. The bands wanted high-paying gigs and lucrative recording contracts, but they didn't want to go the show business route. Show business—its crassness, insincerity, and indifference to the artistic— was the enemy. San Francisco musicians weren't going to churn out two-and-a-half minute bubblegum hits to please record companies and radio programmers; nor were they going to tone down their style so they could appear on *American Bandstand* or be featured in *Sixteen* magazine. They were auteurs, not crowd-pleasing entertainers. When Bill Graham suggested that the Airplane go back onstage and give a bow after a spectacular three-hour performance, Paul Kantner snarled, "Fuck that. That's show business."[106]

DESPITE THEIR HOSTILITY to show business, by late 1966 the San Francisco bands were generating some buzz in the music business. But with the exception of the Jefferson Airplane, whose "Somebody to Love" was the number three single in the nation by June 1967, the bands had not broken out nationally. Everything changed with June 1967's Monterey International Pop Festival. Woodstock grabbed all the headlines two years later, but Monterey, which was attended by anywhere from 55,000 to 90,000 people, was a landmark, the festival that made the "San Francisco sound" and signaled that what was happening on the streets of Haight-Ashbury was going national. America was turning. Otis Redding performed there and marveled at the scene: "They're smoking dope and shit like it's *legal* out here."[107] For Redding and many others, the scene at Monterey looked like nothing short of a "cultural revolution."[108] Although Redding, Jimi Hendrix, Janis Joplin, and the Who gave knockout performances that weekend, the real star of the festival was the San Francisco scene—its music, light shows, and groovy vibe.

Monterey Pop lasted only three days, but its reverberations were still being felt years later. The whole rock juggernaut—not just Woodstock—had its origins in the festival.[109] Within months Jann Wenner launched *Rolling Stone* magazine, featuring, ironically, a cover story lambasting the festival's promoters for lining their own pockets. Record companies that had scorned rock 'n' roll as music that "smells but sells," now courted rock musicians and made *Rolling Stone* required reading for their executives.[110] An especially "happy accident" for the music industry, Monterey Pop spawned "the next billion dollar business," in the words of rock critic Robert Christgau.[111] In 1962, record sales totaled $500 million; by 1996 they grossed over 20 billion, largely on the basis of rock 'n' roll.[112] Until this shift, rock musicians, however popular, were the "low guys on the totem pole," who earned far less money than what they made for others. On tour, rock acts had been consigned to the world of lousy flat rates, while "class" acts like Danny Thomas and Harry Belafonte received 60 percent of the gross, always a more lucrative arrangement. As rock music became more lucrative, booking agents began bucking the system whereby rock was "subsidizing the Thomases and Belafontes." They started demanding 60 percent for the rock acts they represented, not the standard $5,000 flat fee that rock bands received.[113] No longer the "asshole" of the entertainment industry, rock musicians were now in a better position to negotiate with record companies and promoters, and to make money for themselves.[114]

As soon as the San Francisco sound became commercially viable, left-leaning rock journalists began questioning whether the music business wasn't co-opting the Haight-Ashbury rock underground. Within a year of Monterey, critic Christgau complained that "art and social commentary were absorbed, almost painlessly, by the world's schlockiest business." Citing as evidence a trade journal's review of a new single as " 'a highly commercial rock allegory of perishing society,'" he groused, "apparently, society itself would perish before the record industry."[115] Humorist Cynthia Heimel recalls the time in June 1967 that she and her hippie friends spied a press kit for Moby Grape, one of the new San Francisco bands. "It looked psychedelic, yet it was done by ad people. I believe the word 'hype' was coined that very day."[116]

Sixties rockers' refusal of show business and their position within the counterculture led some writers to conclude that the musicians had set out to change the world and were co-opted and transformed instead. However, the commercial takeover of the new rock wasn't the straightforward assault that myth has made of it. The co-optation thesis both exaggerates the bands' hostility to the music industry and minimizes the significance of the cultural revolt wrought by sixties rock musicians.[117] San Francisco bands promoted sex, drugs, and rock 'n' roll and saw themselves as an alternative to AM teenybopper fare, but they were never averse to making money, much less at war with capitalism. In 1967 Bob Weir of the Dead told a reporter that "If the industry is gonna want us, they're gonna take us the way we are. Then, if the money comes in, it'll be a stone gas."[118] Once the money began coming in—and it did for many of the bands—they did what successful performers have always done—they bought fancy cars and expensive homes. The Jefferson Airplane even became flaks for Levi's jeans, though the company's labor practices had come under attack.

The bands may have allowed themselves to be "swallowed by the voracious maw of corporate America," but they nonetheless transformed the country's cultural landscape in the process.[119] The Airplane's manager Bill Thompson recalls the band's gig at Grinnell College's homecoming dance. It was the fall of 1966, and there they were in Iowa: "All the girls were in ruffled dresses all the way down to the ankles with corsages, and their *families* were there. We started the light show and we had three sets to do that night. The first set, it was like we were from Mars. Guys with haircuts like Dobie Gillis were standing there and staring at us." The parents ducked out early, and by the second set "people started dancing a little bit. . . . The third set, people went *nuts*. Off came the corsages. Shoes were coming off. Guys were ripping off their ties. They went *nuts*. It was one of the greatest feelings I ever had. It was like the turning of America in a way. We went out and played everywhere and did that. We were the first band to do that out of San Francisco."[120]

Certainly Janis Joplin saw herself as a cultural provocateur. "Kids from the Midwest, their whole fucking thing is to sit in row Q47 and be still . . . It's never occurred to them that they could *not* go in the army. You know, it's a thing I do . . . If you can get them once, man, get them standing up when they should be sitting down, sweaty when they should be decorous . . . I think you sort of switch on their brain, man, so that makes them say: 'Wait a minute, maybe I can do anything.'"[121] Joplin understood the irony of her situation and relished exploiting it. "People aren't supposed to be like me, sing like me, make out like me, drink like me, live like me; but now they're paying me $50,000 a year for me to be like me. That's what I hope I mean to those kids out there. After they see me, when their mothers are feeding them all that cashmere sweater and girdle ___ [expletive deleted by the *New York Times*], maybe they'll have a second thought—that they can be themselves and win."[122] If the groups didn't manage, or for that matter, set out to overthrow corporate America, they encouraged American youth to entertain that second thought.

HAIGHT-ASHBURY WAS still an insider's secret through much of 1966, but January 1967's Human Be-In solidified its reputation as the capital of weirdness. An effort to unite Bay Area politicos and hippies, the Be-In drew anywhere from ten to twenty thousand people and countless reporters. Almost all the San Francisco rock bands played and speakers included Allen Ginsberg, who chanted, Lenore Kandel, who read from her recently censored poems, *The Love Book*, Timothy Leary, and Berkeley activist Jerry Rubin. The Be-In was widely reported, and some, like longtime boho clothes designer Linda Gravenites, think it marked a watershed, the moment when the Haight turned from a spontaneous expression of the counterculture to a hyped-up caricature. By focusing exclusively on sex, drugs, and rock 'n' roll, the press, many say, pretty much determined what the nature of the Haight would be. "Up until then people came because they were full to overflowing, and were sharing their fullness," Gravenites contends. "After that, it was the empties who came, wanting to be filled."[123]

Once the Haight was flooded with reporters and lost kids, the community began unraveling. The Haight's "renegades, outlaws, misfits, and dropouts" as photographer Bob Seidemann called them, made for a volatile brew. "A cauldron," he says, "that's what this society was."[124] Moreover, the Haight was an interracial neighborhood bordering the black Fillmore district, and tension escalated as it filled up with middle-class young white kids renouncing the nice homes, good schools, and well-paying jobs that remained out of the reach of most blacks. Of course, drugs added to the destabilization. Hippies defended marijuana and psychedelics as mind-expanding "life" drugs, but mind-numbing "death" drugs, such as heroin, speed, and barbiturates, were around the Haight from the beginning, too.[125] Over time, the drug scene got uglier. As journalist Charles Perry points out, the Haight taught many people, especially the Hell's Angels, "that there was a lot of money in the dope trade."[126] In fact, one reason good relations often obtained between Angels and hippies was that the bikers were an important drug connection, especially for grass and speed. Within a few years, the Angels forced many smaller dealers in the Haight out of business. In 1972, California's attorney general concluded that the bikers were actually a huge dope ring; the U.S. Customs Service guessed that the group had shipped thirty-one million dollars worth of drugs to the East Coast since 1969.[127]

Ken Kesey had inaugurated the relationship between freaks and the Angels, perhaps in an effort to demonstrate the transformative power of acid, or maybe just to out-hip everyone else. ("We're in the same business," Kesey told the Angels. "You break people's bones, I break people's heads.")[128] In any case, relations grew a lot cozier between freaks and Angels in Haight-Ashbury, with the Dead and Big Brother leading the way. Janis Joplin insisted that the cover of Big Brother's 1968 album *Cheap Thrills* bear the Angels' emblem and the words: "Approved by Hell's Angels Frisco."[129] The Angels dropped acid, but the counterculture's faith that LSD would transform them into cuddly teddy bears was, more often than not, misplaced. Artist Jack Jackson recalls "biker guys taking acid and smashing heads. It was like climbing in bed with Hitler." Radical journalist Warren Hinckle of *Ramparts* magazine cautioned that the Haight-Ashbury ethos of dropping out, while fun, would "leave the driving to the Hell's Angels."[130]

But politico Hinckle wasn't part of the counterculture, and at the time, people on the inside who were troubled by the Angels were reluctant to voice their concerns lest they be branded uptight and unhip. One defense mounted on the Angels' behalf was that the real villain was large-scale, state-sponsored terror. Poet Michael McClure, for example, argued that President Lyndon Johnson, who was escalating the war in Vietnam, was more evil than a bunch of guys on bikes who express the violence that most of us would rather deny.[131] McClure and Diggers Peter Coyote and Emmet Grogan hung out with the Angels and insisted that the bikers had to be judged individually, not as a group.[132] Yet the Angels, whatever their individual talents, acted as a group. People were killed and women raped, all on the orders of the club. "I can only believe it was the fascination the weak feel for the strong," suggests musician Bob Brown. "Maybe there was some sense that the Establishment had their cops, their thugs, and now we had ours."[133] Except that the Angels often behaved like thugs with hippies, too. Bruce Barthol of Country Joe and the Fish remembers a gig where the Angels handled security. "Their method of clearing the stage was to push people off it. One guy took a bottle and smashed a girl's head with it."[134] Defended as outlaws, the Angels were conservative, even racist. But many of the Haight's musicians and freaks continued to consort with them even after 1969's Altamont rock festival where an Angel stabbed and stomped to death a black man who had drawn a gun.

If the Be-In destabilized Haight-Ashbury, the Summer of Love sent it reeling as many more "empties" flocked to the neighborhood. Rock music didn't make San Francisco, as the Jefferson Starship later boasted in "We Built This City," but rock did make it the capital of hipness. However, this was an honor that veterans of the Haight would have gladly palmed off on any other city during 1967's disastrous Summer of Love. That spring, the crowds in the Haight had grown so thick—and progressively thicker every weekend—that people realized the neighborhood was on the cusp of a much larger influx. The Diggers predicted a hundred thousand newcomers would descend on the district that summer, and along with the Straight Theater, the Oracle, and the Family Dog, they formed the Council for the Summer of Love to organize celebratory events and serve as a liaison to the straight world. The coming invasion of kids also prompted entrepreneurs to convert anything and everything into Love Cafés and Love Burger stands. In a one-month period, immediately after Monterey Pop, fifteen storefronts either changed hands or changed their names to capitalize on the hippie craze.[135] In April, the Gray Line Bus Company began its "Hippie Hop Tour," advertising it as "the only foreign tour within the continental limits of the United States."[136] Pete Townshend of the Who visited the Haight around the time of Monterey and was surprised and saddened by how thoroughly commercialized the area had become.[137]

Increasingly, the crowds at the Fillmore and the Avalon neither knew or cared about the origins of the scene. They cared only about the music. The Red Dog Saloon and Ken Kesey's Acid Tests were largely forgotten. Less than two years after the original 1965 benefits, the Fillmore held another dance for the San Francisco Mime Troupe. "Some of the musicians remembered us from the old days," said its founder Ronny Davis, "but the new rock fans . . . knew the bands but not the Mime Troupe." He tried addressing the audience, but "it was like speaking into a cotton candy machine."[138] By the Summer of Love, the scene had changed, growing, as Ken Kesey observed, "tighter and stranger."[139]

Seventy-five thousand kids spent their summer vacation in the Haight, and by summer's end, "Haight Street was lined with people with problems," wrote *Village Voice* reporter Don McNeil. "Behind the scenes, there were only more problems."[140] The streets of the Haight were "griseous and filthy, psychedelic weirdburger stands springing up in mutant profusion," wrote Ed Sanders in his book about Charles Manson. It was "like a valley of thousands of plump white rabbits surrounded by wounded coyotes."[141] A community that had relied upon long hair and weed as badges of authenticity and cool, found itself vulnerable to the faux-hippie con artists flooding into the neighborhood and other hip enclaves across America. "There was a six month period," recalled folksinger Arlo Guthrie, "when you could look down the street and you could tell who was your friend and who wasn't . . . You knew who had a roach on him . . . but soon after you had guys who looked exactly like you sellin' you *oregano*."[142] Oregano was the least of it: bad drugs, stickups, rape, and venereal disease were increasingly common in Haight-Ashbury. The downward mobility of white hippies further fueled the neighborhood's racial tension. "You could see this animosity developing," remembers Seidemann, who thinks blacks' anger toward white kids of the Haight was aggravated by hippies' deliberately mellow stance. "No matter how uptight and freaked blacks got at the hippies, all they got back was, 'Yeah, brother, peace, love, shit, I can dig it, power to the people.' So it was like yelling at silly putty." Before long, "blacks began showing up on Haight Street and they weren't looking like Jimi Hendrix," Seidemann says. "They were looking like bad guys."[143] And there were the cops, who increasingly made their presence felt in the neighborhood. In early October they began making daily sweeps of Haight Street to pick up runaways.[144] Around the same time, the police busted the Grateful Dead's house on 710 Ashbury Street.[145]

Before long the old Haight habitués either fled or stayed indoors. "Uh oh, the street people have become the house people," Raechel Donahue, a KMPX deejay, recalls her husband Tom saying.[146] The Dead began moving away soon after the bust. Even Janis Joplin, who had loved walking through the neighborhood and hearing the whispers and shouts of recognition, found it unlivable and moved out in early 1968. The Haight's swift and precipitous decline came as something of a shock. To many, the Summer of Love stood as a cautionary tale about the perils of publicity and hype. In fact, in October 1967, some veteran freaks staged a "Death of the Hippie" ceremony. About eighty people showed up for the event, where they urged people to move past the media construction of the "hippie," and become free men instead. However, skeptics charged that the protest reeked of "the same media crap as the Be-In and the Summer of Love."[147] In the end, the story of Haight-Ashbury demonstrated the wrongheadedness of Timothy Leary's mantra, "turn on, tune in, drop out." Where had dropping out gotten the counterculture but the blinding glare of the media, the reification of "hippie," and the ruination of the Haight? The limitations of the drop-out philosophy, especially in the context of heightened police presence, broke down some of the counterculture's aversion to political protest. And the repression of hippie communities also led some politicos to reconsider their earlier dismissal of the "hippy-dippy" counterculture. "A blending of pot and politics . . . a cross-fertilization of the hippie and New Left philosophies," was how leftists Abbie Hoffman and Jerry Rubin and the other leaders of Yippie (Youth International Party) characterized their new group in late 1967.[148]

As the Haight lay in shambles its rock bands simply pulled up stakes and escaped, usually to that "outpost of Nirvana," Marin County.[149] The growing gulf between musicians and the larger counterculture was illustrated by conditions at Woodstock, the 1969 rock festival where the audience was mired in the mud without adequate food while the stars, who stayed dry and dined on steaks and champagne at the Holiday Inn and the Howard Johnson, were helicoptered in and out of the festival site. These stark differences spoke to the distance traveled in the two short years since Monterey Pop, where the line separating performers from audience was still permeable. In the era's lore, Woodstock has become synonymous with the "good sixties," with the beautiful people of the counterculture, while Altamont, the Rolling Stone's free concert just four months later, has come to stand for the decade's underside and the end of all that was hopeful in the hippie subculture. A hastily thrown together open-air concert at a speedway on the outskirts of San Francisco, Altamont reeked of bad vibes as the Angels, who'd been hired to handle security, ran amuck, beating up people at will.[150] Altamont, which occurred fittingly in the last month of the decade, came to symbolize the final gasp of the sixties, but it was Woodstock that put an end to the era which had begun with the Family Dog dances and Mime Troupe benefits.

The lesson of Woodstock for managers and musicians alike was the wisdom of playing one big gig rather than several smaller gigs; ironically, the festival sounded the death knell for electric ballrooms, the cultural spaces that had made Woodstock possible. "Before Woodstock the Jefferson Airplane still played four shows at the Fillmore East and earned $12,000," recalls light show artist Joshua White. "Only really big acts—the Stones and the Doors—played Madison Square Garden. After Woodstock many more played the Garden. I knew—everybody on that stage at Woodstock knew—the future wasn't in rock theaters. The future was in arenas—big, spectacle shows—and the musicians were going to start doing grander acts." Six months after the festival, White left his light show company to start a video projection business. "One of the reasons I got hired was that the bands playing these arenas felt a little guilty. And so they would make up to their audience for playing one show in a 20,000-seat arena by paying me $14,000 to project them up on a giant 20' by 30' screen."[151] The new rock music was already a commodity before Woodstock, but the festival accelerated the process of commercialism by suggesting to corporate executives how they could reap untold profits off of rock and the larger generation gap.

IN WOODSTOCK'S AFTERMATH, radical activist Todd Gitlin asked "whether the youth culture will leave anything behind but a market."[152] His was a question that even some San Francisco musicians may have asked themselves several years later when their careers were stalled and the ballrooms that had nourished their music were shuttered, the victims of stadium rock. Over time, there was no ignoring that the counterculture in many ways did devolve into a market. Peter Coyote never repudiated his past, but he admitted that the Digger philosophy of life-acting "was diluted into the weak tea of *lifestyle*," which in turn "came to mean *spend* any way you choose."[153] And Carol Brightman, a political radical who came much later in life to an appreciation of the counterculture, observed that the "formlessness and chaos" of the '60s led to a "new order," not just in places like the Haight, but in America's corporate boardrooms as well.[154] "All those basement leather shops, hippie massage parlors, tie-dye vats—even Stewart Brand's *Whole Earth Catalog*—were seedbeds for growth industries to come."[155] One could add to that list funky food co-ops, which paved the way for all those pricey and profitable health food emporiums.[156]

But all sixties movements found their rebellion appropriated by capitalists on the lookout for new markets to exploit, new lifestyles to sell. To dismiss these movements because they proved evanescent or were partially absorbed by the dominant culture loses sight of the challenges they once posed. Rock critic Simon Frith is critical of those gloomy, "told-you-so" leftist accounts of youth culture's co-optation. "The exhilaration, the sense of change and purpose, the emotional underpinnings of the experience of liberation are dismissed as fraudulent because of what happened next."[157] Moreover, what happened next was sometimes more than further commodification. As he points out, the counterculture "survives in important interstices of youth and leisure culture." The process of recuperation is also hard work, and doesn't always succeed in stripping ideas entirely of their original meaning. Judy Goldhaft of the Diggers points to the time that the line "Today is the first day of the rest of your life," which had appeared in a Digger broadside, showed up a year later in an ad for a San Francisco bank. Even in the context of a bank ad, the idea still contained a transformative truth, according to Goldhaft.[158] Cultural critic Ellen Willis goes further, arguing that leftist accounts that emphasize the "essential harmony" of corporate and countercultural interests fail to see that "cultural radicalism, with its celebration of freedom and pleasure and its resistance to compulsive, alienated work, is always a potential threat to the corporate system, however profitable its music, art and favored technological toys may be."[159]

It was precisely the counterculture's hedonism that troubled many politicos. Being political didn't preclude sex, drugs, and rock 'n' roll, but it sometimes did require subordinating the self to the larger cause, and this was at odds with the "laissez-faire libertarianism" that prevailed in the counterculture.[160] This is an important difference, but it shouldn't obscure what the counterculture shared with the political movement: the same restless and reckless energy that embraced life on the edge. Growing up in the fifties starved for stimulation, connection, and meaning, activists and hippies turned their backs on the cautious lives of their parents. Nothing defines the generation that came of age in the sixties better than its determination to live outside the parameters of reasonable behavior, which, after all, seemed at the very root of the problem, the cause of America's terrible adventure shortage. People in the counterculture may have had more fun in their pursuit of intensity than those in politics, but they, too, tested themselves and risked their lives. Bob Seidemann admits to having had "fun and a lot of laughs," in the sex-drugs-and-rock 'n' roll world of Haight-Ashbury, but he insists, "It wasn't a party. It was very intense and people were dying among us and all around us. It was exciting to be there because you were literally on the cutting edge, but you *were* the edge of the sword doing the cutting. . . . We all laid our bodies on the line," he ventures.[161]

"Put your body on the line" was a slogan sixties radicals often invoked to inspire themselves and others to greater acts of resistance. "There's a time when the operation of the machine becomes so odious, makes you so sick at heart, that you can't take part," declared Mario Savio of Berkeley's Free Speech Movement in 1964. "And you've got to put your bodies upon the gears and upon the wheels, upon the levers, upon all the apparatus and you've got to make it stop."[162] Hippies and activists often occupied different worlds but they were all involved in high-risk experimentation, often with the self the site of experimentation. To Ken Kesey and the Merry Pranksters, whose Acid Tests helped ignite the counterculture, the goal was simply "Furthur," as their Day-Glo bus proclaimed. Or as one survivor put it, "the feeling then was, if you've got a light, burn it out."[163] As the war escalated and the repression of radicals intensified at home, the Movement moved "from protest to resistance," and in the process plenty of politicos ended up making bombs of their lives. Huey Newton of the Black Panthers advocated "revolutionary suicide" and Weatherman, an SDS splinter group, took up political terror.

Excess was part of the reckless, "superhypermost" sixties life, and some people did succeed in extinguishing their light altogether.[164] Certainly drugs "cut a big swath" through the counterculture and the world of sixties rock.[165] Everyone knows the big names—Jimi Hendrix, Janis Joplin, and Jim Morrison—but there were so many more losses, including those who ended up in hospitals, halfway houses, or on the streets. Between 1965 and 1975 Peter Coyote lost eighteen friends, many of them to drugs and dope deals gone sour. His fellow Digger Emmett Grogan's OD in a subway car at the end of the line in America's first playground, Coney Island, seemed eerily appropriate. Darby Slick had been among the first San Francisco rockers to use heroin, and years later he'd write, "This was our Vietnam, the Battle of the Brain Cells, and drugs were the weapons and the transport ships, the airplanes, and people were the weapons too."[166] In 1977 novelist Philip K. Dick, who had been addicted to amphetamines, wrote of drugs as a "dreadful war," one whose losses he doubted the larger culture would ever fully comprehend or acknowledge.[167]

The losses, especially because they've been condemned rather than understood or mourned, make it hard to claim the pleasure, the exhilaration, and the revelations that can come from drugs and life lived close to the edge. But, as Carol Brightman argues, to deny that pleasure erases a large chunk of the sixties. She writes of biker-turned-drug-counselor Skip Workman's reaction upon seeing an old clip of Janis Joplin on TV. He had to fight the impulse to get high because he was so overcome by "the music and the memories" as he watched her sing. "How are you going to tell the kids about that?" he asks. "You can't lie to 'em and say you didn't have a good time."[168] Writer Carl Gottlieb admits that some of his friends regret the take-it-to-the-limit lives they led in the sixties, but he doesn't share their regret. "If you survived, you had a chance to experience things at a level most people only dream about," he says. "I cherish those memories, and I know I put my life in danger a few times."[169]

Of course, excess did play a role in the unraveling of both these sixties movements. Opposition to the country's knee-jerk anticommunism led to a foolhardy romanticizing of Third World revolutionary governments and movements. Laissez-faire libertarianism sanctioned the use of all kinds of drugs. The celebration of the outlaw encouraged the counterculture's love affair with the Angels and politicos' blind veneration of the Black Panthers. But I would argue that the excesses of the sixties functioned in a more insidious fashion as well. The Viet Cong flags, the militant rhetoric, the turn to violence, like the outrageous hair, clothes, drugs, and music, blinded rebels and observers alike to the ways that both movements failed to break through many of the conventions and customs of mainstream America. The sheer outrageousness of hippies and radical activists masked how tied both groups were to the dominant culture, particularly as regards gender and homosexuality. And by decade's end, young women, inspired by the go-for-broke risktaking and antiauthoritarianism of cultural and political radicals but angry at the old-timey gender relations that prevailed in both groups, would come together to form the sixties' most far-reaching social movement—women's liberation.

2

THE IKE AGE: RETHINKING THE 1950S

"TEENAGERS ARE LIKE AIRPLANES," explained President Dwight Eisenhower, "you only hear about the ones that crash."[1] Ike's airplane analogy, designed to avert a national panic about juvenile delinquency, may apply to decades, too. Certainly America's crash-and-burn decade, the sixties, continues to haunt us some forty years later. The front burner issues of the last few years—welfare reform, abortion, affirmative action, gay and lesbian rights, and the so-called culture wars—always manage to provoke yet another round of fighting about those tumultuous years. So have Bill Clinton and his entire triangulated presidency, particularly in the wake of Monicagate. Christian Coalition founder Pat Robertson spoke for many on the Right when he excoriated Clinton as "the poster child of the 1960s."[2] Clinton's transgressions fall far short of the prodigious proportions required of that era's legendary poster children—think Jimi Hendrix, Abbie Hoffman, and Janis Joplin. But despite his fondness for Kenny G and his apparent reluctance to go all the way either with a joint or Ms. Lewinsky, Clinton is indisputably a boomer.

Opportunistic politicians and finger-wagging political pundits aren't the only ones obsessed with the sixties.[3] Each year has brought a new crop of documentaries and memoirs that attempt to unravel the mysteries of that decade. Even among tweedy historians, who usually believe that the dustier the past the better, the sixties has overshadowed the fifties. Colleges routinely offer courses on the period, a distinction not bestowed on most other

---

This essay is a revised version of "Fiftiesomething," which appeared in the September 20, 1994, issue of the *Village Voice*.

decades—not the apparently dull and empty fifties, and certainly not the seventies, that seemingly shallow decade of polyester, promiscuity, and disco.

However, the tide seems to be turning as some scholars have taken to arguing against the idea that the sixties was an exceptional decade.[4] Historian Thomas Sugrue, for one, contends that we "misread other decades if we focus on the sixties as this moment of rupture or apocalypse," and proposes that we study the postwar period as a whole.[5] He argues, for example, that the race riots of the '60s grew out of job discrimination, housing practices, and deindustrialization that date back to the forties and fifties. And others have pointed out that the fifties was not exactly a time of cultural and political quiescence. After all, the fifties mark the beginning of meaningful dissent as the civil rights movement (and rock 'n' roll) took on the politics of Jim Crow, and the Beats challenged the country's craven materialism and its worship of bureaucratic rationality.

Most of this revisionist history concerns the "Ike Age," although conservative historian David Frum has recently argued that the seedbed of much that's wrong with the country—hedonism, the erosion of civility and decline in literacy—was the 1970s, not the 1960s.[6] Historians Casey Blake and Ken Cmeil don't share Frum's right-wing politics, but they agree that our lives today are more affected by the seventies than the sixties.[7] As proof, they point to such seventies phenomena as the growing cynicism about public institutions, the emergence of postmodernism in the arts, homelessness, the deinstitutionalization of mental patients, and the birth of both the New Right and the gay rights movement. I would include disco, which despite its low cultural standing helped give birth to today's most popular music—rap, house, electronica, and techno.

The shift away from sixties exceptionalism may seem like a recent trend—the *New York Times* spotted it only last year—but for some time now scholars have been questioning the tendency to treat the period as though it were utterly anomalous and disconnected from the fifties. In fact, the first studies to chip away at the foundation of sixties exceptionalism appeared in the mid-eighties, almost ten years before the publication of David Halberstam's best-selling tome *The Fifties* and that other great cultural marker—The Gap's rehabilitation of khaki.[8]

What follows is my ambivalent reaction to this revisionist literature. Much of this work effectively debunks the idea that the fifties can be summarily dismissed as America's "Dark Ages," a wasteland of hula hoops, panty raids, and poodle skirts. However, it sometimes overstates the extent of continuity across decades. Take the case of Janis Joplin. She might have ended up the Port Arthur schoolteacher of her mother's dreams had the Beats and the folk revival of the fifties not held out other possibilities, but her unlikely success, her transformation from misfit rebel to rock superstar, speaks volumes about the seismic changes that rocked America in the 1960s.

SOCIOLOGIST ALDON MORRIS was among the first to challenge the idea that the sixties began on February 1, 1960, at the Woolworth's counter in Greensboro, North Carolina. Morris's 1984 book, *The Origins of the Civil Rights Movement*, argued that the movement was not a spontaneous eruption, but rather the result of determined organizing stretching back to the late forties. Even Rosa Parks, whose defiance of Jim Crow laws sparked the Montgomery bus boycott, was an experienced NAACP activist, and not, as legend has it, some "quiet, dignified older lady" who'd simply "had enough."[9] Likewise, John D'Emilio's 1983 monograph, *Sexual Politics, Sexual Communities* revealed the ways that fifties homophile activists paved the way for the gay and lesbian liberationists of the '70s, though he was careful to admit the "glaring and undeniable" differences between pre- and post-Stonewall activists.[10]

In the prodigiously researched *If I Had a Hammer*, Maurice Isserman locates the organizational and intellectual roots of the New Left in Max Schachtman's Young People's Socialist League, the crowd at Irving Howe's journal *Dissent*, and the radical-pacifist groups led by A. J. Muste. Isserman goes so far as to contend that the New Left emerged from the old left "in ways that made it difficult to perceive exactly where the one ended and the other began."[11] Isserman has unearthed a fascinating range of left activism and writing in these years. As James Miller and Todd Gitlin have argued, some of the ideas put forward by the New Left were first advanced by C. Wright Mills, Dwight MacDonald, and Paul Goodman. But most old leftists had limited appeal to new leftists chasing a political high. Who needed the *Dissent* crowd's tired defeatism masquerading as sober realism, or their knee-jerk anticommunism? Although the rift between the old and new left widened considerably during the decade, substantial differences existed from the beginning. There's no better example than the tensions between the sixties' leading New Left group, Students for a Democratic Society (SDS), and its parent organization, the economistic League for Industrial Democracy (LID), which are ably documented by Isserman. The fact that the LID board paid no attention to the "values" section of SDS's 1962 Port Huron Statement—the meat of the document, at least in author Tom Hayden's view—suggests the magnitude of the generational divide. To SDSers like Gitlin, LID was nothing more than a "musty relic of a bygone past." In fact, SDSers took to calling their parent group the *lid*.[12]

Isserman's own evidence suggests that old leftists failed in their efforts to clone themselves, or even to influence appreciably the new generation of activists. Indeed, the old left's most lasting contribution to the New Left was probably negative. The old left's rigid anticommunism put SDS on a "political trajectory leading first toward anti-anti-communism," writes Isserman, "and then onward toward an identification with Third World Communist movements and governments."[13] Isserman is understandably critical of this development, but he fails to adequately acknowledge the extent to which anticommunism had become, as Alan Wald argues, "an ideological mask for discrediting movements for radical social change and supporting the status quo."[14]

Just as Isserman looked for the connections between old and new leftists, so have feminist scholars searched for the roots of second-wave feminism in organizations like the stubbornly elitist National Women's Party and the early sixties pacifist group, Women Strike for Peace. In *Survival in the Doldrums*, historian Leila Rupp and sociologist Verta Taylor argue for the connection between famous suffragist Alice Paul's organization, the National Women's Party, and the women's liberation movement that arose in the late sixties. As evidence, Rupp and Taylor point to second-wave feminists' enthusiastic support for the Equal Rights Amendment, which the NWP had been fighting for since the 1920s.[15] Although the liberal feminists of NOW did come to embrace the ERA once unionists were won over, many younger women, especially radical and socialist feminists, initially opposed the reform. Rather than reform a social order built on racial, class, and gender inequality, rather than seek an equal piece of an inherently unequal pie, feminists, they argued, ought to dismantle the system altogether. In fact, some women's liberationists went so far as to denounce woman suffrage,

which had been won in 1920, as a "sop" for women, designed to buy them off
and shut them up. The women of the NWP were appalled by younger feminists' breezy dismissal of suffrage. And they were mystified by younger
women's concern with private life, especially their preoccupation with sexual pleasure. How could orgasms possibly matter as much as the ERA?

The NWP was not particularly effective in the years before feminism's
revival, but the same wasn't true of Women Strike for Peace. Historian Amy
Swerdlow argues that WSP not only nudged public opinion in favor of 1963's
partial test ban treaty, but also inflicted permanent damage on the Red
hunters of HUAC.[16] Most of the women in WSP had been liberals, radicals,
or pacifists in the 1940s, but they crafted a very different image: apolitical
housewives. Trading on their image as concerned mothers, the group not
only pulled off the largest national women's peace protest of the twentieth
century, involving 50,000 women in sixty communities, they also made a
brilliant end run around the anti-Communism and the antifeminism of the
period. WSP mainstreamed pacifism so successfully that within a year of its
November 1961 demonstration the House Committee on Un-American Activities (HUAC) decided to investigate the organization for possible Communist infiltration. From the very first day of the hearings, however, the
mild-mannered, well-dressed women of WSP had the Congressmen wish-
ing they had left the group alone. With the committee solemnly asking wit-
nesses questions like, "Did you wear a colored paper daisy to identify yourself as a member of the Women Strike for Peace?" HUAC became a joke.
Asked if she would permit Communists in the group, WSPer Dagmar Wilson
giggled and explained she had no control over who joined their demonstrations, but added, "I would like to say that unless everybody in the whole
world joins us in this fight, then God help us." Confounded by WSP's studied guilelessness and unassailable motherist politics, HUAC emerged from
the hearing looking, to columnist Russell Baker, "less like dashing Red-
hunters than like men trapped in a bargain basement on a sale day."

Swerdlow argues convincingly that the WSP's strategic structurelessness
and its rejection of the knee-jerk anti-Communism so typical of the non-
Communist left prefigured the political culture of the New Left. However,
less persuasive is her contention that in their deployment of femininity the
maternalist pacifists of WSP foreshadowed feminism. In fact, younger
women's liberationists were intolerant of the WSP's selfless moral mother

politics, especially its privileging of the Vietnam war over women's issues. After all, this was several years before "difference feminism" became the vogue. For their part, WSPers were outraged by the younger women's efforts to put sexism "on a par with social issues such as war, poverty, and racism."

Neither Swerdlow nor Rupp and Taylor upend the usual interpretation of the fifties as a dark time for women, but that's what Joanne Meyerowitz sets out to do in *Not June Cleaver: Women and Gender in Postwar America, 1945– 1960*. Meyerowitz organized this lively anthology around the idea that most women's historians, misled by their "unrelenting focus on female subordination" and their obliviousness to women who weren't white and middle-class, got the fifties all wrong.[17] In her own contribution, Meyerowitz demonstrates that the feminine mystique was not nearly as pervasive as previously imagined. Popular magazines geared to African Americans, she argues, often encouraged women's independence and professional aspirations. But too often this volume tries to displace the "domestic stereotype" and complicate the fifties by presenting us with stories of women who weren't June—Communist Party members, Mexican-American community activists, and those protesting air raid drills and nuclear "preparedness."[18] After all, the idea that the "feminine mystique" was more prescriptive than descriptive is hardly new; ideology always falls short of its mark. The issue is that women were generally expected to embrace domesticity. Although there are exceptions (Wini Breines, Ruth Feldstein, Donna Penn, Rickie Solinger, and Meyerowitz herself), too many of the essayists here mistake the fissures of the fifties for the outright rebellion of the sixties. One contributor even claims that her research on civil defense protests proves that McCarthyism and the feminine mystique were desperate and failed attempts to "stave off a massive revolt against the Cold War state and the older gender roles." In fact, she continues, "it now seems evident that 'The Sixties' actually began in the middle of the 1950s."[19]

Anyone who thinks the fifties lasted five years should read Hettie Jones and Sally Belfrage. In her wonderfully evocative memoir, *Unamerican Activities*, Belfrage recounts her 1954 campaign to remake herself into an "AAG," or all-American girl.[20] Daughter of leftist journalist Cedric Belfrage whose deportation to Britain under the McCarran-Walter Act made headlines, Belfrage struggled to make herself invisible by doing "all the regulation things, wear spike rollers to bed, stuff tissues down my bra, starve." She recalls not knowing "which is the tightest, my panty girdle, my cinch belt, my pointy heels, or that smile fixed to my face to disguise all the pain."[21]

Talk about a culture of constraints! Even the red diaper babies she met were "goody-goody . . . naturals at the jargon . . . and up on all ten stanzas to the Red version of "Green Grow the Rushes-Ho."[22] Belfrage rebelled by getting pinned to a West Point cadet who years later became one of the architects of Star Wars. She didn't turn patriotic; her father's incarceration and deportation ("This is interesting. No evidence, no charge, no bail."[23]) wouldn't permit that. Although her days as an AAG were shortlived (she soon got involved in the civil rights movement), Belfrage didn't feel much affinity for her father's bohemian Village friends who all seemed "oddball in the same way." The mothers all "wear leotards and Capezios, black or beige, with natural leather bags and sandals, their hair straight and long and smoothed into buns and ponytails, and no lipstick, only mascara."[24]

Belfrage forgot about the tights, which Hettie Jones lists as a crucial Beat-girl accessory in *How I Became Hettie Jones*. New York's bohemian scene provided a refuge of sorts for an outsider like Jones, who as a college student had felt like a "mutation" and yearned to "*become* something"—an ambition that led her to Greenwich Village where she met and married Amiri Baraka (né Leroi Jones).[25] Although Jones thought the Beats "*looked* okay," neither she nor her husband had the "B-movie graininess, saintly disaffection," or the "wild head of hair" required to be truly Beat.[26] Moreover, she was a girl in a rebel world where that great enemy of bohemia, conventionality, was inscribed as feminine, and where marriage, like everywhere else in postwar America, resulted in the man being "augmented" and the woman diminished.[27]

Containment defined postwar America, as these memoirs by Belfrage and Jones demonstrate. Historian Elaine Tyler May makes this point as well in *Homeward Bound*.[28] Although the U.S. wasn't facing anything like a massive revolt, entrenched interests wanted to check the power of certain groups. In these years the country was structured around controlling black veterans, unionists, women, and gays, all of whom were emboldened in various ways by the wartime mobilization. The containment of women followed from the disruptiveness of the Great Depression and World War II. In the waning days of the war, the media was obsessed with whether women would cooperate with the national interest and go back to being mothers and wives. As anthropologist Margaret Mead noted, this "continuous harping" on women's domesticity reflected deep-seated anxieties.[29] The Cold War intensified these anxieties by making family stability and traditional gender roles critical to the war against communism. Labor's containment is among the more dramatic stories of postwar America. Had Operation Dixie, the CIO's abortive attempt to organize the South succeeded, unionism could have grown into a national movement rather than remaining a regional— and crushable—movement. Racism played a critical role in its defeat, as it did in the gradual unraveling of the New Deal coalition, a development which is usually laid at the doorstep of the sixties. Recent work by Thomas Sugrue shows Franklin Roosevelt's coalition coming apart as early as the late '40s, when fair-housing policies in Northern cities provoked a grass-roots rebellion against liberalism among the urban white working class, the very backbone of the coalition.[30]

Just as there emerged in the postwar years a newly assertive working-class whiteness committed to residential segregation, white youth—irrespective of class—were violating America's racial line by going to rock 'n' roll shows. George Lipsitz connects the development of rock 'n' roll to World War II, which brought large numbers of white and black Southerners to industrial cities. In his view, extreme overcrowding broke down residential segregation and made for unprecedented cultural exchanges across the color line. The war also gave migrants greater purchasing power, a fact not lost on small-time entrepreneurs, who began meeting the newcomers' demand for country, blues, and R&B records. In the aftermath of World War II, over four hundred record companies were formed. Radio stations, hungry to attract listeners now that many of their most popular programs had moved to TV, began trying to attract specific listening groups, including blacks. Alan Freed was just one of many deejays who noticed that white kids were tuning into stations playing rhythm and blues. Lipsitz ties white kids' fascination with early rock 'n' roll—and the truck drivers, dishwashers, and factory workers who became its first stars—to their discontent with the newly formed white-bread suburbs in which they found themselves marooned. White youth, he contends, were drawn to the "cultures of the dying industrial city" because they longed for a "connection to the past, for emotional expression, and a set of values that explained and justified rebellion."[31]

By the mid-'60s the tensions and contradictions of the postwar period could no longer be contained. White middle-class youth fled suburbia for the cities, often the inner cities that their parents had escaped in the great postwar migration to the suburbs. Fearful of ever becoming Jim Bakkus or˙ June Cleaver many young people avoided settling down at all costs. White, middle-class kids' restlessness and their search for meaning and stimulation was a reaction to their parents' preoccupation with comfort and security—itself a response to the uncertainties and insecurities of the Depression and war years. Efforts to make up for the blandness of suburban life, the dearth of stimulation, helped provoke the risk-taking of baby boomers eager to experiment with sex, drugs, new sounds, and something other than Cold Warrior-style politics. While the sixties may have been a revolt against mindless consumption, sixties hedonism was very much the product of postwar consumer capitalism and its promotion of uninhibited pleasure.[32] It didn't take much to get from advertising slogans that promised "satisfaction guaranteed" to the Rolling Stones' incendiary 1965 number one hit, "I Can't Get No Satisfaction," which inveighed against the false promises of consumer capitalism, but from a position of lustful hedonism. Finally, as Wini Breines demonstrated in *Young, White, and Miserable*, the contradiction between the feminine mystique and the emancipatory possibilities of the fifties (higher education, more democratic marriages, paid work, and better sex) created "dry tinder" for the spark of women's liberation.[33]

And then there was television, the much-maligned boob tube, which brought the civil rights movement into practically every American home. In his vivid memoir, *Colored People*, Henry Louis Gates remembers watching the 1957 battle to integrate Central High in Little Rock, Arkansas. "*All* the colored people in America watched together, with one set of eyes. We'd watch it in the morning, on the *Today* show; we'd watch it in the evening, on the news."[34] TV revealed the viciousness of Jim Crow and the audacious bravery of those whose eyes were on the prize. Writer Dorothy Allison felt "awed" by this movement, which seemed to offer the possibility of "freedom for all of us."[35] Even the rhetoric of the Cold War with those predictable buzzwords "democracy," "freedom," and "self-determination," could encourage a critical consciousness in the context of high-power hoses and police dogs.[36] "There's a town in Mississippi called Liberty. There's a department in Washington called Justice," read the sign in one Mississippi

civil rights office during 1964's Freedom Summer.[37] The government finally moved against segregation in large measure because the necessities of
the Cold War required it. If the U.S. was going to prove the virtues of
democracy and capitalism over Communism, especially in its struggle with
Russia to win the Third World, it was going to have to dismantle segregation
and close the credibility gap with regard to America's commitment to freedom and democracy.

Despite all these contradictions, the spirit of the fifties proved remarkably tenacious. In early 1963, before Kennedy's assassination, the escalation of the Vietnam War, and the British Invasion that the Beatles spearheaded, there was little hint of the unrest to come. Culturally, the country
still felt and looked crew-cut conservative. Of course, once the country unraveled, it did so with dizzying speed, and America, which had seemed, in
Allen Ginsberg's words, "as solid as the Empire State Building," turned out
to be less solid than almost anyone had imagined.[38] But fissures are not
tremors, which is to say that although the fifties gave rise to the sixties in all
sorts of unexpected ways, the fifties weren't the sixties. No amount of revisionism will change that.

3

"WE GOTTA GET OUT OF THIS PLACE":
NOTES TOWARD A REMAPPING OF THE SIXTIES

NO PERIOD IN RECENT U.S. HISTORY stands in greater contrast to the present, or seems to have held more possibilities for radical transformation, than the sixties. This is no doubt why the sixties remains the site of intense ideological contestation more than thirty years after it all began. While liberals have typically reacted to the sixties as an enormous embarrassment, conservatives have used the period to great political effect, deploying a version of the sixties that emphasizes disorder, permissiveness, and black as well as female assertiveness in such a way that accelerating poverty, crime, drug use, and even AIDS can be laid at the decade's doorstep. The right's vilification of the period has, of course, served the strategic function of obscuring the connection between the aforementioned social ills and the policies of the Reagan and Bush administrations.

But if the right's version of the sixties has prevailed in the realm of formal politics, it has been a different story in the cultural and intellectual arenas of American life. Here we find rap musicians like Public Enemy disrupting the mainstream construction of the black freedom movement as a "friendly crusade for racial integration" by claiming for Malcolm X a critical role in that struggle.[1] Documentary films such as *Berkeley in the Sixties*, and two television series, *Eyes on the Prize* and *Making Sense of the Sixties*, chronicle the achievements (and, to a lesser extent, the missteps) of various sixties movements in a largely unrepentant manner.

This essay is reprinted with revisions from an article of the same title in *Socialist Review* 22, no. 2 (1992): 9–34, by permission of the *Socialist Review*.

Predictably, Hollywood's record is more mixed. But certainly Oliver Stone, who has directed four films on various aspects of the sixties (*Platoon, The Doors, Born on the Fourth of July,* and *JFK*), has offered audiences cynical appraisals of the government and sympathetic depictions of the antiwar and youth movements. Finally, within publishing the sixties has become a kind of growth industry as intellectuals and former activists have produced a host of memoirs, histories, and anthologies, most of which affirm the democratic and egalitarian vision of the sixties movements.

However, women often play a larger role in the conservatives' demonizing scripts of the sixties—predictably, as welfare cheats or selfish feminists—than in progressive accounts of the period. Most egregious of all are Oliver Stone's sixties films, in which citizenship, principled protest, and rock 'n' roll genius are assumed to be the unique preserve of men.[2] Stone's masculinist formulations of the period are particularly disturbing because he has become a kind of de facto historian of the sixties.[3] But even *Eyes on the Prize,* which in many ways is a model of documentary filmmaking, devotes little attention to the pivotal role of women in the civil rights movement or to that critical figure, Ella Baker. Especially troubling to me as a historian of the women's liberation movement is that virtually all recently published books about the sixties fail to effectively integrate that movement into their reconstructions of the period.[4] In fact, much of this work replicates the position of women in the male-dominated Movement—that is, the women's liberation movement remains on the periphery, far from the core of the narrative. Curiously, through their narrative containment of women these writers have managed to marginalize women more effectively than could the movements they write about, because, of course, women did succeed in taking center stage by the end of the decade.

In this essay I criticize how "the sixties" has been mapped in the many books that purport to tell its story, and I offer some thoughts on how we might remap it. My criticisms will center not only on the failure to embed women and the women's liberation movement within the history of the sixties, but also on the failure to engender the New Left—the focus, after all, of most of these sixties books. The remapping I envision would make the women's liberation movement an integral part of the sixties by demonstrating its considerable philosophical connections to the New Left and the black freedom movement—without, of course, denying its originality. This remapping should be understood as a political intervention, one that seeks to disrupt the accepted version of the sixties, which too often depicts the women's liberation movement and the New Left, in particular, as philosophically opposed. I am concerned that people understand that conflicts between the New Left and the women's liberation movement were a consequence of specific historical circumstances and not, as most sixties books (and many feminist accounts) would have it, the result of some inevitable and chronic antagonism—an interpretation that makes all feminist and left collaborations seem doomed. In this sense, the revisioning I call for shares much with Ellen DuBois's recent work challenging the idea that in the early twentieth century the woman suffrage movement and socialism were fundamentally and irreconcilably antagonistic.[5]

My remapping also involves locating sixties radicalism in the postwar period and exploring the ways that both the white New Left and the white women's liberation movement represented a rebellion against the dominant gender constructions of the ultradomestic fifties.[6] I contend that future studies would benefit from exploring the contested terrain of masculinity in postwar America and its relation to sixties radicalism. I suggest that counterhegemonic constructions of masculinity, especially those advanced by Beats and rock 'n' rollers, may not only have inspired white male new leftists but, in their appropriation of a "black" style, may also have helped destabilize racial boundaries in the United States.

THE MARGINALIZATION OF the women's liberation movement in sixties books has several sources, but it has been facilitated by the scarcity of memoirs or autobiographies by women's liberation activists. While it sometimes seems as if every male leader of Students for a Democratic Society has either written a memoir or is in the process of writing one (the latest being Mark Rudd), only Mary King, Angela Davis, and Jane Alpert have published book-length memoirs about their movement experiences. Moreover, neither King nor Davis was active in the women's liberation movement, while Alpert, as a cultural feminist, presents her conversion to feminism as following from her rejection of the left.[7] (It is also distressing that there have been few recent autobiographies by African-American men or women active in the radical black freedom struggle. James Forman's, Cleveland Sellers's and Anne Moody's compelling memoirs are more than twenty years old.[8])

Not unrelated to this fact is that books by white male new leftists stand as representative of "the sixties." Their experiences are presented as universal, as defining the era, whereas the experiences of women and people of color (two overlapping categories, of course) are constructed as particularistic. There is a depressingly familiar metonymy at work here. For instance, Todd Gitlin's and Tom Hayden's books claim to be about "the sixties," and despite the incompleteness of their accounts most reviewers have agreed. Yet had Carlos Muñoz, the author of *Youth Identity, Power: The Chicano Movement*, used "The Sixties" as the subtitle of his book and still focused primarily on Chicanos, as Gitlin and Hayden do on white men, most reviewers would have thought it odd at the very least.[9]

I suspect the textual subordination of women's liberation also reflects a certain reluctance to part with what has become the conventional sixties story line whereby radicalism emerges on February 1, 1960, with the Greensboro lunch-counter sit-in, and ends with the February 1970 Greenwich Village townhouse explosion or the Kent State killings later that year. If one's narrative is conceptualized around the idea that radicalism was simply played out by the decade's end, then there really is only token narrative space available for women's liberation (or for the Chicano, Native American, or gay and lesbian movements). Thus, most sixties books, while they do note the problem of sexism on the left and acknowledge the considerable achievements of the women's liberation movement, fail to provide any substantive discussion of that movement, including the ways in which it carried on and extended the radicalism of the era. The film *Berkeley in the Sixties*, for instance, devotes astonishingly little time to the women's liberation movement. Indeed, by ignoring or downplaying the connections between the women's liberation movement and the New Left and the black freedom movements, these accounts create the impression that the women's liberation movement was a breed apart.

But if women's liberation generally constitutes an interruption in the narrative flow, it is nonetheless presented as a significant interlude in two very important retrospectives of the sixties, Todd Gitlin's often brilliant *The Sixties: Years of Hope, Days of Rage* and Tom Hayden's wonderfully evocative *Reunion: A Memoir*.[10] In both books women's liberation is associated with the male-dominated Movement's unraveling and with each man's personal pain and turmoil.[11] In his brief chapter on women's liberation, for example,

Gitlin analyzes with great perceptiveness the emotional divide separating left men and women in the late sixties. He observes that men who were not a part of hardline sects "were miserable with the crumbling of their onetime movement, [while] women were riding high." But he doesn't discuss the source of women's "high" in any depth. In fact, while his discussions of the New Left are marked by analytic rigor, his observations about the women's liberation movement are glib, if not diminishing—as in "there were a myriad of ways to be 'in the movement,' from sexual experimentation as 'political lesbians' . . . to journal-keeping à la Anaïs Nin."[12] (Of course, as anyone with even the most glancing knowledge of lesbian feminism knows, sexual experimentation was not exactly its driving force.) After this obligatory chapter on the women's liberation movement, Gitlin returns to the tale of the left's continued collapse and his own personal pain, much of it apparently caused by the women's movement.

Tom Hayden, too, associates women's liberation with the fragmentation of sixties radicalism. In fact, Hayden characterizes the period when black power and women's liberation were in ascent as a "Dostoyevskian nightmare."[13] For him, feminism's rise (and black power's as well) is inseparable from the disintegration of the "beloved community" and his own personal anguish. The lengthiest passage on the women's movement concerns the men's consciousness-raising group to which Hayden belonged and what he calls the "torture sessions" he and the others endured in an effort to undo their sexism.[14] (Although both Hayden and Gitlin were living in the Bay Area at the time, they apparently were not in the same group, since Gitlin remembers his men's group degenerating into gripe sessions about women rather than attacks on male members.)[15]

It is true that the emergence of the women's liberation movement coincided with the disintegration of much of the New Left and SDS in particular. I would go even further and suggest that the rise of women's liberation is related to the collapse of the left as a national movement. The New Left's repudiation of prefigurative politics, which had emphasized creating in the present the desired community of the future, and its reversion to a tired old left politic not only guaranteed its irrelevance to most people in the United States but also contributed to the development of feminist consciousness.[16] But that isn't the point either of these authors are making. For Hayden and Gitlin (although Gitlin is more self-reflexive), women's liberation is the final nail in the coffin of the "beloved community" and it is remembered with sadness and not a little petulance. This attitude plays a role, I believe, in the diminished narrative status accorded the women's liberation movement in sixties books.

As Wini Breines has pointed out, a lot of sixties books (including these two) dichotomize the era into the "good" and "bad" sixties.[17] In the case of SDS, of course, it seems justified: After all, SDS did self-destruct in a spectacularly awful way. But this demonizing of the late sixties confuses SDS with all of sixties radicalism, which was recombining in some interesting and constructive ways at that time, as the case of women's liberation demonstrates.[18] My point is that when the sixties is recast so that the New Left no longer occupies the privileged narrative core, the record of the late sixties is somewhat more mixed than the reigning interpretation of destructive disintegration would suggest.[19]

This formulation of the "good" and "bad" sixties has something to do with the writers' own positions as SDS "heavies"—the sixties equivalents of what Josephine Herbst derisively termed "the head boys" to describe the male luminaries of the thirties literary left.[20] This conflation of the sixties and SDS confuses the fortunes of the Movement with these writers' own status, which, as Breines points out, was in serious decline by the late sixties. Inattention to their own circumstances is a factor as well in Gitlin and Hayden's failure to explore the ways in which the New Left was gendered, and in particular how masculinity was constructed in SDS. No one, with the exception of Barbara Epstein, has really grappled with SDS's androcentrism, except perhaps to suggest that it reflected the chasm separating the New from the old left, which, it is explained, at least acknowledged male chauvinism as a problem.[21] It is as though SDS's androcentrism requires acknowledgment and a few mea culpas, but no serious engagement.

My reading of the New Left suggests that while it failed to problematize gender inequality, it did call into question at least some of the prevailing cultural assumptions about masculinity. Indeed, I see the androcentrism of the New Left as, in part, a response to the domesticated, attenuated sort of masculinity critiqued by William Whyte in his book *The Organization Man*. Anxiety about masculinity was not confined to new leftists. Pop culture abounded with images of "small dads." Social critics expounded on the dangers of the Organization Man and the "other-directed personality," attributing this new and untraditional form of masculinity to the expanding white-collar, corporate work world and sometimes to suburban matriarchs as well.[22] (As an aside, it's interesting how fears of emasculation figure in the radicalism of both the sixties and the thirties. While sixties white male radicals were rebelling against a spiritually depleted masculinity, male literary radicals in the thirties were outraged by the way in which masculinity had become physically depleted. As Paula Rabinowitz points out, the image of the male body diminished by hunger and unemployment was central to the radical iconography of the thirties.)[23]

By advancing an untamed masculinity, one that took risks and dared to gamble, the New Left was in some sense promoting a counterhegemonic (though not feminist) understanding of masculinity.[24] I suspect male new leftists' admiration for the radical sociologist C. Wright Mills had as much to do with his leather jacket and BMW motorcycle and their evocation of an unfettered, unmanaged masculinity as it did with his excoriation of the white-collar world and his trenchant critiques of functionalism and anticommunism.[25] Similarly, this factor may explain why what Maurice Isserman has called the "tired heroism" of those old leftists associated with the journal *Dissent* had so little appeal to most new leftists.[26] Gitlin notes Mills's maverick appeal and mentions in passing that Hayden's master's thesis on Mills was subtitled "Radical Nomad."[27] Hayden notes that his own father seemed the embodiment of Mills's white-collar worker.[28] But neither of them (nor James Miller, who spends considerable time on Mills in his book *Democracy Is in the Streets*) discusses the relation of Mills and masculinity to the politics they themselves forged and the lives they led.

The dissatisfaction of white New Left men with domesticated masculinity led them to identify with those on the margins of white U.S. culture, particularly African-American men, or what they imagined them to be.[29] Todd Gitlin has written that in spheres of both music and justice, "white America was drawing its juice from blacks."[30] But for white male radicals (and perhaps others too) the attraction went well beyond music and justice to include masculinity and sexuality. White leftist men's admiration of African-American men seems related to their romanticized view of these men as unencumbered by domestic constraints and therefore somehow more authentically masculine. This dynamic was at work in community-organizing projects such as SDS's Economic Research and Action Projects (ERAP), where white New Left men tried to cop a "black" or a white Appalachian style, depending upon the neighborhood.

Writing in 1970, Gitlin observed that ERAPers like himself romanticized the poor, whom they saw as "involuntarily insulated from the treadmill consumerism of the middle classes from which the organizers had come."[31] But while most ERAPers shared an antimaterialist stance and a desire to transcend their class through downward mobility, the very different responses of New Left men and women to the poor communities they entered suggest that these communities may have held different attractions for men than for women. According to Sara Evans's *Personal Politics*, former ERAPers agree that New Left women made significant progress in organizing poor women, while their male counterparts made little headway because they spent most of their time hanging out in bars and on street corners trying to emulate (or compete with) the most marginal men in the community. While ERAP women were attracted to the self-sufficiency and assertiveness of neighborhood women, the men were often drawn to the renegade and antidomestic masculinity of the most marginal men. Rennie Davis recalls that in order to be accepted by the gang in his neighborhood, he spent his whole first week drunk and, in what must have been one especially drunken moment, boasted that he would "beat every mean son of a bitch" in the local bar.[32] Steve Max remembers the ideologically inclined men "always kind of hanging back . . . trying to develop southern accents."[33]

Sara Evans has suggested that the macho posturing of ERAP men was compensatory. She contends that "their commitment to the movement and their identification with the very poor required a break with the traditional avenues of success—money, prestigious jobs, respectability." Denied these avenues for "proving their 'manhood,'" they turned to the avenues provided by community organizing, including sexual conquest.[34] But it strikes me that this "break" Evans speaks of was fundamental rather than incidental to their radicalism. While they were undoubtedly committed to the poor and to the Movement, they were also committed to seeking alternatives to the prevailing model of masculinity in which men were ostensibly prisoners of their wives, their jobs, and the American Dream of achieving the good life through consumption.

IF NEW LEFT MEN have produced a problematic rendering of the sixties, so have women's liberationists. Feminist recollections often formulate the relationship between the women's liberation movement and the larger Movement in entirely negative terms. Although there are exceptions, what emerges from many feminist recollections, especially from about 1973 onward, is not the way in which the Movement empowered women (however unintentionally) but the ways in which it exploited them.[35] The idea that women might have learned anything from their Movement experience—except, of course, a well-developed cynicism about leftist men—is disallowed. In many such accounts New Left men appear as possibly even more cretinous and patriarchal than the men they sought to supplant. For example, Robin Morgan, editor of the best-selling anthology *Sisterhood Is Powerful* (and a recent editor of *Ms.* magazine), denounced the "ejaculatory politics" of the New Left.[36] And Andrea Dworkin has written that what distinguished New Left men from others was that they "wanted to wield penises, not guns, as emblems of manhood."[37]

Although I disagree with these assessments, feminist cynicism was not unwarranted. The male-dominated New Left was almost willfully blind to sexism. After all, this was a movement where slogans like "Girls Say Yes to Guys Who Say No" went uncontested.[38] This was a movement where some men reportedly said "the movement hangs together on the head of a penis."[39] In other words, this was a movement where gender inequality was seen, just as in the larger culture, as unremarkable. As feminists pointed out at the time, in this respect the Movement mirrored the larger culture all too accurately. But if it offered young white middle-class men a different version of masculinity than was available in the dominant culture, it offered different possibilities for their female counterparts as well. The Movement both was and wasn't the larger culture for white women. As Sara Evans has shown, it was in the New Left and the black freedom movement that white women acquired the skills, confidence, and political savvy necessary to discern the disjuncture between those movements' egalitarian rhetoric and their own subordination. It was here that they encountered black women whose self-reliance and assertiveness were at odds with the "feminine mystique." It was here, in the Movement, not in the larger culture. Although some feminist memoirs, especially those by Ellen Willis, Elinor Langer, and Kathie Sarachild, acknowledge this complicated history,[40] most depict the New Left in particular as unremittingly sexist.[41]

I don't dispute that the women's liberation movement caused many male leftists pain or that the New Left resisted feminism. But too many left and feminist reconstructions of the sixties misremember the past by treating the antagonism between these movements as somehow inevitable. Initially, even radical feminists, who were at the time often wrongly accused of being antileft, saw feminism as involving an expansion rather than a rejection of left analysis. They imagined themselves building a feminist radicalism and continuing to work on both left and feminist political projects.[42] Had the New Left not been in retreat from prefigurative politics, the relationship between these two movements might have developed very differently.

But the relentlessness of the war machine in Vietnam, the government's all-out war against black radicalism, and growing feelings of impotence among white radicals exiled from the black movement and unable or unprepared to fight white racism where it lived, led white new leftists toward a politics of desperation.[43] This politics took different forms as some, embracing the (only recently) repudiated labor metaphysic, took jobs in factories in order to organize the white working class while others cast themselves as auxiliaries to the Black Panther Party or hoped to ignite a youth revolt. What all of these strategies shared was the conviction that authentic radicalism could not emerge among middle-class white students from college campuses. The idea that genuine radicalism (as opposed to mere liberalism) involved acknowledging and fighting one's own oppression, not struggling exclusively on behalf of other more downtrodden groups, was discredited just at the moment when women, empowered by that idea, were raising the issue of male dominance.[44] New Leftists dismissed the idea that women (much less the white middle-class women in the ranks of the New Left) were oppressed. Their trivialization and derogation of women's liberation as bourgeois and/or diversionary resulted not only from a desire to hold onto male privilege but also from the way in which class and race were now enshrined as the privileged categories. Women's liberationists responded by appropriating critiques of colonialism and the logic of black power to describe women's oppression and legitimate their struggle. Over time, and with the ascendance of cultural feminism—a strand that grew out of radical feminism but diverged from it in significant ways—anger at the left often solidified into an antileft politics. Under these circumstances a feminist radicalism simply could not grow.

Leftist and feminist constructions of this period not only fail to histori- cize the conflict between women's liberation and the New Left but also ob- scure what these two movements had in common, including the historical moment they shared. If New Left men were rebelling against the domesti- cated masculinity of their postwar fathers, women's liberationists were re- belling against the domesticated femininity of their mothers. If New Left men were drawn to C. Wright Mills, women's liberationists were drawn to Simone de Beauvoir, most obviously because of *The Second Sex* but also be- cause of the independent female characters in her fiction and her own un- conventional relationship with Sartre.[45] New Left men and women were in flight from both the nuclear family and the gender conventions of their day. What neither could know was that the "breadwinner/homemaker nuclear family" was an "aberrant and highly fragile" family system, one "already passing from the scene" by the late sixties, as Judith Stacey and Deborah Rosenfelt have argued.[46]

Feminist and leftist accounts of the period also elide other connections between women's liberation and the larger Movement. Although it is true that the women's movement has persisted (albeit in weakened form) while much of the U.S. New Left burned up and out in a spectacular fashion, often leaving little trace of itself in the larger culture, the two experienced many of the same dilemmas. Both movements discovered that creating group structures that were at once democratic and efficient was no mean feat. Both tended to conflate reform and reformism, a move that resulted in a too-total rejection of all reform. Nor was either able to acknowledge difference or own up to the inequalities that existed, whether in the "beloved communi- ty" or the "sisterhood." And, finally, both found it difficult not to succumb to the idea that somebody *else* out there—African Americans, the working class, or lesbians—must be the revolutionary agent of change.

More importantly, it is difficult to imagine women's liberation establish- ing itself as a radical force *without* the philosophical breakthroughs made by new leftists and black radicals. While the left was often antagonistic to feminism, it nevertheless gave women considerable intellectual ammunition in building their own movement. This is, of course, the paradox at the core of the relationship between these two movements. The conviction that radicalism involved fighting one's own oppression, the commitment to both prefigurative politics and participatory democracy, the genesis of identity politics, and most importantly, the idea that the "personal is political"—all originated in the New Left and the civil rights movement.

THE REMAPPING OF THE SIXTIES that I envision would involve a narrative decentering of the New Left. It would acknowledge the women's liberation movement as a quintessentially sixties movement and would emphasize just how significant its redefinition of the political has been in the larger culture. It would be exciting to see histories of the sixties written in what Elsa Barkley Brown calls a "multivocal" style, so that we understand more about the variety of sixties radical movements and their often interrelated histories.[47] Finally, any remapping must necessarily involve a greater effort to locate sixties radicalism within the postwar United States. Resource mobilization theorists were perhaps the first to pursue this path.[48] But I would like to see more attention paid to official and oppositional discourses and the popular culture of the postwar period. For instance, recently it has been argued persuasively that the discourse of the Cold War, with its strategic rhetoric of democracy, may have unintentionally helped ignite the civil rights movement.[49] As I've already suggested, I think we could also benefit from an exploration into the ways that, for young white people in the United States, the sixties represented a gendered generational revolt against the ultradomestic fifties.

As others have pointed out, masculinity became a contested terrain in the postwar United States as the breadwinner ethic came under attack from a variety of sources.[50] I would expand the typical list of rebels to include fifties rock 'n' rollers and sixties new leftists. I am struck by the way in which the domesticated masculinity of the postwar period is challenged repeatedly by the Beats, rock 'n' roll culture, and white new leftists. Disaffected white men in all these examples come to identify, I think, with those forced to live on the margins of America, especially African-American men. (Think, for instance, of the centrality and recurrence of the phrase "rolling stone(s)" to the sixties. It was the old proverb "a rolling stone gathers no moss" that inspired blues singer Muddy Waters to first use the phrase as the title of one of his songs, which was how the phrase came to be appropriated by the Rolling Stones. On this side of the Atlantic, Bob Dylan had his first Top 40 hit with "Like a Rolling Stone." Finally, the aboveground magazine that best reflected the sixties was, of course, called *Rolling Stone*.)[51]

What interests me here is the way in which these revolts against domesticated masculinity did sometimes call into question racial categories. (The Organization Man and the white-collar worker were both racially marked concepts.) One can certainly see this in relation to rock 'n' roll, where what is most threatening about the genre is the way in which it is perceived by much of white America as disrupting racial boundaries, not only by bringing different racial groups into contact with one another but by promoting "jungle rhythms."[52] Rock changes the meaning of "whiteness" as white men, especially, strive to emulate a "black" musical style and stance, thereby challenging the cultural devaluation of "black" music. This is why Elvis, the "Hillbilly Cat" with his pomaded, dyed hair and "black"-inspired dress, moves, and vocal style, was so revolutionary. He violated and confounded the racial boundaries of the fifties.[53] (Of course, it was business as usual in the sense that once again a white person was reaping the profits from this appropriation of "black" music.)

What I want to suggest is that white rock 'n' rollers' revolt against domesticated masculinity, by leading them to identify with black men whom they perceived as both unencumbered by domesticity and having (in the words of the writer Claude Brown) "masculinity to spare" (or "the juice," as Gitlin put it), may have contributed to a shift in America's color line. Over twenty years ago, in *Soul on Ice*, Eldridge Cleaver called the Twist "a guided missile, launched from the ghetto into the very heart of suburbia."[54] Rock did have a profound impact, desegregating the radio waves and much of the music charts, bringing together different racial and ethnic groups at dances and concerts, and changing blacks' and whites' self-perceptions. In ways we don't yet know, rock 'n' roll reconstructed the meanings of "whiteness" and "blackness," which as Tom Holt has argued are, of course, absolutely interdependent.[55] This is not to say that racial boundaries are not constantly rearticulated—they are, as in the gradual construction of rock itself as a "white" music. But if we want to get at the sixties, we will have to consider that Cleaver may be right that rock 'n' roll helped prepare the ground.

Still, what is missing from Cleaver's analysis (and what it shares with the sixties books under discussion here) is any acknowledgment of gender's role in the transformations of the sixties. This is especially striking since it was dissatisfaction with the dominant model of masculinity that in part fueled the birth of rock 'n' roll. Moreover, as rock 'n' roll destabilized the categories of whiteness and blackness, so did it necessarily destabilize notions of masculinity and femininity. In fact, rock 'n' roll allows us to see the ways in which race, gender, class, and sexuality exist not as abstract and distinct categories, but are, rather, mutually constitutive identities. While it seems that rock 'n' roll did involve, at least initially, a greater challenge to domesticated masculinity than to domesticated femininity, further research may reveal that this is to some extent a function of the way in which histories of rock, like histories of the sixties, place women on the sidelines. Future studies may very well uncover ways in which young white women and girls also harnessed rock's subversive and rebellious possibilities. Then we may have a better understanding of the white women's side of the sixties generational revolt—the women's liberation movement—that is so vital a part of the sixties story.

4

"NOTHING DISTANT ABOUT IT": WOMEN'S LIBERATION AND SIXTIES RADICALISM

O N SEPTEMBER 7, 1968, THE SIXTIES came to that most apple-pie of American institutions, the Miss America Pageant. One hundred women's liberation activists descended upon Atlantic City to protest the pageant's promotion of physical attractiveness as the primary measure of women's worth. Carrying signs that read, "Miss America Is a Big Falsie," "Miss America Sells It," and "Up Against the Wall, Miss America," they formed a picket line on the boardwalk, sang anti-Miss America songs in three-part harmony, and performed guerrilla theater. Later that day, they crowned a live sheep Miss America and paraded it on the boardwalk to parody the way the contestants, and, by extension, all women, "are appraised and judged like animals at a county fair." They tried to convince women in the crowd that the tyranny of beauty was but one of the many ways that women's bodies were colonized. By announcing beforehand that they would not speak to male reporters (or to any man for that matter), the demonstrators challenged the sexual division of labor that consigned female reporters to the "soft" stories while reserving for male reporters the coveted "hard" news stories. Newspaper editors who wanted to cover the protest were thus forced to pull their women reporters from the society pages.[1]

The protesters set up a "Freedom Trash Can" and filled it with various "instruments of torture"—high-heeled shoes, bras, girdles, hair curlers,

This essay was published in David Farber, ed., *The Sixties: From Memory to History* (Chapel Hill: University of North Carolina Press, 1994). Used by permission of the publisher.

false eyelashes, typing books, and representative copies of *Cosmopolitan*, *Playboy*, and *Ladies Home Journal*. They had wanted to burn the contents of the Freedom Trash Can, but they were thwarted by a city ordinance prohibiting bonfires on the boardwalk. However, word had been leaked to the press that the protest would include a symbolic bra-burning, and, as a consequence, reporters were everywhere.[2] Although they burned no bras that day on the boardwalk, the image of the bra-burning, militant feminist remains part of our popular mythology about the women's liberation movement.

The activists also managed to make their presence felt inside the auditorium during that night's live broadcast of the pageant. Pageant officials must have known that they were in for a long night when early in the evening one protester sprayed Toni Home Permanent Spray (one of the pageant's sponsors) at the mayor's booth. She was charged with disorderly conduct and "emanating a noxious odor," an irony that women's liberationists understandably savored. The more spectacular action occurred later that night. As the outgoing Miss America read her farewell speech, four women unfurled a banner that read, "Women's Liberation," and all sixteen protesters shouted "Freedom for Women" and "No More Miss America" before security guards could eject them. The television audience heard the commotion and could see it register on Miss America's face as she stumbled through the remainder of her speech. But the program's producer prevented the cameramen from covering the cause of Miss America's consternation.[3] The TV audience did not remain in the dark for long, because Monday's newspapers described the protest in some detail. As the first major demonstration of the fledgling women's liberation movement, it had been designed to make a big splash, and after Monday morning no one could doubt that it had.

In its wit, passion, and irreverence, not to mention its expansive formulation of politics (to include the politics of beauty, no less!), the Miss America protest resembled other sixties demonstrations. Just as women's liberationists used a sheep to make a statement about conventional femininity, so had the Yippies a week earlier lampooned the political process by nominating a pig, Pegasus, for the presidency at the Democratic National Convention.[4] Although Atlantic City witnessed none of the violence that had occurred in Chicago, the protest generated plenty of hostility among the six hundred or so onlookers who gathered on the boardwalk. Judging from their response, this new thing, "women's liberation," was about as popular as the antiwar movement. The protesters were jeered, harassed, and called "man-haters" and "commies." One man suggested that "it would be a lot more useful" if the demonstrators threw themselves, and not their bras, girdles, and make-up, into the trash can.[5]

But nothing—not even the verbal abuse they encountered on the board-walk—could diminish the euphoria women's liberationists felt as they start-ed to mobilize around their own, rather than other people's, oppression. Ann Snitow speaks for many when she recalls that in contrast to her experi-ence in the larger, male-dominated protest Movement,[6] where she had felt sort of "blank and peripheral," women's liberation was like "an ecstasy of discussion." Precisely because it was about one's own life, there was, she says, "nothing distant about it."[7] Robin Morgan has claimed that the Miss America protest "announced our existence to the world."[8] That is only a slight exaggeration, for as a consequence of the protest, women's liberation achieved the status of a movement both to its participants and to the media; as such, the Miss America demonstration represents an important moment in the history of the sixties.[9]

Although the women's liberation movement only began to take shape toward the end of the decade, it was a quintessentially sixties movement. It is not just that many early women's liberation activists had prior involve-ments in other sixties movements, although that was certainly true, as has been ably documented by Sara Evans.[10] And it is not just that, of all the six-ties movements, the women's liberation movement alone carried on and extended into the 1970s that decade's political radicalism and rethinking of fundamental social organization. Although that is true as well. Rather, it is also that the larger, male-dominated protest Movement, despite its con-siderable sexism, provided much of the intellectual foundation and cultur-al orientation for the women's liberation movement, many of whose ideas and approaches—especially its concern with revitalizing democratic process and reformulating "politics" to include the personal—were refined and recast versions of those already present in the New Left and the black freedom movement.

Moreover, like other sixties radicals, women's liberationists were re-sponding at least in part to particular features of the postwar landscape. For instance, both the New Left and the women's liberation movement can be understood as part of a gendered generational revolt against the ultra-domesticity of that aberrant decade, the 1950s. Sixties radicals, white and black, were also responding to the hegemonic position of liberalism and its promotion of government expansion both at home and abroad—the welfare/warfare state. Although sixties radicals came to define themselves in opposition to liberalism, their relation to liberalism was nonetheless complicated and ambivalent. They saw in big government not only a way of achieving greater economic and social justice, but also the possibility of an increasingly manipulated society and an ever more remote government.

In this essay I will attempt to evaluate some of the more important features of sixties radicalism by focusing on the specific example of the women's liberation movement. Although my accounting of the sixties is in some respects critical, I nonetheless believe that there was much in sixties radicalism that was original and hopeful, including its challenge to established authority and expertise, its commitment to refashioning democracy and "politics," and its interrogation of such naturalized categories as gender and race.

WOMEN'S DISCONTENT with their place in America in the 1960s was, of course, produced by a broad range of causes. Crucial in reigniting feminist consciousness in the 1960s was the unprecedented number of women (especially married white women) being drawn into the paid labor force, as the service sector of the economy expanded and rising consumer aspirations fueled the desire of many families for a second income.[11] As Alice Kessler-Harris has pointed out, "homes and cars, refrigerators and washing machines, telephones and multiple televisions required higher incomes." So did providing a college education for one's children. These new patterns of consumption were made possible in large part through the emergence of the two-income family as wives increasingly "sought to aid their husbands in the quest for the good life." By 1960, 30.5 percent of all wives worked for wages.[12] Women's growing labor force participation also reflected larger structural shifts in the U.S. economy. Sara Evans has argued that the "reestablishment of labor force segregation following World War II ironically reserved for women a large proportion of the new jobs created in the fifties due to the fact that the fastest growing sector of the economy was no longer industry but services."[13] Women's increasing labor force participation was facilitated as well by the growing number of women graduating from college and the introduction of the birth control pill in 1960.

Despite the fact that women's "place" was increasingly in the paid work force (or perhaps because of it), ideas about women's proper role in American society were quite conventional throughout the fifties and the early sixties, held there by a resurgent ideology of domesticity—what Betty Friedan coined the "feminine mystique." But, as Jane De Hart-Mathews has observed, "the bad fit was there: the unfairness of unequal pay for the same work, the low value placed on jobs women performed, the double burden of housework and wage work."[14] By the mid-sixties at least some American women felt that the contradiction between the realities of paid work and higher education on the one hand, and the still pervasive ideology of domesticity on the other, had become irreconcilable.

However, without the presence of other oppositional movements the women's liberation movement might not have developed at all as an organized force for social change. It certainly would have developed along vastly different lines. The climate of protest encouraged women, even those not directly involved in the black movement and the New Left, to question conventional gender arrangements. Moreover, as already noted, many of the women who helped form the women's liberation movement had been involved as well in the male-dominated Movement. If the larger Movement was typically indifferent, or worse, hostile, to women's liberation, it was nonetheless through their experiences in that Movement that the young and predominantly white and middle-class women who initially formed the women's liberation movement became politicized. The relationship between women's liberation and the larger Movement was at its core paradoxical. The Movement was a site of sexism, but it also provided white women a space in which they could develop political skills and self-confidence, a space in which they could violate the injunction against female self-assertion.[15] Most important, it gave them no small part of the intellectual ammunition—the language and the ideas—with which to fight their own oppression.

Sixties radicals struggled to reformulate politics and power. Their struggle confounded many who lived through the sixties as well as those trying to make sense of the period some thirty years later. One of the most striking characteristics of sixties radicals was their ever-expanding opposition to liberalism. Radicals' theoretical disavowal of liberalism developed gradually and in large part in response to liberals' specific defaults—their failure to repudiate the segregationists at the 1964 Democratic National Convention, their lack of vigor in pressing for greater federal intervention in support of civil rights workers, and their readiness (with few exceptions) to support President Lyndon B. Johnson's escalation of the Vietnam War. But initially some radicals had argued that the Movement should acknowledge that liberalism was not monolithic but contained two discernible strands—"corporate" and "humanist" liberalism. For instance, in 1965 Carl Oglesby, an early leader of the Students for a Democratic Society (SDS), contrasted *corporate liberals*, whose identification with the system made them "illiberal liberals," with *humanist liberals*, who he hoped might yet see that "it is this movement with which their own best hopes are most in tune,"[16]

But by 1967 radicals were no longer making the distinction between humanist and corporate liberals that they once had. This represented an important political shift for early new leftists in particular, who once had felt an affinity of sorts with liberalism.[17] Black radicals were the first to decisively reject liberalism, and their move had an enormous impact on white radicals. With the ascendancy of black power many black militants maintained that liberalism was intrinsically paternalistic, and that black liberation required that the struggle be free of white involvement. This was elaborated by white radicals, who soon developed the argument that authentic radicalism involved organizing around one's own oppression rather than becoming involved, as a "liberal" would, in someone else's struggle for freedom. For instance, in 1967 Gregory Calvert, another SDS leader, argued that the "student movement has to develop an image of its own revolution . . . instead of believing that you're a revolutionary because you're related to Fidel's struggle, Stokely's struggle, always someone else's struggle."[18] Black radicals were also the first to conclude that nothing short of revolution—certainly not Johnson's Great Society programs and a few pieces of civil rights legislation—could undo racism. As leftist journalist Andrew Kopkind remembered it, the rhetoric of revolution proved impossible for white new leftists to resist. "With black revolution raging in America and world revolution directed against America, it was hardly possible for white radicals to think themselves anything less than revolutionaries."[19]

Radicals' repudiation of liberalism also grew out of their fear that liberalism could "co-opt" and thereby contain dissent. Thus, in 1965 when President Johnson concluded a nationally televised speech on civil rights by proclaiming, "And we *shall* overcome," radicals saw in this nothing more than a calculated move to appropriate Movement rhetoric in order to blunt protest. By contrast, more established civil rights leaders reportedly cheered the president on, believing that his declaration constituted a significant "affirmation of the movement."[20] Liberalism, then, was seen as both compromised and compromising. In this, young radicals were influenced by philosopher Herbert Marcuse, who emphasized the system's ability to reproduce itself through its recuperation of dissent.[21]

Just as radicals' critique of materialism developed in the context of relative economic abundance so did their critique of liberalism develop at a time of liberalism's greatest political strength. The idea that conservativism might supplant liberalism at some point in the near future was simply unimaginable to them. (To be fair, this view wasn't entirely unreasonable given Johnson's trouncing of Barry Goldwater in the 1964 presidential election.)

This was just one of many things which distinguished new leftists from old leftists, who, having lived through McCarthyism, were far more concerned about the possibility of a conservative resurgence. For if sixties radicals grew worlds apart from liberals, they often found themselves in conflict with old leftists as well. In general, new leftists rejected the economism and virulent anticommunism of the noncommunist old left. In contrast to old leftists whose target was "class-based economic oppression," new leftists (at least before 1969 when some new leftists did embrace dogmatic versions of Marxism) focused on "how late capitalist society creates mechanisms of psychological and cultural domination over *everyone*."[22] For young radicals the problem went beyond capitalism and included not only the alienation engendered by mass society, but also other systems of hierarchy based on race, gender, and age. Indeed, they were often more influenced by existentialists like Camus, or social critics like C. Wright Mills or Herbert Marcuse, both of whom doubted the working class's potential for radical action, than by Marx or Lenin. For instance, SDS president Paul Potter contended it would be "through the experience of the middle class and the anesthetic of bureaucracy and mass society that the vision and program of participatory democracy will come."[23] This rejection of what Mills dubbed the "labor metaphysic" had everything to do with the different circumstances radicals confronted in the sixties. As Arthur Miller observed, "The radical of the thirties came out of a system that had stopped and the important job was to organize new production relations which would start it up again. The sixties radical opened his eyes to a system pouring its junk over everybody, or nearly everybody, and the problem was to stop just that, to escape being overwhelmed by a mindless, goalless flood which marooned each individual on his little island of commodities."[24]

Sixties radicals initially rejected orthodox versions of Marxism, but over time many did appropriate, expand, and recast Marxist categories in an effort to understand the experiences of oppressed and marginalized groups. Thus exponents of what was termed "new working-class theory" claimed that people with technical, clerical, and professional jobs should be seen as constituting a new sector of the working class, better educated than the traditional working class, but working class nonetheless. According to this view, students were not members of the privileged middle class, but rather "trainees" for the new working class. And many women's liberationists (even radical feminists who rejected Marxist theorizing about women's condition) often tried to use Marxist methodology to understand women's oppression. For example, Shulamith Firestone argued that just as the elimination of "economic classes" would require the revolt of the proletariat and their seizure of the means of production, so would the elimination of "sexual classes" require women's revolt and their "seizure of control of reproduction."[25]

Young radicals often assumed an arrogant stance toward those remnants of the old left that survived the fifties, but they were by the late sixties unambiguously contemptuous of liberals. Women's liberationists shared new leftists' and black radicals' rejection of liberalism, and, as a consequence, they often went to great lengths to distinguish themselves from the liberal feminists of the National Organization for Women (NOW). (In fact, their disillusionment with liberalism was more thorough during the early stages of their movement-building than had been the case for either new leftists or civil rights activists because they had lived through the earlier betrayals around the the War and civil rights. Male radicals' frequent denunciations of feminism as "bourgeois" also encouraged women's liberationists to distance themselves from NOW.) NOW had been formed in 1966 to push the federal government to enforce the provisions of the 1964 Civil Rights Act outlawing sex discrimination—a paradigmatic liberal agenda focused on public access and the prohibition of employment discrimination. To women's liberationists, NOW's integrationist, access-oriented approach ignored the racial and class inequalities that were the very foundation of the "mainstream" that the feminists of NOW were dedicated to integrating. In the introduction to the 1970 bestseller she edited, *Sisterhood Is Powerful*, Robin Morgan declared that "NOW is essentially an organization that wants reforms [in the] second-class citizenship of women—and this is where it differs drastically from the rest of the Women's Liberation Movement."[26] In *The Dialectic of Sex* Shulamith Firestone described NOW's political stance as "untenable even in terms of immediate political gains" and deemed it "more a leftover of the old feminism rather than a model of the new."[27] Radical feminist Ti-Grace Atkinson went even further, characterizing many in NOW as only wanting "women to have the same opportunity to be oppressors, too."[28]

Women's liberationists also took issue with liberal feminists' formulation of women's problem as their exclusion from the public sphere. Younger activists argued instead that women's exclusion from public life was inextricable from their subordination in the family, and would persist until this larger problem was addressed. For instance, Firestone claimed the solution to women's oppression wasn't inclusion in the mainstream, but rather the eradication of the biological family, which she argued was the "tapeworm of exploitation."[29]

Of course, younger activists' alienation from NOW was often more than matched by NOW members' annoyance with them. Many liberal feminists' were appalled (at least initially) by women's liberationists' politicization of personal life. NOW founder Betty Friedan frequently railed against women's liberationists for waging a "bedroom war" that diverted women from the real struggle of integrating the public sphere.[30]

Women's liberationists believed that they had embarked upon a much more ambitious project—the virtual remaking of the world.[31] Nothing short of radically transforming society was sufficient to deal with what they were discovering: that gender inequality was thoroughly embedded in everyday life. As Shulamith Firestone put it, "sex-class is so deep as to be invisible."[32] The pervasiveness of sexism and gender's status as a naturalized category demonstrated to women's liberationists the inadequacy, the shallowness, of NOW's legislative and judicial remedies and the necessity of thoroughgoing social transformation. Thus, whereas liberal feminists talked of ending sex discrimination, women's liberationists called for nothing less than the destruction of patriarchy and capitalism. As defined by feminists, patriarchy, in contrast to sex discrimination, defied reform. For example, Adrienne Rich contended: "Patriarchy is the power of the fathers: a familial-social, ideological, political system by force, direct pressure, or through ritual, tradition, law and language, customs, etiquette, education, and the division of labor, determine what part women shall or shall not play, and in which the female is subsumed under the male."[33]

Women's liberationists typically indicted capitalism as well. Ellen Willis, for instance, maintained that "the American system consists of two interdependent but distinct parts—the capitalist state, and the patriarchal family." Willis argued that capitalism succeeded in exploiting women as cheap labor and consumers "primarily by taking advantage of women's subordinate position in the family and our historical domination by man."[34]

Central to the revisionary project of the women's liberation movement was the desire to render gender meaningless, to explode it as a significant category. In the movement's view, both masculinity and femininity represented not timeless essences, but rather "patriarchal" constructs. (Of course, even as the movement sought to deconstruct gender, it was, paradoxically, as many have noted, trying to mobilize women precisely on the basis of their gender.[35]) This explains in part the significance abortion rights held for women's liberationists, who believed that until abortion was decriminalized biology would remain women's destiny, thus foreclosing the possibility of women's self-determination.[36]

Indeed, the women's liberation movement made women's bodies the site of political contestation. The "colonized" status of women's bodies became the focus of much movement activism. The discourse of colonization originated in Third World national liberation movements, but in an act of First World appropriation was taken up by black radicals who claimed that African Americans constituted an "internal colony" in the U.S. Radical women trying to persuade the Movement of the legitimacy of their cause soon followed suit by deploying the discourse to expose women's subordinate position in relation to men. This appropriation represented an important move, and one characteristic of radicalism in the *late* sixties, that is, the borrowing of conceptual frameworks and discourses from other movements to comprehend the situation of oppressed groups in the U.S.—with mixed results at best. In fact, women's liberationists challenged not only tyrannical beauty standards, but also violence against women, women's sexual alienation, the compulsory character of heterosexuality and its organization around male pleasure (inscribed in the privileging of the vaginal over the clitoral orgasm), the health hazards associated with the birth control pill, the definition of contraception as women's responsibility, and, of course, women's lack of reproductive control. They also challenged the sexual division of labor in the home, employment discrimination, and the absence of quality child-care facilities. Finally, women's liberationists recognized the power of language to shape culture.

The totalism of their vision would have been difficult to translate into a concrete reform package, even had they been interested in doing so. But electoral politics and the legislative and judicial reforms that engaged the energies of liberal feminists did little to animate most women's liberationists. Like other sixties radicals, they were instead taken with the idea of developing forms that would prefigure the utopian community of the imagined future.[37] Anxious to avoid the "manipulated consent" that they believed characterized American politics, sixties radicals struggled to develop alternatives to hierarchy and centralized decision-making.[38] They spoke often of creating "participatory democracy" in an effort to maximize individual participation and equalize power. Their attempts to build a "democracy of individual participation" often confounded outsiders, who found Movement meetings exhausting and tedious affairs.[39] But to those radicals who craved political engagement, "freedom" was, as one radical group enthused, "an endless meeting."[40] According to Gregory Calvert, participatory democracy appealed to the "deep anti-authoritarianism of the new generation in addition to offering them the immediate concretization of the values of openness, honesty, and community in human relationships."[41] Women's liberationists, still smarting from their first-hand discovery that the larger Movement's much-stated commitment to egalitarianism did not apply equally to all, often took extraordinary measures to try to ensure egalitarianism. They employed a variety of measures in an effort to equalize power, including consensus decision-making, rotating chairs, and the sharing of both creative and routine movement work.

Fundamental to this "prefigurative politics," as sociologist Wini Breines terms it, was the commitment to developing counterinstitutions that would anticipate the desired society of the future.[42] Staughton Lynd, director of the Mississippi Freedom Schools and a prominent new leftist, likened sixties radicals to the Wobblies (labor radicals of the early twentieth century) in their commitment to building "the new society within the shell of the old."[43] According to two early SDSers, "What we are working for is far more than changes in the structure of society and its institutions or the people who are now making the decisions. . . . The stress should rather be on wrenching people out of the system both physically and spiritually."[44]

Radicals believed that alternative institutions would not only satisfy needs unmet by the present system but also, perhaps, by dramatizing the failures of the system, radicalize those not served by it but currently outside the Movement. Tom Hayden proposed that radicals "build our own free institutions—community organizations, newspapers, coffeehouses—at points of strain within the system where human needs are denied. These institutions become centers of identity, points of contact, building blocks of a new society from which we confront the system more intensely."[45]

Among the earliest and best known of such efforts were the Mississippi Freedom Democratic Party and the accompanying Freedom Schools formed during Freedom Summer of 1964. In the aftermath of that summer's Democratic National Convention, Bob Moses [Parris] of the Student Nonviolent Coordinating Committee (SNCC) even suggested that the Movement abandon its efforts to integrate the Democratic Party and try instead to establish its own state government in Mississippi. And as early as 1966 SNCC's Atlanta Project called on blacks to "form our own institutions, credit unions, co-ops, political parties."[46] This came to be the preferred strategy as the sixties progressed and disillusionment with traditional politics grew. Rather than working from within the system, new leftists and black radicals instead formed alternative political parties, media, schools, universities, and assemblies of oppressed and unrepresented people.

Women's liberationists elaborated on this idea, creating an amazing panoply of counterinstitutions. In the years before the 1973 Supreme Court decision decriminalizing abortion, feminists established abortion referral services in most cities of any size. Women's liberationists in Chicago even operated an underground abortion clinic, "Jane," where they performed about one hundred abortions each week.[47] By the mid-seventies most big cities had a low-cost feminist health clinic, a rape crisis center, and a feminist bookstore. In Detroit after "a long struggle to translate feminism into federalese" two women succeeded in convincing the National Credit Union Administration that feminism was a legitimate field from which to draw credit union members. Within three years of its founding in 1973, the Detroit credit union could claim assets of almost one million dollars. Feminists in other cities soon followed suit. Women's liberation activists in Washington, D.C., formed an all-women's record company, Olivia Records, which by 1978 was supporting a paid staff of fourteen and producing four records a year.[48] By the mid-seventies there existed in most cities of any size a politicized feminist counterculture, or a "women's community."

The popularity of alternative institutions was that they seemed to hold out the promise of political effectiveness without co-optation. Writing in 1969, Amiri Baraka (formerly LeRoi Jones), an accomplished poet and black nationalist, maintained, "But you must have the cultural revolution.... We cannot fight a war, an actual physical war with the forces of evil just because we're angry. We can begin to build. We must build black institutions . . . all based on a value system that is beneficial to black people."[49]

Jennifer Woodul, one of the founders of Olivia Records, argued that ventures like Olivia represented a move toward gaining "economic power" for women. "We feel it's useless to advocate more and more 'political action' if some of it doesn't result in the permanent material improvement of the lives of women."[50] Robin Morgan termed feminist counterinstitutions "concrete moves toward self-determination and power."[51] The situation, it turned out, was much more complicated. Women involved in nonprofit feminist institutions such as rape crisis centers and shelters for battered women found that their need for state or private funding sometimes militated against adherence to feminist principles.

Feminist businesses, by contrast, discovered that while they were rarely the objects of co-optation, the problem of recuperation remained. In many cases the founders of these institutions became the victims of their own success, as mainstream presses, recording companies, credit unions, and banks encroached upon a market they had originally discovered and tapped.[52] For instance, by the end of the seventies, Olivia was forced to reduce its staff almost by half and to scuttle its collective structure.[53] Today k.d. lang, Tracy Chapman, Michelle Shocked, and Sinead O'Connor are among those androgynous women singers enjoying great commercial success, but on major labels.

Although Olivia helped lay the groundwork for their achievements, it finds its records, as Arlene Stein has observed, "languishing in the 'women's music' section in the rear [of the record store] if they're there at all."[54]

The move toward building counterinstitutions was part of a larger strategy to build new societies "within the shell of the old," but this shift sometimes had unintended consequences. While feminist counterinstitutions were originally conceived as part of an active culture of resistance, over time they often became more absorbed in sustaining themselves than in confronting male supremacy, especially as their services were duplicated by mainstream businesses. In the early years of the women's liberation movement this alternative feminist culture did provide the sort of "free space" women needed to critically confront sexism. But as it was further developed in the mid-seventies, it ironically often came to promote insularity instead—becoming, as Adrienne Rich has observed, "a place of emigration, an end in itself," where patriarchy was evaded rather than confronted.[55] In practice, feminist communities were small, self-contained subcultures that proved hard to penetrate, especially to newcomers unaccustomed to their norms and conventions. The shift in favor of alternative communities may have sometimes impeded efforts at outreach for the women's liberationists, new leftists, and black radicals who attempted it.

On a related issue, the larger protest Movement's pessimism about reform—the tendency to interpret every success as a defeat resulting in the Movement's further recuperation (what Robin Morgan called "futilitarianism")—encouraged a too-global rejection of reform among sixties radicals. For instance, some women's liberationists actually opposed the Equal Rights Amendment (ERA) when NOW revived it. In September 1970, The Feminists, a group based in New York, denounced the ERA and advised feminists against "squandering invaluable time and energy on it."[56] A delegation of Washington, D.C. women's liberationist activists invited to appear before the senate subcommittee considering the ERA testified: "We are aware that the system will try to appease us with their [sic] paper offerings. We will not be appeased. Our demands can only be met by a total transformation of society which you cannot legislate, you cannot co-opt, you cannot *control.*"[57] And in *The Dialectic of Sex,* Firestone went so far as to dismiss child-care centers as attempts to "buy women off" because they "ease the immediate pressure without asking why the pressure is on *women.*"[58]

Similarly, many SDS leaders opposed the National Conference for New Politics (NCNP), an abortive attempt to form a national progressive organization oriented around electoral politics, and to launch an antiwar presidential ticket headed by Martin Luther King and Benjamin Spock. Immediately following NCNP's first and only convention, in 1967, the SDS paper *New Left Notes* published two front-page articles criticizing NCNP organizers. One writer contended that "people who recognize the political process as perverted will not seek change through the institutions that process has created."[59] The failure of sixties radicals to distinguish between reform and reformism meant that while they defined the issues, they often did very little to develop policy initiatives around those issues.[60] Moreover, the preoccupation of women's liberationists with questions of internal democracy (fueled in part by their desire to succeed where the men had failed) sometimes had the effect of focusing attention away from the larger struggle in an effort to create the perfect movement. As feminist activist Frances Chapman points out, women's liberation was "like a generator that got things going, cut out and left it to the larger reform engine which made a lot of mistakes."[61] In eschewing traditional politics rather than entering them skeptically, women's liberationists, like other sixties radicals, may have lost an opportunity to foster critical debate in the larger arena.

Young radicals eschewed the world of conventional politics, but they nonetheless had a profound impact upon it, especially by redefining what is understood as "political." Although the women's liberation movement popularized the slogan "the personal is political," the idea that there is a political dimension to personal life was first embraced by early SDSers who had encountered it in the writings of C. Wright Mills.[62] Rebelling against a social order whose public and private spheres were highly differentiated, new leftists called for a reintegration of the personal with the political. They reconceptualized apparently personal problems—specifically their alienation from a campus cultural milieu characterized by sororities and fraternities, husband and wife hunting, sports, and careerism, and their powerlessness as college students without a voice in campus governance or curriculum—as political problems. Thus, SDS's founding Port Huron Statement of 1962 suggested that for an American New Left to succeed, it would have to "give form to . . . feelings of helplessness and indifference, so that people may see the political, social, and economic sources of their private troubles and organize to change society."[63] Theirs was a more expansive formulation of politics than what prevailed in the old left.[64] Power was conceptualized as relational and by no means reducible to electoral politics.

By expanding political discourse to include personal relations, new leftists unintentionally paved the way for women's liberationists to develop critiques of the family, marriage, and the construction of sexuality. (Of course, nonfeminist critiques of the family and sexual repressiveness were hardly in short supply in the fifties and sixties, as evidenced by *Rebel Without a Cause*, *Catcher in the Rye*, and Paul Goodman's *Growing Up Absurd*, to mention but a few.) Women's liberationists developed an understanding of power's capillary-like nature, which in some respects anticipated those being formulated by Michel Foucault and other poststructuralists.[65] Power was conceptualized as occupying multiple sites, and as lodging everywhere, even in those private places assumed to be the most removed from or impervious to politics—the home, and more particularly, the bedroom.

The belief of sixties radicals that the personal is political also suggested its converse—that the political is personal. Young radicals typically felt it was not enough to sign leaflets or participate in a march if one returned to the safety and comfort of a middle-class existence. Politics was supposed to unsettle life and its routines—even more, to transform life. For radicals the challenge was to discover underneath all the layers of social conditioning the "real" self unburdened by social expectations and conventions. Thus, SNCC leader Stokely Carmichael advanced the slogan, "Every Negro is a potential black man."[66] And Shulamith Firestone and Anne Koedt argued that among the "most exciting things to come out of the women's movement so far is a new daring . . . to tear down old structures and assumptions and let real thought and feeling flow."[67] Life would not be comfortable, but who wanted comfort in the midst of so much deadening complacency? For a great many radicals, the individual became a site of political activism in the sixties. In the black freedom movement the task was very much to discover the black inside the Negro, and in the women's liberation movement it was to unlearn niceness, to challenge the taboo against female self-assertion.[68]

Sixties radicalism proved compelling to many precisely because it promised to transform life. Politics was not about the subordination of self to a larger political cause; instead it was the path to self-fulfillment. This ultimately was the power of sixties radicalism. As Stanley Aronowitz notes, sixties radicalism was in large measure about "infus[ing] life with a secular spiritual and moral content," and "fill[ing] the quotidian with personal meaning and purpose."[69] But "the personal is political" was one of those ideas whose rhetorical power sometimes seemed to work against or undermine its explication. It could encourage a solipsistic preoccupation with self-transformation. As new leftist Richard Flacks presciently noted in 1965, this kind of politics could lead to "a search for personally satisfying modes of life while abandoning the possibility of helping others to change theirs."[70] Thus the idea that "politics is how you live your life, not who you vote for," as Yippie leader Jerry Rubin put it, could and did lead to a subordination of politics to lifestyle.[71] But if the idea led some to confuse personal liberation for political struggle, it led others to embrace an asceticism that sacrificed personal needs and desires to political imperatives. Some women's liberation activists followed this course, interpreting the idea that the personal is political to mean that one's personal life should conform to some abstract standard of political correctness. At first this tendency was mitigated by the founders' insistence that there were no personal solutions, only collective solutions, to women's oppression. However, over time one's self-presentation, marital status, and sexual preference frequently came to determine one's standing or ranking in the movement. The most notorious example of this involved the New York radical group, The Feminists, who established a quota to limit the number of married women in the group.[72] Policies such as these prompted Barbara Ehrenreich to question "a feminism which talks about universal sisterhood, but is horrified by women who wear spiked heels or call their friends 'girls.'"[73] At the same time, what was personally satisfying was sometimes upheld as politically correct. In the end, both the women's liberation movement and the larger protest Movement suffered, as the idea that the personal is political was often interpreted in ways that made questions of lifestyle absolutely central.

The social movements of the sixties signaled the beginning of what has come to be known as "identity politics," the idea that politics is rooted in identity.[74] Although some New Left groups by the late sixties did come to endorse an orthodox Marxism whereby class was privileged, class was not the pivotal category for these new social movements.[75] (Even those New Left groups which reverted to the "labor metaphysic" lacked meaningful working-class participation.) Rather, race, ethnicity, gender, youth, and, eventually, sexual orientation/preference were the salient categories for most sixties activists. In the women's liberation movement, what was termed "consciousness-raising" was the tool used to develop women's group identity.

As women's liberationists started to organize a movement, they confronted American women who identified unambiguously as women, but who typically had little of what historian Nancy Cott would call "we-ness," or "some level of identification with 'the group called women.'"[76] Moreover, both the pervasiveness of gender inequality and the cultural understanding of gender as a natural rather than a social construct made it difficult to cultivate a critical consciousness about gender even among women. To engender this sense of sisterhood or "we-ness," women's liberationists developed consciousness-raising, a practice involving "the political reinterpretation of personal life."[77] According to its principal architects, its purpose was to "awaken the latent consciousness that . . . all women have about our oppression." In talking about their personal experiences, it was argued, women would come to understand that what they had believed were personal problems were, in fact, "social problems that must become social issues and fought together rather than with personal solutions."[78]

New York women's liberationist Kathie Sarachild was reportedly the person who coined the term *consciousness-raising.* However, the technique originated in other social movements. As Sarachild noted in 1973, those who promoted consciousness-raising "were applying to women and to ourselves as women's liberation organizers the practice a number of us had learned in the civil rights movement in the South in the early 1960s."[79] There they had seen that the sharing of personal problems, grievances, and aspirations—"telling it like it is"—could be a radicalizing experience. Moreover, for some women's liberationists consciousness-raising was a way to avoid the tendency of some in the movement to try to fit women into existing (and often Marxist) theoretical paradigms. By circumventing the "experts" on women and going to women themselves, they would be able not only to construct a theory of women's oppression but to formulate strategy as well. Thus women's liberationists struggled to find the commonalities in women's experiences in order to generate generalizations about women's oppression.

Consciousness-raising was enormously successful in exposing the insidiousness of sexism and in engendering a sense of identity and solidarity among the largely white, middle-class women who participated in "c-r" groups. By the early seventies even NOW, whose founder Betty Friedan had initially derided consciousness-raising as so much "navel-gazing," began sponsoring c-r groups.[80] But the effort to transcend the particular was both the strength and weakness of consciousness-raising. If it encouraged women to locate the common denominators in their lives, it inhibited discussion of women's considerable differences. Despite the particularities of white, middle-class women's experiences, theirs became the basis for feminist theorizing about women's oppression. In a more general sense the identity politics informing consciousness-raising tended to privilege experience in certain problematic ways. It was too often assumed that there existed a kind of core experience, initially articulated as "women's experience." Black and white radicals (the latter in relation to youth) made a similar move as well. When Stokely Carmichael called on blacks to develop an "ideology which speaks to our blackness" he, like other black nationalists, suggested that there was somehow an essential and authentic "blackness."

With the assertion of difference within the women's movement in the eighties, the notion that women constitute a unitary category has been problematized. As a consequence, women's experiences have become ever more discretely defined, as in "the black female experience," "the Jewish female experience," or "the Chicana lesbian experience." But, as Audre Lorde has argued, there remains a way in which, even with greater and greater specificity, the particular is never fully captured.[81] Instead, despite the pluralization of the subject within feminism, identities are often still imagined as monolithic. Finally, the very premise of identity politics—that identity is the basis of politics—has sometimes shut down possibilities for communication as identities are seen as necessarily either conferring or foreclosing critical consciousness. Kobena Mercer, a British film critic, has criticized the rhetorical strategies of "authenticity and authentication" that tend to characterize identity politics. He has observed: "If I preface a point by saying something like, 'as a black gay man, I feel marginalized by your discourse,' it makes a valid point but in such a way that preempts critical dialogue because such a response could be inferred as a criticism not of what I say but of who I am. The problem is replicated in the familiar cop-out clause, 'as a middle-class, white, heterosexual male, what can I say?'"[82]

The problem is that the mere assertion of identity becomes in a very real sense irrefutable. Identity is presented as stable and fixed, and insurmountable. While identity politics gives the oppressed the moral authority to speak (perhaps a dubious ground from which to speak), it can, ironically, absolve those belonging to dominant groups from having to engage in a critical dialogue. In some sense, then, identity politics can unintentionally reinforce Other-ness. Finally, as the antifeminist backlash and the emergence of the New Right should demonstrate, there is nothing inherently progressive about identity. It can be, and has been, mobilized for reactionary as well as well as for radical purposes.[83] For example, the participation of so many women in the antiabortion movement reveals just how problematic the reduction of politics to identity can be.

Accounts of sixties radicalism usually cite its role in bringing about the dismantling of Jim Crow and disfranchisement, the withdrawal of U.S. troops from Vietnam, and greater gender equality. However, equally important, if less frequently noted, was its challenge to politics as usual. Sixties radicals succeeded both in reformulating politics, even mainstream politics, to include personal life, and in challenging the notion that elites alone have the wisdom and expertise to control the political process. For a moment, people who by virtue of their color, age, and gender were far from the sites of formal power became politically engaged, became agents of change.

Given the internal contradictions and shortcomings of sixties radicalism, the repressiveness of the federal government in the late sixties and early seventies, and changing economic conditions in the United States, it is not surprising that the movements built by radicals in the sixties either no longer exist or do so only in attenuated form. Activists in the women's liberation movement, however, helped to bring about a fundamental realignment of gender roles in this country through outrageous protests, tough-minded polemics, and an "ecstasy of discussion." Indeed, those of us who came of age in the days before the resurgence of feminism know that the world today, while hardly a feminist utopia, is nonetheless a far different, and in many respects a far fairer, world than what we confronted in 1967.

Part 2

Feminism, Sexual Freedom, and Identity Politics

Some readers might find my linking of feminism and sexual freedom peculiar, but many second-wave feminists believed the two were inextricably connected. Ellen Willis, for instance, once quipped that many early radical feminists like herself "felt about the sexual revolution what Ghandi reputedly thought of Western civilization—that it would be a good idea." My 1984 essay, "The Taming of the Id," which was published in *Pleasure and Danger*, both criticizes the feminist antipornography movement and argues for that strain of feminism that believes sexual repression is the problem, not the solution. (An earlier version of this essay, which I wrote in 1981, was published as "The New Feminism of Yin and Yang" in the 1983 collection *Powers of Desire.*) "The Taming of the Id" was written for the 1982 Barnard conference on sexuality, and it is an uncompromising polemic. The tone of the piece is so indignant and unforgiving that it makes me cringe. However, at the time the antipornography movement felt like a juggernaut. I was convinced that it represented the culmination of a larger process of retrenchment and accommodation that threatened to empty feminism of its maverick-like vision. It's safe to say that this didn't happen, at least when it came to sex, because most women, thank God, were not ready to condemn their desires to the dustbin of false consciousness.

Although I think many of my criticisms of cultural feminism are on the nose, I want to amend and clarify certain parts of my argument. In the early eighties when this was written, it was widely assumed that the best way to make sense of feminism's heterogeneity was to break it down into competing camps, or theoretical strands—usually liberal, socialist, and radical. In arguing for a new category, cultural feminism, I was, I suppose, encouraging the further taxonomizing of feminism, though that was hardly my aim. My effort to capture the broad outlines of this shift within the movement led me to attribute more ideological coherence to cultural feminism than was there. Susan Brownmiller and Catharine MacKinnon were antiporn and in some ways even antileft, but they couldn't have been less interested in celebrating the Goddess or women's culture. Although the term cultural feminism was initially resisted, it has become commonplace, at least in the work of feminist scholars. Yet I would argue that this schema of cultural, radical, liberal, and socialist feminism, while a useful road map in understanding second-wave feminism, has virtually no explanatory power in making sense of today's women's movement.

It's become almost axiomatic that 1970s feminists were unstylish, humorless, and prudish, and my work is sometimes cited as proof that this was so. In truth, as I tried to make clear in "Taming," feminism was not monolithic in regards to sexuality. Moreover, despite the initial knee-jerk acceptance of antiporn thinking by much of the feminist community, there was always a dissonance between theory and practice when it came to sex.

In 1993 I began writing journalistic pieces—at first book reviews for the *Village Voice* and *The Nation*. In 1993 the *Voice* asked me to review Shulamith Firestone's great, eccentric 1970 book *The Dialectic of Sex*, which had just been reprinted. I used the opportunity to contextualize her work, which is in so many ways at odds with feminism today. Most people would find Catharine MacKinnon's work more recognizably feminist than Firestone's. In 1994 I returned to the porn wars when I reviewed MacKinnon's 1993 book of essays *Only Words* for the *Voice*. The rest of the articles in this section have never before been published. I wrote "Gender Disobedience, Academia, and Popular Culture" in 1995 for a special issue of the *L.A. Weekly* on "gender fuck" that was scuttled. " 'Thousands of Men and a Few Hundred Women,'" began as a 1995 talk about rock singer Janis Joplin's ambiguous, much-talked-about, sexuality. I have revised it substantially in light of all I learned from Joplin's many friends and lovers in the course of researching her life. I wrote "Queer Like Us?" for this collection, but it began as a series of book reviews on recent titles in gay and lesbian history that I'd done for *The Nation*. Rather than reprint those reviews I have written an essay that aims to acquaint readers with the critical issues raised by gay and lesbian historians over the past twenty-five years.

5
THE DWORKINIZATION OF
CATHARINE MACKINNON

WITH *ONLY WORDS*, CATHARINE MacKinnon has issued a rant worthy of her longtime collaborator, Andrea Dworkin. While MacKinnon's ideas about the perniciousness of pornography are indistinguishable from those of her sidekick, she has always struck a very different pose in her writing and self-presentation. In fact, Dworkin and MacKinnon owe much of their success as antiporn divas to their act as feminism's Odd Couple. Whereas MacKinnon favors the sort of elegant power suits Susan Dey once sported on *L.A. Law*, Dworkin is attached to overalls and T-shirts, giving her the look of an unreconstructed '70s lesbian feminist. In their public appearances MacKinnon was the cool, clever, erudite legal scholar, Dworkin the barnstormer—the proverbial wild-eyed radical.

While both have written passionate fulminations against women's oppression, MacKinnon has, until now, labored to give hers a scholarly patina. Pick up the article that established her as a force to be reckoned with in women's studies, her 1982 essay in *Signs*—"Feminism, Marxism, Method, and the State: An Agenda for Theory"—and you'll discover a text dwarfed by fat footnotes displaying her familiarity with writers as diverse as Georg Lukacs, Helene Cixous and Michel Foucault.[1] While MacKinnon never shied away from extreme formulations such as "Man fucks woman; subject verb object," she embedded her zingers in the turgid prose for which academics

This essay was previously published as "Sex and the Single-Minded: The Dworkinization of Catharine MacKinnon" in the *Village Voice Literary Supplement*, March 1994.

have become famous.[2] MacKinnon has been rewarded very nicely for this scholarly drag. She has tenure at the University of Michigan Law School and publishes with Harvard University Press. Dworkin, by contrast, publishes with nonscholarly presses, enjoys no academic affiliation, and is regarded by many as a crackpot.

However, in this exceedingly slender collection of her recent essays MacKinnon seems determined to beat Dworkin at her own game. Gone are the apparently logical arguments and learned asides. *Only Words* opens with a nightmarish description of "women's reality":

Imagine that for hundreds of years your most formative traumas, your daily suffering and pain, the abuse you live through, the terror you live with, are unspeakable—not the basis of literature. You grow up with your father holding you down and covering your mouth so another man can make a horrible searing pain between your legs. When you are older, your husband ties you to the bed and drips hot wax on your nipples and brings in other men to watch and makes you smile through it. Your doctor will not give you drugs he has addicted you to unless you suck his penis.[3]

This lurid composite—what MacKinnon calls "facts" she's "adapted" from two court cases and drawn from her own "confidential consultations with women who have been used in pornography"—is classic, over-the-top Dworkin.[4] But by playing Dworkin's role so well, MacKinnon has screwed up the Good Cop/Bad Cop routine that made her seem the reasonable alternative.

It remains to be seen whether MacKinnon has abandoned the old duet permanently. Certainly it has served her well, not only with Dworkin but in relation to those early radical feminists whose ideas her work builds on. Whereas some radical feminists like Kate Millett became movement stars, MacKinnon is the only radical feminist to achieve superstardom in the academy. Yet anyone familiar with contemporary feminist theory knows that her notions about gender and sexuality are just dressed-up versions of a particular strand of radical feminism; *Only Words* has a long history.

The idea that (hetero)sexuality reinforces women's oppression, for example, was a truism among radical feminists in the late '60s and early '70s.

This insight suggested wildly different possibilities to those feminists for whom it was axiomatic. If feminism encouraged the pursuit of sexual pleasure for some, for others it was about getting women out of the bedroom. Where you came down on the issue had a lot to do with what you believed to be the bigger culprit—sexual repression or sexual liberation.

To the radical feminists who influenced MacKinnon, sexuality was a place of domination and subordination, something women needed to be liberated from. This position was most fully articulated by Ti-Grace Atkinson, dubbed the movement's "haute thinker" twenty-five years ago by the *New York Times*.[5] Atkinson claimed that heterosexuality acts as a "reassuring reminder" to men of their "class supremacy" and as a "convenient reminder to the female of her class inferiority."[6] In *Signs*, MacKinnon took this idea further, arguing that "sexuality is the linchpin of gender inequality."[7] Gender doesn't determine sexuality, as other radical feminists had imagined; it's the other way around. MacKinnon even contended that women actually are gendered through the experience of " 'having sex.'"[8] Just as the "organized expropriation of the work of some for the benefit of others defines a class—workers—[so] the organized expropriation of the sexuality of some for the use of others defines the sex—woman."[9]

For MacKinnon sexuality will remain an arena of male domination and female subordination until gender equality is achieved. Not surprisingly, she has argued that, under conditions of male supremacy, "consent" is highly overrated. Although MacKinnon admitted in *Feminism Unmodified: Discourses on Life and Law* that sex might feel good, might even involve the "glimpsing of freedom," she rejected any thought that it might be empowering for women.[10] She has sneered at feminists who had the nerve to write about women as historical agents: "In the law, agent means someone whose strings are being pulled by someone else."[11]

It is just this gloomy depiction of women as perpetually at the mercy of others—pimps, pornographers, civil libertarians, and anticensorship feminists who are themselves the pawns of pimps—that's made Katie Roiphe and Camille Paglia overnight sensations. Who *wouldn't* find "postfeminism" attractive when prominent feminists treat women as history's favorite victims, snookered time and again? The media have played a role in the postfeminist turn, too. By ignoring saucy anticensorship feminists, the media have made feminism synonymous with MacKinnonism. Indeed, most reviews of *Only Words* fail to even mention that MacKinnon's views are by no means gospel among feminists.

MacKinnon's conviction that women's strings are always being pulled and that sexuality is never in their own interest led her to criticize *Roe v Wade* for "facilitating women's heterosexual availability" and "freeing male aggression" by removing one of the very few "legitimized reasons women have had for refusing sex."[12] Before Anita Hill went public, MacKinnon scolded women's groups for opposing Clarence Thomas's nomination simply because of "scanty evidence about his views on abortion," and stressed that, as a conservative, he might be more comprehending of the "real injury pornography causes women."[13]

Feminists who disagree with MacKinnon are "elitist," "idealist," or, worst of all, "liberal."[14] To critics who point out that many women don't experience sex as unrelieved oppression, MacKinnon has countered that "a worker can sometimes have a good day or even a good job," but that "does not mean . . . the work is not exploited labor, structurally speaking."[15] She chides those who disagree for being radical on every other subject but liberal on sex (not that this has ever stopped MacKinnon, as her own position on Thomas makes clear). MacKinnon's use of the worker-boss relationship to make sense of heterosexuality assumed not only that the personal is political but that power works the same way in both arenas. This worker-woman analogy recalls the crudest socialist-feminism, which imagined, as Barbara Ehrenreich put it, that every time "a mother kissed her children good night she was 'reproducing labor power.'"[16]

MacKinnon the theorist has become MacKinnon the celebrity feminist largely because of her work on pornography; *Only Words* is its perverse culmination. But MacKinnon was a latecomer to the antiporn struggle. Until the law professor signed on, antiporn feminists had succeeded in accomplishing one thing: creating acrimonious, crippling conflict within the women's movement. MacKinnon's genius lay in making an end run around her feminist opponents, whom she must have despaired of ever persuading, and going directly to legislators and the courts. She and Dworkin drafted an antiporn ordinance for Indianapolis that skirted the censorship problem by making pornography actionable as a civil-rights violation. In contrast to conservatives, who fought pornography on obscenity grounds, the duo emphasized its role in women's subordination. Although U.S. courts have rejected this approach, the Canadian Supreme Court has been more receptive. Its recent *Butler* ruling affirmed MacKinnon's logic, with the result that Dworkin's own *Pornography: Men Possessing Women*, was seized at the border.

In *Only Words* MacKinnon struggles to make sexual-harassment law, which she helped define, a leading wedge in her struggle against porn. She notes that, as a consequence of harassment law, porn in the workplace is understood to create a "hostile unequal working environment." Unfortunately, "there is no law against a hostile unequal living environment, so everywhere else [pornography] is protected speech." Some of you may wonder how it is that a man whacking off to *Juggs* in his bathroom is engaged in a public act of sex discrimination. What about private space? Or fantasy?

MacKinnon maintains that "sooner or later, in one way or another, the consumers [of porn] want to live out the pornography further in three dimensions. . . . *It* makes them want to."[17] Pornography's central message—"'get her'"—is "addressed directly to the penis, delivered through an erection, and taken out on women in the real world."[18] Porn is an "unconscious mental intrusion and physical manipulation . . . giving men erections that support aggression against women."[19] Pornography makes the man. In earlier work, MacKinnon discussed porn as both cause and effect of male supremacy; here, she comes close to indicting porn as wholly responsible for male domination. The idea that pornography circumvents thought by acting directly on the penis—a revival of postwar hysteria about subliminal messages?—allows MacKinnon to counter both her First Amendment critics who define porn as speech and her many feminist opponents who question why she focuses so relentlessly on sexually explicit material when there is so much misogyny elsewhere.

For the first time, MacKinnon situates her argument against pornography in a larger discussion about free speech and gender and racial equality. She claims the First and Fourteenth Amendments are on a "collision course": "Fourteenth Amendment equality . . . has grown as if equality could be achieved while the First Amendment protected the speech of inequality."[20] For MacKinnon, the solution is simple enough. "Wherever equality is mandated, racial and sexual epithets, vilification, and abuse should be able to be prohibited, unprotected by the First Amendment."[21] She acknowledges that "distinguishing talk about inferiority from verbal imposition of inferiority may be complicated at the edges." But, she reassures us, "it is clear enough at the center with sexual and racial harassment, pornography, and hate propaganda."[22] She declines to "spell out all the policy implications of such a view," but argues that "those who wish to keep materials that promote inequality from being imposed on students . . . especially without critical commentary, should not be legally precluded from trying. . . . No teacher should be forced to teach falsehoods."[23]

But a falsehood for whom? Just as one person's pornography is another's erotica, so is one person's falsehood another's truth. Would histories of prostitution that take into account the agency of prostitutes be verboten on the grounds that this somehow nullifies or ignores their oppression? Would Khalid Abdul Muhammad's remarks at Kean College be regarded as hate speech or a salutary blow against white supremacy?

Recently I was helping a women's studies student decipher the comments I'd scribbled on her term paper. She was puzzled that I had circled her phrase "low-income status persons." I explained that it was awkward, to which she replied, "But what should I say?" I suggested "poor." She was silent for a few seconds before informing me she could never use that word. I told her about Martin Luther King's Poor People's Campaign, but to no avail; the word was beyond the pale of political rectitude. Later, in talking with a friend, it occurred to me that the banishing of "poor" from her vocabulary involved an unintended banishment of poverty itself.

Like *Only Words,* this underscores the depressing reality that for some people politics has come to mean the policing of attitudes through the suppression of speech—an impoverished practice that replaces political vision with political purity, analysis with moralizing, and hopefulness with despair.

6

"TOTaLLY ReaDY TO GO": SHULamITH Firestone anD *THE DIaLeCTIC OF seX*

LONG BEFORE OTHERS, SHULAMITH Firestone understood the radical possibilities of badness. Almost twenty-five years ago she urged women to "dare to be bad." For Firestone, risking badness meant refusing femininity. It meant resisting the cultural imperative that white girls always be nice and their lives small and circumscribed. Firestone was determined to eliminate all vestiges of her own (admittedly minimal) good-girlism, and this sometimes got her into trouble, even in the movement she helped found. At a time when sharing the "shit-work" was doctrine, Firestone balked. Asked at a meeting to help with typing, Firestone reportedly refused, explaining she had already done a lifetime's worth of typing and hadn't joined the movement to do more. Even her friend Ellen Willis admits, "Shulie could be snarky about that."

The movement's commitment to remaining leaderless, what Jo Freeman called its "tyranny of structurelessness," presented problems for everyone, but especially for those who weren't good girls. They found themselves, as Firestone put it, in the "peculiar position of having to eradicate, at the same time, not only their submissive natures, but their dominant natures as well, thus burning their candle at both ends."[1] This proved to be an insurmountable problem for Firestone, who, not coincidentally, left the women's movement at the very moment she could have become one of its leading spokeswomen. By the time *The Dialectic of Sex* hit bookstores, in October 1970, Firestone had already retired.

This essay was previously published as "Like a Hurricane: Shulamith Firestone's Wild Ride" in the *Village Voice Literary Supplement*, October 1993.

Her retreat was a tragedy for the movement. There was nothing like *The Dialectic of Sex*. Kate Millett's pioneering *Sexual Politics* was a sober tome. Germaine Greer's *The Female Eunuch* was provocative but annoyingly coy. From its opening line—"Sex class is so deep as to be invisible"—*The Dialectic of Sex* is a passionate, brilliant, and uncompromising book. Now that it has been reissued, people can marvel at the intelligence and irreverence of this woman who in her midtwenties tried to develop a new dialectical materialism based on gender.[2]

Firestone's feminist reworkings of Marx, Engels, and Freud were always bold, sometimes breathtaking, and occasionally weird. Her reclamation of Freud was especially nervy. If U.S. feminists were united on anything it was their contempt for Freud. Ever the maverick, Firestone declared Freud of even greater relevance than Marx and Engels. She argued that feminism and Freudianism were both responses to the "increasing privatization of family life, its extreme subjugation of women, and the sex repressions and subsequent neuroses this caused." Over time, however, Freudianism "flourished at the expense of Feminism" as it "acted as a container of [feminism's] shattering force." Firestone's analysis of feminism's historical relationship to psychoanalysis is intriguing, and more interesting than her reinterpretation of Freud. As Juliet Mitchell noted, Firestone's revision of Freud denied the very existence of the unconscious—when the very fact of the unconscious was, after all, Freud's point.

Whereas many feminists writing at the time went to great lengths to prove that Marxism really did explain sexism, Firestone declared that Marx and Engels "knew next to nothing" about women. What she did appreciate, and appropriate, was their analytic method—dialectical materialism. If socialism required the elimination of "economic class" through "the revolt of the underclass and their seizure of *production*," so feminism required "the elimination of sexual classes" through the "revolt of women and the seizure of control of *reproduction*." Just as socialism would end the class distinction, so would feminism end the "sex distinction." Although Firestone was a socialist, she believed the dialectic of sex, not class, was the great motor of history.

Firestone located male supremacy, or "sex-class," in the "natural reproductive difference between the sexes." Given antifeminists' fondness for biological explanations of male supremacy, her argument was quite startling. But where they proclaimed biology destiny, Firestone called for artificial reproduction, or as she bluntly put it, "getting rid of nature." By eliminating pregnancy, cybernation would end the sexual division of labor, and the "tyranny of the biological family."

All radical feminists attacked the family as a site of women's subordination, but Firestone went further. She argued that families are where dominance and submission are learned and come to feel familiar. She maintained that Marx "was onto something more profound than he knew when he observed that the family contained within itself in embryo all the antagonisms that later develop on a wide scale within society."[3] For Firestone the cause of racism, class exploitation, and the oppression of women and children was the "psychology of power." And the family was its incubator.

Even then Firestone's ideas were controversial. To many feminists, Firestone's biological account of patriarchy seemed too bleak and her cybernetic solution facile. Some wondered why biology couldn't be reconceived rather than gotten rid of. Feminist anthropologists argued strenuously that the problem was the cultural interpretation of biology, not biology itself. Sherry Ortner, for one, suggested the roots of male dominance were cultural, the result of the apparently universal identification of men with culture and women with nature. Ortner didn't believe women actually were closer to nature, a fact lost on the growing number of feminists committed to reclaiming femaleness.

In the mid-'70s as radical feminism devolved into celebrations of the Goddess and Mother-Right, Ortner was sometimes invoked to prove the superiority of femaleness. Firestone was invoked too, but unfavorably. Her detractors judged her "male-identified." You could see it in her repudiation of gender, they said, not to mention her promotion of those "male" inventions—socialism, polymorphous sexuality, and technology. Then there was her strange conviction that women's intimate relations with men encouraged rather than retarded feminism by putting a "revolutionary in every bedroom." Worse still, Firestone had pronounced pregnancy "barbaric."[4] By 1975 Firestone was rapidly becoming the negative referent, the bad girl who harbored a contempt for all things "woman-identified." Ten very long years would pass before Donna Haraway's heretical declaration, "I would rather be a cyborg than a goddess."

I remember how confounded my women's studies students were when they read Firestone. Who was this strange woman who advocated getting rid of nature, and who believed feminism would actually be advanced by hetero-sexuality? How could she have been one of the founders of radical feminism? Despite my best efforts, they often saw her as a historical curiosity, a relic of a less evolved feminism. What their reaction revealed was the extent to which radical feminism was becoming ossified in certain predictable ways.

By the early '80s, mainstream feminists, never big fans of Firestone's, began attacking her and other radical feminists for having advanced a mas-culinist vision of women's equality. Betty Friedan accused feminists of ex-pressing a "lack of reverence for childbearing," and of fighting for "equality in terms of male power." Jean Elshtain hit Firestone more directly, calling her utopia a "cybernetic Brave New World." Friedan and Elshtain, advocates of a kinder and gentler feminism, argued that the family was the final outpost of compassion and nurturance in an otherwise heartless world and not, as radical feminists believed, a locus of oppression. However, in opposing the family, Firestone and other early radical feminists were not rejecting nur-turance. They were calling for a reorganization of personal life so that care and compassion would become the domain of both men and women.

Firestone knew she would be accused of creating a Brave New World where "women had become like men, crippled in the identical way." But, she insisted, "we are suggesting the opposite: rather than concentrating the female principle into a 'private' retreat, into which men periodically duck for relief, we want to rediffuse it."[5] Firestone was quite clear on this—the point was not the "drafting of women into a *male* world," but the "elimina-tion of the sex class distinction altogether." However, it was to no avail be-cause Firestone's radical feminism provoked and revealed an enormous cultural anxiety about who would provide the caretaking were women to stop being "women." Tellingly, her harshest critic, Elshtain, advised feminists to follow the example of "the handicapped movement," which she hailed for having "transcended a politics of self-interest."

Although Firestone didn't want to make men of women, she did want to escape femininity. It was her nightmare, and mine too. And why not, given the hyperdomestic '50s that consigned middle-class white girls to what Friedan called "the comfortable concentration camp" of suburban homes, or to virtual oblivion as single women? For Firestone, and many other early radical feminists, liberation lay in the unashamed refusal of gender differ-ence. This is what attracted me to radical feminism, and why celebrations of "woman-identification" have always felt like a capitulation—a return to the familiar prison of gender. Of course, it is more complicated than that. Writing on the equality-difference divide in modern feminism, Ann Snitow points out that no one gets to "stay firmly on her side of the divide." She notes that even feminist activists who want women to be bad, "nonetheless warn them there's a price to pay for daring to defy men in public space."[6] And they are right. Yet, after years of "difference" feminism, I long for what attracted me in the first place: the refusal of femininity.

No one practiced this better than Firestone, whose " 'dream'" action for women's liberation was a *"smile boycott,"* in which "all women would instantly abandon their 'pleasing' smiles, henceforth smiling only when something pleased *them*." "In my own case," Firestone explained, "I had to train myself out of that phony smile, which is like a nervous tic on every teenage girl." For women, smiling is the "equivalent of the shuffle; it indicates acquiescence of the victim to [her] own oppression." When it's not forthcoming, men respond violently; because "it makes them uncomfortable to know that the woman or the child or the black or the workman is grumbling, the oppressed groups must also appear to *like* their oppression."[7]

In *The Dialectic of Sex*, Firestone seemed "totally ready to go," which is how Patti Smith described herself on her 1975 debut album, "Horses." Firestone and Smith, the white girl visionaries of women's liberation and punk rock, respectively. Sure, there were differences. Firestone was committed to analyzing gender, while Smith ignored it as she tried to live outside its confines. But both had chutzpah at a time when it was still reserved for men. Both were subjected to enormous critical abuse. And both opted for retirement. In *Without You I'm Nothing*, Sandra Bernhard observes that Patti Smith "saw so far into the future she could afford to take 10 years off and not say another word." Smith, however, continued to write, whereas Firestone's silence was only occasionally interrupted by a letter to *Ms.* or the *Village Voice* in the 1970s.

But if Firestone disappeared from the movement, at least her book is available again. How it will fare in the women's studies programs where it was once a staple, is another matter. The truth is that, even if Firestone was ahead of her time in 1970, the book is far from hip now. Firestone's quest was for the truth, not "standpoints." Moreover, in contrast to some of today's feminist theorists whose impenetrable prose and ritual genuflections to

Lacan, Derrida, and Foucault have become depressingly familiar (and may be the academic expression of good-girlism), Firestone wrote without obfuscation and took risks. Of course, it was a different era. Firestone, like many '60s theorists, wrestled with Marx and Freud—two thinkers who've been relegated to theory's bargain basement. Moreover, Firestone wrote for a movement, not a tenure committee. As feminism found harbor inside the academy, theoretical moves too often became career moves; the risk-taking that characterized Firestone's work was the casualty.

Then there's the likely resistance of students who would rather condemn feminism as irrevocably racist than analyze the reasons for its racism. Firestone's book, which is both remarkably astute and painfully obtuse about race, would be an ideal text for getting at what Adrienne Rich called the "snow blindness" of white feminists. On the one hand, just as new leftists emulated black men, feminists like Firestone clearly took much of their inspiration from black women, whose self-reliance they envied and romanticized. They considered themselves antiracist and were puzzled when women of color stayed away from the movement. On the other hand, Firestone and other white feminists were unable to see their many mechanisms of exclusion, beginning with the assumption that their "woman" was everywoman. Nor did they understand that their treatment of all other systems of hierarchy as mere "extensions of sexism" seemed a way of subsuming, and thus ignoring, race—the very maneuver that had been used against feminism.

Like so many '60s books, searching for grand syntheses, *The Dialectic of Sex* is simultaneously profound and flaky. Talk of totalizing politics and mechanistic solutions! But one reads it not for prescriptions, but for Firestone's insights into the operations of gender and the family. Rereading *The Dialectic of Sex* makes me wonder if the movement's trajectory might not have been different had Firestone stuck around. What if bad-girl feminism hadn't been overwhelmed by its good girl variant? Would "women's music" have rocked instead of bored? What if Firestone had continued pointing to the difficulties in developing a feminist critique of sexuality? Would feminists have paid greater attention to sexual pleasure? It was Firestone, after all, who observed that feminism's goal wasn't the "elimination of sexual joy and excitement," but rather its "rediffusion" over "the spectrum of our lives." Who knows, maybe even Patti Smith would have felt an affinity with feminism had Shulie stuck around.

7
THE TAMING OF THE ID:
FEMINIST SEXUAL POLITICS, 1968–1983

I N REVIEWING THE LAST FIFTEEN
years of radical feminist sexual
politics, it seems that one element
has remained constant—sex is as difficult and contested an area for feminists in 1983 as it was in the earliest days of the movement. Although it often
seems as though we have been engaged in one long, seamless debate all
these years, radical feminist sexual politics have changed in very fundamental ways over the decade. For instance, while early radical feminists
were hardly uninterested in identifying particular sexual expressions as
feminist and others patriarchal, today's radical feminists have developed a
more highly prescriptive understanding of sexuality—one which in some
crucial respects is antithetical to early radical feminist sexual politics. In the
following pages, I will explore the permutations in radical feminist sexual
politics since the late 1960s so that we might better appreciate the theoretical distance we have traveled.

However, it is impossible to understand current feminist views on sexuality without first analyzing broader shifts in feminist thinking on gender
over the past decade. In fact, our understanding of gender really informs
our analysis of sexuality. Early radical feminists believed that women's oppression derived from the very construction of gender and sought its elimination as a meaningful social category. Today's radical feminists, by contrast, claim that our oppression stems from the repression of female values
and treat gender differences as though they reflect deep truths about the

---

This essay first appeared in Carole Vance, ed., *Pleasure and Danger: Exploring Female Sexuality* (New York: Routledge, 1984).

intractability of maleness and femaleness. For instance, in 1972 Bonnie Kreps argued that women's oppression "is based on the corrupt notion of 'maleness vs. femaleness,'" yet in 1979 Janice Raymond asks ominously what feminists "can hope to agree on . . . if [we] cannot agree on the boundaries of what constitutes femaleness?"[1]

For any oppressed group it is tempting to seek solace in the reclaiming of that identity which the larger culture has systematically denigrated. This approach becomes especially compelling when the possibilities for radical change seem remote, and the only alternative seems to be assimilation into an oppressive and inegalitarian system. Unfortunately, as recent feminism has become synonymous with the rehabilitation of female values, it has come to reflect and reproduce dominant cultural assumptions about women. For instance, antipornography feminists suggest that women's sexual inhibition is further confirmation of women's superiority rather than emblematic of our oppression. And, in contradiction to early radical feminists who maintained that the identification of women with nature is a patriarchal construct, many ecofeminists and pacifist feminists claim not only that women are closer to nature, but that our "bond with the natural order" makes us uniquely qualified to save the planet from nuclear holocaust and ecological ruination.[2]

I believe that what we have come to identify as radical feminism represents such a fundamental departure from its roots that it requires renaming. To this end, I will refer to this more recent strain of feminism as cultural feminism, because it equates women's liberation with the nurturance of a female counter culture which it is hoped will supersede the dominant culture.[3] Cultural feminism's polarization of male and female sexuality and its demonization of the former and idealization of the latter has its political incarnation in the antipornography movement. By the end of the 1970s, cultural feminism had achieved hegemony within the movement and its celebration of femaleness, which has led some to label it "femininism," not only informs the antipornography campaign, but ecofeminism and the feminist peace movement as well. Like its French counterpart, *néoféminité,* cultural feminism is "an ideal bound up through symmetrical opposition in the very ideological system feminists want to destroy."[4] Of course, to propose that there exists a theoretical coherence to cultural feminism is not to suggest that it is monolithic.

While cultural feminists are committed to preserving rather than challenging gender differences, some demonstrate a cavalier disregard for whether these differences are biological or cultural in origin. In *The Transsexual Empire*, Janice Raymond argues:

> Yet there are differences, and some feminists have come to realize that those differences are important whether they spring from socialization, from biology, or from the total history of existing as a woman in a patriarchal society.

RAYMOND CONSIDERS THE SOURCE of these differences irrelevant, because she reasons that, as women, "we know who *we* are." (her italics)[5]

Even more troubling than equivocation of this sort is the growing tendency among other cultural feminists to invoke biological explanations of gender differences. This is a particularly ironic development, given radical feminists' opposition to precultural explanations of gender asymmetry.[6] These cultural feminists generally attribute male dominance to the rapaciousness or barrenness of male biology. Thus Susan Brownmiller accepts that rape is a function of male biology, while Mary Daly argues that the "emptiness" of male biology explains male supremacy. As though it proves her point, Daly cites archconservative George Gilder's view that "while the female body is full of internal potentiality, the male is internally barren."[7] While Daly suggests that men are "mutants [who may like other mutations] manage to kill themselves off eventually," Sally Gearhart insists that the preservation of the planet requires that the "proportion of men must be reduced to and maintained at approximately 10% of the human race."[8]

Although radical feminists viewed female biology as a liability and thus in some cases mirrored the culture's devaluation of the female body, cultural feminists have overreacted to this earlier position in arguing that female biology is a powerful resource.[9] While Jane Alpert's 1973 article, "Mother-Right," is the earliest articulation of this revisionism, Adrienne Rich is its most eloquent exponent:

> I have come to believe, as will be clear throughout this book, that female biology . . . has far more radical implications than we have yet come to appreciate. Patriarchal thought has limited female biology to its own narrow specifications. The feminist vision has recoiled from female biology for these reasons; it will, I believe, come to view our

physicality as a resource, rather than a destiny. In order to live a truly human life we require not only *control* of our bodies . . . we must touch the unity and resonance of our physicality, our bond with the natural order, the corporeal ground of our intelligence. (her italics)[10]

ALTHOUGH RICH FAILS to acknowledge that feminist biological determinism might reproduce dominant cultural assumptions about women, Gearhart admits that it does:

> But if by believing that women are by nature less violent we reinforce the sex roles that have held women down for so long, then perhaps it is time to dare to admit that some of the sex-role mythology is in fact true and to insist that the qualities attributed to women (specifically empathy, nurturance and cooperativeness) be affirmed as human qualities capable of cultivation by men even if denied them by nature.[11]

Not all cultural feminists are enthusiastic supporters of biologically-based explanations of gender. Both Florence Rush and Andrea Dworkin have criticized biological determinism. However, for others, like Robin Morgan, the danger lies less in the concept itself than in the control of its application. Morgan has advised feminists against accepting "biological-determination theories . . . until we have enough feminists to right the current imbalance and bias and to create a genuinely value-free science."[12]

This new feminist biological determinism, like its antifeminist counterpart, is fraught with contradictions. For instance, cultural feminists distinguish between patriarchally conditioned femininity which they associate with passivity and submissiveness, and female nature which they assume to be nurturant, tender, and egalitarian. However, no such distinction is made between patriarchally conditioned masculinity and biologically determined maleness. So while female passivity is believed to be socially constructed, male violence is seen as intrinsic and the crystallization of maleness.

Although radical feminists often stressed the psychological dimension of women's oppression, they understood the importance of analyzing and challenging the material basis of patriarchy. By contrast, cultural feminists have demonstrated less interest in effecting structural change than in nurturing an alternative female consciousness, or what Mary Daly terms "the spring into free space."[13] Cultural feminists believe that the struggle against male supremacy begins with women exorcizing the male within us and maximizing our femaleness. And while radical feminists were generally careful to distinguish between individual and political solutions, cultural feminists typically believe that individual solutions are political solutions. Cultural feminism's validation of individual solutions not only encouraged the scrutiny of personal behavior rather than ideas but contributed to the development of standards of "liberated" behavior. It has also fostered a blamatory and elitist attitude among those who consider themselves "woman-identified." In one of the most egregious examples of this, Daly has suggested that heterosexual women could get themselves "off the hook of the . . . contraceptive dilemma" were they to follow the example of "Spinsters"—"women who choose to be agents of be-ing"—and elect "Misterectomy."[14]

Finally, whereas radical feminists like Shulamith Firestone believed that a "sexual revolution much larger than—inclusive of—a socialist one [was needed] to truly eradicate all class systems," cultural feminists see capitalism and socialism as equally injurious to women.[15] While radical feminists "criticized the left *from the left* for refusing to broaden its analysis to account for women's oppression," cultural feminists insist that feminism and the left are intrinsically incompatible.[16] For cultural feminists, the left, like pornography, is an intrusive and contaminating force which prevents us from fully "dispossessing ourselves" of our patriarchal past.[17] In fact, cultural feminism began to emerge as philosophically distinct from radical feminism in early 1975 with the creation of the Circle of Support for Jane Alpert. Rather than deny the charge that Alpert had supplied the FBI with information about fellow members of the underground, the Circle rejoiced in her defection from the left and her conversion to feminism.[18]

But it was in the mid-1970s phenomenon of feminist capitalism that cultural feminism really took shape. These early cultural feminists treated capitalism as a relatively benign system that could be enlisted in the struggle to defeat patriarchy.[19] Some even embraced capitalism while repudiating democratic process and rationalized this position by invoking women's superiority and commonality of interests.[20] Those feminists who criticized their attempt to wed capitalism with feminism were characterized as "aping" the "correct-line politics" and "trashing" style of the male left.[21] Antipornography feminists have tried to silence their intramovement critics with the same red-baiting tactics used against critics of feminist capitalism. Recently, Kathy Barry characterized the feminist opposition to the antipornography movement as a cabal of leftist women—lesbian and heterosexual alike—who want to destroy the movement so that "male leftists can continue their sexual abuse of women without fear of censure."[22]

Cultural feminists vilify the left because its analysis so completely contravenes their belief system, especially their faith that truly radical change will be achieved only when the culture "returns" to female values and that race and class are merely ancillary to gender hierarchy. Just as some socialists argue that socialism will eliminate women's oppression, cultural feminists maintain that feminism will eradicate race and class oppression. Cultural feminist faith in women's superiority and commonality not only encourages them to label dissent "unsisterly" or left-inspired, but it promotes political expediency as well.[23]

Given this theoretical incompatibility, how did radical feminism devolve into cultural feminism? In part the fragmentation within our ranks and the erosion of feminist gains in the recent past have made cultural feminism, with its promise of female unity, especially attractive. More specifically, the debate around the relationship of lesbianism to feminism was, to a great extent, responsible for promoting the assumptions which underlie cultural feminism. The struggle for lesbian visibility and recognition in the 1970s was extremely important because it forced feminists to acknowledge that sexuality is socially conditioned and that heterosexuality is culturally, rather than biologically, mandated. But the homophobia, and, to a lesser extent, the antisex attitudes within certain elements of the movement precluded lesbian feminists from promoting lesbianism as a sexual rather than a political choice. Initially, some heterosexual feminists, reflecting dominant cultural assumptions, defined and dismissed lesbianism as a solely sexual experience. And for Ti-Grace Atkinson, founder of the New York group The Feminists, and Abby Rockefeller of the Boston group Cell 16, who believed that sex is the foundation of women's oppression, lesbianism was particularly threatening. For instance, Atkinson cautioned:

A case could be made that lesbianism, in fact *all* sex, is reactionary, and that feminism is revolutionary. . . . Because lesbianism involves role-playing and more important, because it is based on the primary assumption of male oppression, that is, sex, lesbianism reinforces the sex class system. (her italics)[24]

AND ROCKEFELLER ARGUED that lesbianism "muddles what is the real issue for women by making it appear that women really like sex as much as men—that they just don't like sex *with* men." (her italics)[25] Even Anne Koedt, whose politics could hardly be characterized as erotophobic, hedged her approval of lesbianism:

> Two lesbians who have chosen not to fall into imitative roles, but are instead exploring the positive aspects of both "masculine" and "feminine" behavior beyond roles—forming something new and equal in the process—would in my opinion probably be healthy.[26]

GIVEN THIS CONTEXT, it is understandable that many lesbian feminists found it easier to justify their sexuality on exclusively political grounds.

Lesbian recognition was achieved by locating the discourse within the already established framework of separatism. The conviction that feminism is conditional upon separation from men predated lesbian separatism. For example, The Feminists established a quota system at the time of their founding in 1969 to limit women living with men to one-third of the group's membership.[27] Lesbian separatists, like the Washington, D.C., Furies collective, argued further that heterosexual women were impeding the movement's progress. Furies member Rita Mae Brown opined:

> Straight women are confused by men, don't put women first. They betray lesbians and in its deepest form, they betray their own selves. You can't build a strong movement if your sisters are out there fucking with the oppressor.[28]

BY DEFINING LESBIANISM as a political choice and encouraging an idealization of female sexuality, lesbian feminists deprived heterosexual feminists of one of their favorite charges against lesbianism—that it was male-identified.[29] However, this assumption that sexual relationships with men are inevitably debilitating while those with women are automatically liberating has had, as we shall see, serious consequences for lesbian sexuality.

Furthermore, in establishing lesbianism as a true measure of one's commitment to feminism, lesbian separatists distorted the meaning of "the personal is political," giving it a prescriptive rather than a descriptive meaning. Of course, the tendency to judge a woman on the basis of her sexual preference, marital status, or hair length did not originate with lesbian separatism, but it was further legitimated by it.[30]

Lesbian separatism's open hostility to heterosexual feminists guaranteed that it would remain a minority view. However, in its reincarnation as cultural feminism, lesbian separatism has been modified and refined in such a way as to make it more acceptable to a wider audience. Whereas lesbian separatists advocated separation from men, cultural feminists advocate separation from male values. And rather than promote lesbianism, cultural feminists encourage woman-bonding and thus avoid estranging heterosexual feminists.

With the rise of cultural feminism, relations between lesbian and heterosexual feminists have become more cordial. However, the very terms of this reconciliation have ensured that suspicion and acrimony would be preserved, though often below the surface. First, lesbian recognition has been achieved by further abstracting it from the realm of sexuality—cloaking it as female bonding. And lesbian acceptance is contingent upon the extent to which our relationships conform to standards of egalitarianism. Second, although they are more likely to be defined now as victims rather than traitors, heterosexual feminists remain objects of suspicion, for their acceptance depends upon how completely they conceal or renounce heterosexual desire. Ironically, heterosexual feminists are still made to feel like the movement's backsliders by virtue of their proximity to contaminating maleness. Occasionally hostility surfaces, as it did at the 1979 Women Against Pornography conference when a lesbian separatist denounced Susan Brownmiller as a "cocksucker." Brownmiller retaliated by pointing out that her critic "even dresses like a man."[31] But, with the antipornography movement, cultural feminism has succeeded in mobilizing feminists regardless of sexual preference, however fragile the alliance.

Radical feminists embraced a dualistic approach to sexuality—one which acknowledged both the danger and the pleasure associated with sexual exploration for women in this culture. For instance, the popularity of feminist sex manuals was not believed to undermine the effectiveness of the antirape movement. While radical feminists recognized that the ideology of the sexual revolution discriminated against women, they did not conclude from this, as have cultural feminists, that sexual liberation and women's liberation are mutually exclusive. For instance, in *The Dialectic of Sex*, Shulamith Firestone argued that "in our new society, humanity could finally revert to its natural polymorphous sexuality—all forms of sexuality would be allowed and indulged."[32] In a 1971 article, "Thoughts on Promiscuity," Karen Lindsey claimed that men's continued acceptance of the sexual double standard had sabotaged the sexual revolution. Moreover, she warned that:

> unless we understand, very exactly, what is at the heart of the failure in our sexual experimenting, we are, in fact, in danger of reverting to a rejection of sex without love—with all the self-denial, smugness, guilt, and dishonesty that goes with such a rejection.[33]

Radical feminists did not idealize women's sexual conservatism, but rather would have agreed with Muriel Dimen that "female sexual turf and male emotional range need expansion."[34] For instance, Karen Durbin contended that rock music encouraged female sexual assertion:

> Rock music . . . provided me and a lot of women with a channel for saying, "I want," for asserting our sexuality without apologies and without having to pretty up every passion with the traditionally "feminine" desire for true love and marriage, and that was a useful step toward liberation.[35]

Radical feminists understood that women's sexual inhibition is related in large part to the absence of safe, accessible, and effective contraception, which renders women sexually vulnerable. They attributed women's attachment to traditional morality not to the innately spiritual quality of women's sexuality, but rather to our socialization which encourages sexual alienation and guilt. This consciousness informed the radical feminist struggle for reproductive rights. Radical feminists understood, as does the New Right, that the fight for reproductive freedom is the struggle for sexual self-determination.

Of course, from the earliest days of the women's movement there were those radical feminists whose views on sexuality anticipated cultural feminist sexual politics. Ti-Grace Atkinson declared that "*all* sex is reactionary." Dana Densmore suggested that celibacy is preferable to "making love to a man who despises you."[36] And Abby Rockefeller claimed that "women *don't* like [sex] either with the same frequency or in the same way as men." (her italics)[37] But these views represented a minority opinion within the ranks of radical feminists.

However, in some crucial respects radical feminist thinking on sexuality did contribute to the development of cultural feminist sexual politics. Radical feminists' skepticism toward individual solutions disinclined them from defining "the personal is political" prescriptively. However, this same wariness encouraged them to trivialize individual attempts toward sexual empowerment. For instance, two reporters for the feminist newspaper *off our backs* criticized NOW's 1974 Conference on Sexuality for focusing upon sexual technique rather than political analysis:

> Viewing [the conference] from . . . a strictly radical feminist per-
> spective . . . we react with anger and disappointment. We went hop-
> ing to hear some feminist analyses of women's sexuality. Instead, we
> were inundated with tales of organic masturbation parties, bisexual
> chic, and why whips can be fun.[38]

WHILE RADICAL FEMINISTS disparaged personal solutions, they nonethe-less believed that one's sexuality should mirror one's politics—a conviction that promoted prescriptivism. In their desire to develop a genuinely femi-nist sexuality, radical feminists subordinated sexuality to politics in what Deirdre English has suggested is a feminist version of "sexuality in service to society."[39] Most importantly, by envisioning feminist sexuality as requir-ing the elimination of power, radical feminism encouraged us to renounce our sexuality as it is now. In assuming that a liberated sexuality demanded the disentanglement of power and sexuality, radical feminists, quite unin-tentionally, contributed to our alienation from psychological and social sources of sexual power.

On the whole, however, cultural feminist thinking on sexuality repre-sents a significant deviation from radical feminist sexual politics. In the cul-tural feminist analysis, sexual danger so defines women's lives that it pre-cludes a consideration of sexual pleasure. Unlike radical feminists, who generally located the source of women's oppression in the nuclear family, cultural feminists agree with Andrea Dworkin that "the heart of sex oppression [is] the use of women as pornography, pornography as what women *are*."[40] The argument that "pornography is the theory, rape the practice," represents cultural feminism's contribution to the domino theory of sexuality.[41] It identifies pornography as the scourge which leads inexorably to violence against women. More recently, antipornography feminists have extended their critique to encompass fantasy, which they claim is dangerous because it entails the substitution of an illusion for the "social-sexual reality" of another person. In rejecting as so much "male-identified mind-body dualism" the belief that fantasy is the repository of our ambivalent and conflictual feelings, cultural feminists have developed a highly mechanistic, behaviorist analysis that conflates fantasy with reality and pornography with violence. "Integrity," their answer to patriarchy's dangerous dualism, entails the transformation of all aspects of our lives into one seamless, unambiguous reflection of our politics.[42] Such a view assumes that we can and should be held accountable for our desires. And if we fail to banish those tainted fantasies, we can console ourselves with Julia Penelope's suggestion that fantasy may be another "phallocentric 'need' from which we are not yet free."[43]

Cultural feminists define male and female sexuality as though they were polar opposites. Male sexuality is driven, irresponsible, genitally oriented, and potentially lethal. Female sexuality is muted, diffuse, interpersonally-oriented, and benign. Men crave power and orgasm, while women seek reciprocity and intimacy. Although cultural feminists often assume the immutability of male and female sexuality, the prescriptivism which permeates their writing reflects an underlying fear about their mutability. For instance, in her 1973 West Coast Lesbian Feminist Conference address, Robin Morgan warned that lesbian feminists who advocated nonmonogamy, accepted transvestites, and listened to the Rolling Stones had adopted a "male style [which] could be a destroyer from within" the women's movement.[44] By defining the pursuit of relationships as female and the pursuit of sex as male, Morgan tried to intimidate her lesbian audience back into the familiar terrain of romantic love:

Every woman here knows in her gut the vast differences between her sexuality and that of any patriarchally trained male's—gay or straight . . . that the emphasis on genital sexuality, objectification, promiscuity, emotional noninvolvement, and coarse invulnerability was the *male style*, and that we, as women, placed greater trust in love, sensuality, humor, tenderness, commitment. (her italics)[45]

UNLIKE RADICAL FEMINISTS who attacked romantic love, cultural feminists apotheosize it.[46]

For cultural feminists, male sexuality is not only compulsive, but, as Dworkin has described it, "the stuff of murder, not love."[47] Thus, for men, sexuality and violence are inextricably linked and find their cultural expression in pornography. Cultural feminists are so convinced that male sexuality is, at its core, lethal, that they reduce it to its most alienated and violent expressions. The actions of de Sade or Son of Sam come to symbolize the murderousness of male sexuality, and sexual intercourse becomes a mere euphemism for rape.[48] Liberal and leftist men who oppose censorship are characterized as having a prurient interest in pornography. And men's growing interest in their partner's sexual satisfaction is said simply to demonstrate men's obsession with sexual performance. Everything, no matter how contradictory, confirms the premise that male sexuality is selfish, violent, and woman-hating. Their characterization of male sexuality is so uniformly unflattering and overwhelmingly bleak that one wonders what would be accomplished by the restriction or elimination of pornography.[49]

By contrast, women's sexuality is assumed to be more spiritual than sexual, and considerably less central to their lives than is sexuality to men's. For instance, Adrienne Rich describes female sexuality as an "energy which is unconfined to any single part of the body or solely to the body itself."[50] And Ethel Person maintains that "many women have the capacity to abstain from sex without negative psychological consequences." For Person, women's more highly developed "capacity for abstinence, repression, or suppression [has] adaptive advantages" over male hypersexuality.[51] Person fails to understand that women's apparent mental health in the face of anorgasmia or abstention testifies to women's conditioning to subordinate and repress sexual drive. Unfortunately, sexual repression may very well become adaptive for women once again if the Human Life Amendment and Family Protection Act are enacted into law.[52] In fact, cultural feminism feeds what one feminist has described as "our society's treasured illusion that male sexuality is like a bludgeon or a speeding train," and its equally cherished corollary that women seek affection rather than orgasm in their sexual encounters.[53]

It follows from this that cultural feminists would see heterosexuality as a metaphor for male rapaciousness and female victimization. In contrast to lesbian feminists for whom heterosexuality generally represented collaboration with the enemy, cultural feminists appear to take a more sympathetic position toward heterosexual women. They understand women's participation in heterosexuality as more apparent than real, and suggest that women are coerced and bribed into compliance with heterosexual norms. For instance, Adrienne Rich cites Barry's *Female Sexual Slavery* as evidence that "for women heterosexuality may not be a 'preference' at all but something that has to be imposed, managed, organized, propagandized, and maintained by force."[54] Although specific explanations vary, cultural feminists believe that for women heterosexuality is neither fully chosen nor truly pleasurable. It is worth noting that heterosexual cultural feminists seem to accept this understanding of their sexuality, although to do so would appear to involve guilt and self-depreciation, if not self-flagellation.

If the cultural feminist view of heterosexuality is overdetermined, their position on sexual minorities is myopic. Janice Raymond maintains that "all transsexuals rape women's bodies by reducing the real female form to an artifact, appropriating this body for themselves."[55] The contradiction of transsexualism is that it both undermines and reinforces gender as a significant category. However, cultural feminists, especially those who favor biological determinism, find transsexualism troubling, because it confounds the boundaries between maleness and femaleness. But cultural feminists' real contempt is reserved for male-to-female lesbian-feminist transsexuals who seduce lesbians, they argue, by appealing to their vestigial heterosexuality. Mary Daly complains that their "whole presence becomes a 'member' invading women's presence and dividing us once more from each other."[56]

Cultural feminists believe that the centrality of public and anonymous sex to the gay male sexual landscape merely demonstrates that heterosexual men have no monopoly on sexual callousness. They maintain that the gay male subculture of s/m and cross-generational sex is further evidence of male rapacity.[57] NOW endorsed this view at its 1980 convention, which adopted the infamous resolution designed to ensure that NOW not work with any groups that might misconstrue pornography, s/m, cross-generational sex, and public sex as "Lesbian Rights issues."[58] Ironically, the resolution was introduced by the chair of NOW's Sexual Preference Task Force.[59]

How has it come to pass that some lesbians are in the forefront of a movement which has resurrected terms like "sexual deviance" and "perversion"—terms which one would have thought the feminist movement made anachronistic a decade ago? Lesbian cultural feminists would, however, explain, as does Adrienne Rich, that lesbianism is a "profoundly female experience" which needs to be dissociated from "male homosexual values and allegiances."[60] Lesbian cultural feminists' insistence that lesbianism is an issue of "radical female friendship" rather than sexual preference reflects an unwillingness to admit that within the larger culture lesbianism is viewed as a "perversion."[61] For instance, Sally Gearhart suggests that lesbian sexuality is wholesome:

> In being part of the word "gay" weary lesbians have spent untold hours explaining to Middle America that lesbians do not worry about venereal disease, do not have sex in public bathrooms . . . and do not want to go to the barricades fighting for the lowering of the age of consent.[62]

Even more, this hostility toward other sexual minorities reflects their fear that male sexuality as it is symbolized to them in s/m, cross-generational sex, transsexualism, and pornography is polluting the "women's community." Adrienne Rich maintains that pornography impairs the "potential of loving and being loved by women in mutuality and integrity."[63] Raymond cautions us against accepting lesbian-feminist male-to-female transsexuals into our communities, for she fears they might "seduce" us back into heterosexuality.[64] And Gearhart complains:

> I am frustrated and angry that . . . many gay men remain totally oblivious to the effect on women of their objectification of each other, their obsession with youth and beauty, their camped-up consumerism, and their demand for freer sexual expression.[65]

STATEMENTS LIKE THESE betray an apprehension that women's sexuality may not be innately ethereal and that lesbianism may not offer the uncomplicated refuge from what Rita Mae Brown in 1972 termed the "silly, stupid, harmful games that men and women play."[66] But rather than acknowledge that the quest for completely egalitarian relationships and politically-correct sex has proved difficult at best, lesbian cultural feminists have retreated from the ambiguities of sexuality and have used ideological justifications to de-emphasize sex. The growing number of lesbian feminists experimenting with s/m, butch-femme roles, and bisexuality only demonstrates to lesbian cultural feminists that we must be more vigilant in the struggle against the residual heterosexuality which they believe informs these "deviations." They see in the growth of the lesbian-feminist sexual fringe the corrupting influence of male-identified sexuality rather than a rebellion against the ever-narrowing standard for politically permissible sexuality.[67]

This admonition that our sexuality mirror our politics may have originated with radical feminists, but for lesbian cultural feminists it has become the justification for a destructive sexual prescriptivism. The sexual repressiveness of the lesbian cultural feminist orthodoxy has contributed to the heterophobia which is in turn vented in the antipornography movement. Perhaps the movement's success in enlisting the support of certain sectors of the lesbian community reflects the extent to which the movement validates lesbianism through its demonization of maleness and heterosexuality.

For cultural feminists the proliferation of pornography, the apparent increase in rape and incest, and the growing assertiveness of the sexual fringe testify to the evils of sexual permissiveness. They indict pornography for eroding the traditional boundary separating the virgin from the whore. Morgan argues that pornography has contributed to a "new 'all women are really whores' attitude, thus erasing the last vestige of (even corrupted) respect for women."[68] Although pornography is obviously the focus of their struggle, cultural feminists believe that the real villain is the sexual revolution rather than its "propaganda" tool, pornography. Cultural feminists never seem to consider that the apparent growth in violence against women might demonstrate the effectiveness of the feminist movement in challenging the heretofore closeted and uncontested nature of rape, battery, and incest rather than the success of the sexual revolution in promoting these crimes.[69] Instead they maintain that the sexual revolution allowed men to choose "swinging" over commitment, pornographic images over real people, and violence over love.

More importantly, cultural feminists argue that the sexual revolution's affirmation of male sexual values encouraged women to abandon female sexual values in a misguided quest for assimilation. According to Barry, who here sounds disturbingly like Phyllis Schlafly, many women have rejected intimacy only to discover that "new problems arose as they escaped from male power into self-centeredness, and as they tried to depersonalize their sexual being."[70] Cultural feminists also accuse rampant individualism of discouraging intimacy by encouraging us to become selfishly absorbed in meeting our own needs. Barry has even vilified democracy for breeding a "pluralistic notion of cultural diversity" which in turn encourages a perilous tolerance toward "sexual perversion."[71] For cultural feminists sexual freedom is a reactionary, rather than a subversive, force which secures social order by numbing us into political apathy.[72]

This analysis fails to explain why the Reagan administration is more intent upon ushering us back into the sexual repressiveness of the 1950s than in promoting sexual liberation. This equation of sexual freedom with irresponsibility, selfishness, and dehumanization has, in fact, already been used by the New Right in its struggle against feminism, abortion, and gay rights. This analysis further denies the extent to which early radical feminism was a rebellion against traditional sexual morality. The sexual revolution's failure to challenge gender asymmetry hardly justifies cultural feminists' promotion of a traditional sexual standard—albeit modified to include those lesbians and gay men whose sexuality appears to be orthodox. And by fingering individualism as the enemy, cultural feminism ignores the role individualism played in the emergence of the women's movement. Individualism may be bourgeois, but it is precisely the breakdown of a familial orientation and the development of individualism which gave birth to feminism.[73]

To curb the promiscuity and rapacity spawned by the sexual revolution, cultural feminists propose that we impose upon the culture a female sexual standard—a standard which seems to correspond to their understanding of their mothers' sexual values. Thus Morgan argues that in repudiating sexual liberation she is affirming her identification with her mother.[74] And Barry suggests:

In going back into new sexual values we are really going back to the values women have always attached to sexuality, values that have been robbed from us, and destroyed as we have been colonized through both sexual violence and so-called liberation.[75]

Cultural feminist sexual politics really offer us nothing more than women's traditional sexual values disguised as radical feminist sexual values. Moreover, these values derive not from our biology, as Barry suggests, but from our powerlessness. In promoting romantic love as an authentically female and thus feminist sexuality, cultural feminists endorse the same constraining sexuality to which our mothers were condemned. Rather than develop a feminist understanding of sexual liberation, cultural feminists reject it as inherently antifeminist and instead endorse a sexual code which drastically circumscribes the sorts of sexual expressions considered acceptable. And, in demanding "respect," rather than challenging the terms upon which women are granted "respect," cultural feminists reinforce the distinction between the virgin and the whore.

In fact their solution to violence against women is nothing more than a return to the spurious "respect" traditionally reserved for women. This analysis confuses "respect" for liberation and fails to recognize that "respect" is merely the flip side of violation. More importantly, this view suggests that sexual repression is a satisfactory solution to violence against women. Antipornography feminist Diana Russell has admitted that censorship would only push pornography underground, but she reasons this is preferable to seeing it "flourish as an accepted part of the culture."[76]

Cultural feminists seem nostalgic for the old days when men "respected" some women, women acknowledged that love was female and sex was male, and pornography was kept behind the counter. Although cultural feminists blame the sexual revolution for destroying the old sexual order, radical feminists' attack on marriage, romantic love, puritan morality, and respect certainly hastened its downfall. In fact, the cultural feminist analysis of sexuality constitutes an unacknowledged repudiation of radical feminist sexual politics. The radical feminist critiques of the nuclear family, sexual repression, the State and religion have disappeared from the cultural feminist analysis, which focuses instead upon the "pornographic mind" and sexual permissiveness. And as we have seen, cultural feminists are in

the process of rehabilitating much of what radical feminists found most oppressive to women.

Why do cultural feminists, while recognizing that they cannot eliminate
pornography, continue to define it as the overriding feminist issue? On one
level the antipornography campaign represents a calculated attempt to
unify and fortify a movement seriously divided by the issues of race, class,
and sexual preference and badly demoralized by the antifeminist backlash.
In their desperate efforts to construct a mass women's movement to combat
male lust, antipornography feminists abandon feminism for female moral
outrage.[77] For instance, antipornography activist Judith Bat-Ada insists that
a "coalition of all women . . . regardless of race, color, creed, religion, or *political persuasion*" should be formed to fight pornography (emphasis
mine).[78] Unfortunately, in advocating sexual repression as a solution to violence against women, cultural feminists resort to mobilizing women
around their fears rather than their visions.[79]

On a less obvious level, the antipornography movement's insistence
upon the incorrigibility of male sexuality suggests that it is concerned with
something other than its reformation. This movement is as much an attempt to regulate female sexuality as it is an effort to curb men's sexuality.
The movement's monomaniacal concern with sexual danger, epitomized by
Barry's claim that "sexual slavery lurks in the corners of every woman's
life," and its disinterest in developing strategies for sexual empowerment
discourage women from struggling toward sexual self-definition.[80] It has
become a vehicle to establish the proper parameters of lesbian sexuality so
as to diminish the possibility that lesbians will defect to "male-identified"
sexual expressions, whether these be s/m, roles, or heterosexuality. Perhaps antipornography feminists prefer to foreclose on sexuality rather than
to explore it and to risk discovering the disjuncture between their desires
and their politics.

Although the movement's villainization of heterosexuality seems to
offer heterosexual feminists very little but self-denial and guilt, it should be
understood that they do achieve a measure of political legitimacy by virtue
of their status as victims of male lust. For lesbian and heterosexual feminists alike, the antipornography crusade functions as the feminist equivalent to the antiabortion movement—reinforcing and validating women's
sexual alienation and manipulating women's sense of themselves as the cul-

ture's victims as well as its moral guardians. The antipornography movement, like the antiabortion movement, represents a rebellion against the
new sexual order. In acknowledging women's right to sexual pleasure while
ignoring the risks associated with sexual exploration for women, the sexual
revolution has heightened women's sense of sexual vulnerability.[81] But do
we really want to return to the old sexual order whereby women were accorded male protection in exchange for sexual circumspection?

On a more profound level, I suspect that the sexual problematic is related to the mother-daughter problematic. The cultural feminist injunction
against "going too far" sexually may also be an injunction against going too
far, or becoming too differentiated, from our mothers. Whereas radical feminism represented a rebellion against the mother in which identification
with the mother was suppressed, cultural feminism represents fusion with
the mother in which differences between mother and daughter are suppressed. Perhaps cultural feminists advise us to embrace our mother's puta-
tive sexual values because they fear that the sexual empowerment and self-
definition implicit in radical feminism involve a betrayal of our mothers?[82]

In conclusion, I suggest that we reclaim the radical feminist vision that
joined sexual liberation with women's liberation. The struggle for sexual
pleasure is legitimate and need not imply a callous disregard of sexual
danger. In order to develop a truly transformative sexual politics we must
once again resist the familiarity of sexual repression and the platitudes
about male and female sexuality. But we must also break with the radical
feminist tradition which encourages us to subordinate sexuality to politics
in an effort to make our sexuality conform to our political ideology, treating our sexuality as an ugly blemish which with vigilance and time might be
overcome. We must abandon the belief so deeply entrenched in the feminist community that particular sexual expressions are intrinsically liberated or intrinsically degraded. Inequality can exist in relationships where
the lovemaking is assiduously egalitarian as well as in relationships where
the polarized roles of top and bottom are carefully cultivated.[83] We should
acknowledge the possibility that power inheres in sexuality rather than assume that power simply withers away in egalitarian relationships. Perhaps
we might achieve more equality were we to negotiate rather than deny
power. The solution is not to reprivatize sexuality or eschew a critical
analysis of sexuality. Nor is our sexuality so hopelessly conditioned that

our efforts to transform it are misguided and futile. Instead we need to develop a feminist understanding of sexuality which is not predicated upon denial
and repression, but which acknowledges the complexities and ambiguities of
sexuality. Above all, we should admit that we know far too little about sexuality to embark upon a crusade to circumscribe it. Rather than foreclose on
sexuality we should identify what conditions will best afford women sexual
autonomy, safety, and pleasure and work toward their realization.

8

queer like us?

ENTERED GRADUATE SCHOOL JUST AS the reverberations of gay liberation began to be felt in the academy. However, in history, a particularly hidebound discipline, the tremors barely registered. It is no accident that the first substantial effort to write gays into U.S. history, *Gay American History*, which appeared in 1976, was written by an independent scholar, Jonathan Ned Katz.[1] The skepticism, even hostility, of many traditional historians toward this new enterprise ensured that many of the academic historians who pioneered the field were well established, or at least tenured. Although gay and lesbian history hasn't achieved the mainstream success of women's history, it is no longer a pariah field. Many colleges and universities now offer courses in lesbian and gay history and even conventional history journals publish articles in the field. What follows is not a comprehensive review essay, but rather an effort to chart the broad trajectory of the field, and explore some of the challenges that queer theory poses for historians of lesbians and gays.

IN 1977 WHEN I BEGAN teaching women's studies, lesbianism was smuggled into the curriculum under the rubric of "woman-identification." In our hands, lesbianism wasn't a sexual choice (and certainly not an orientation) but rather a matter of political principle: putting women first, thereby challenging the patriarchal imperative that women prioritize men. We ignored—even denied—the connections between lesbians and gay men, whose sexuality lacked such lofty aims and too often smacked of the very power relations that lesbian-feminism was refusing. When the issue of role-playing lesbians came up, as it inevitably did among women's studies students eager to pounce on any and all inconsistencies, we took evasive action. We admitted that older lesbians sometimes did adopt butch and femme roles, but we ventured that male-identified roles would go the way of patriarchy itself—vanquished to the dustbin of history. We offered lesbian-feminists as models of liberated androgyny and hoped that Carroll Smith-Rosenberg's groundbreaking article "The Female World of Love and Ritual" would help get students past their squeamishness about lesbianism.[2] Smith-Rosenberg's 1975 essay, which revisioned the Victorian period as a time when passionate romantic friendships between women were considered completely normal and unremarkable, was powerful ammunition in our struggle to normalize lesbianism.

Undergraduates usually were won over by the wholesomeness of these Victorian ladies, but they were nonetheless perplexed by the murkiness of their sexuality. What did those love letters between them mean? And why did they sometimes dislodge their husbands from their beds and sleep instead with their girlfriends? Smith-Rosenberg admonished readers not to ask whether these women had sex together because "theirs was an entirely different construction of sexuality from ours, sensuous not genital," but, as Christine Stansell observed, this is precisely the question that gets lodged in just about every reader's brain.[3] Smith-Rosenberg's cheeky article advanced the then-radical idea that sexuality isn't a timeless essence, that it changes over time. Even more, she found nothing wrong with the fact that the Victorian era inhibited heterosexual leanings rather than homosocial ties. Go girls! was the intoxicating subtext of the piece.

At first the difficulties of educating undergraduates about lesbianism convinced me that de-emphasizing sexuality as Smith-Rosenberg had was probably not a bad idea, pedagogically speaking. But almost immediately I began to question its utility for scholars outside of the classroom. Smith-Rosenberg's essay had much to recommend it—for one, she took these relationships and "private" life seriously—but it was also problematic, particularly her claim that the Victorian sexual landscape afforded people considerable latitude in moving across the spectrum from heterosexuality to homosexuality. Although she demonstrated that homosocial relationships were commonplace and accepted, she didn't prove that the same tolerance was accorded homosexual relationships. But, then, the entire essay had a hyperbolic, even infatuated, quality to it. It was not only a great time to be homosexual, apparently it was also a swell time to be female. Smith-

Rosenberg went so far as to argue that these passionate friendships proved that women "did not form an isolated and oppressed subcategory" in nineteenth-century America.[4] Why, I wondered, wasn't it possible that these women both enjoyed intense relationships with one another and were still oppressed? What of the feminist complaint, put forward most eloquently by Elizabeth Cady Stanton, that this world was, at bottom, claustrophobic, stultifying, even deadening? In the end, I suspected that female intimacy was tolerated because of the repressiveness of the Victorian gender system—in other words, because women had virtually no other options outside of marriage.[5]

Blanche Wiesen Cook's 1979 article "The Historical Denial of Lesbianism" made Smith-Rosenberg's work seem a model of circumspection. Cook, who went on to write an important and acclaimed two-volume biography of Eleanor Roosevelt, argued here that historians shouldn't base their determination of lesbianism on whether a woman defined herself as a lesbian or whether she had sex with another woman. Why, she asked, were historians of women-loving-women required to find "genital proofs" of lesbianism when the same standard of evidence was not required when studying heterosexuals?[6] No one doubted that Dwight D. Eisenhower and his friend Kay Summersby were heterosexual, she pointed out, although they didn't "consummate" their love.[7] For Cook, historians' obstinate insistence that women not be named lesbian without some evidence that they were sexually drawn to other women was an intolerable erasure of lesbian history. Her solution: redefine lesbianism so that "women who love women, who choose women to nurture and support and to create a living environment in which to work creatively and independently are [seen as] lesbians."[8] To that end, she declared Hull House founder Jane Addams a lesbian, a controversial move for sure.

In her influential essay "Compulsory Heterosexuality and Lesbian Existence" lesbian poet Adrienne Rich went even further than Cook. Rich not only attacked the heterosexist underpinnings of much feminist scholarship, she argued that were it not for the coerciveness of patriarchy, homosexuality, not heterosexuality, would be the norm among women. Like Cook, Rich redefined lesbianism as a political act: female solidarity. And just as Cooke named all kinds of women lesbian, so did Rich characterize a number of women writers and fictional characters—from Virginia Woolf's Chloe and Olivia to Toni Morrison's Sula—as part of what she called the "lesbian continuum," which she defined as "a range—through each woman's life and throughout history—of woman-identified experience." Rich wanted to embrace more "forms of primary intensity between and among women" than the term lesbianism suggested. However, when confronted with actually existing lesbian and bisexual women, Rich was sometimes less than enthusiastic. She judged bisexual writer Colette a "far less reliable source on lesbian existence" than Charlotte Brontë," on the grounds that Colette was male-identified whereas Brontë was woman-identified.[9]

The effort to expand the definition of lesbianism resulted in an ironic elision: by the early eighties, lesbian history was devoid of self-identified, sexually active lesbians. Scholars who understood their own lesbianism as an outgrowth of their feminism (and leading lesbian scholar Lillian Faderman went so far as to argue that lesbianism was not primarily a sexual phenomenon) were in no hurry to claim women whose lesbianism was unambiguously and unabashedly sexual. In fact, the emergence of modern lesbian identity in the early twentieth century was characterized by some scholars, most notably Faderman in *Surpassing the Love of Men*, as a tragedy in which medical professionals stigmatized women's romantic friendships and made them over into perversion. The "medical discourse" may have made lesbian identity possible—by naming what had been previously invisible, even unimaginable—but at a terrible cost, argued Faderman, because romantic friendships between women acquired a "new outlaw status."[10]

Thankfully, the absence of real live lesbians from lesbian history didn't continue much longer. The feminist Sex Wars of the early eighties helped bring about a shift away from the desexualized, woman-identified-woman model of lesbianism by encouraging a reconsideration of feminism, sexuality and power.[11] Joan Nestle, Amber Hollibaugh, Esther Newton, and Cherrie Moraga, all of whom contributed to the revisionism about butch and femme roles, took part in the Barnard Conference of 1984, where they and others advanced the then-controversial idea that playing with power and difference in the bedroom could be sexy rather than oppressive. In the field of lesbian history the impact of the Sex Wars was remarkable, in part because those fighting for a reconsideration of roles also had class on their side; correctly or not, butch-femme was understood to be a largely working-class phenomenon.[12]

Indeed, it wasn't the Sex Wars, but the desire to represent the lives of working-class lesbians, that led Elizabeth Kennedy and Madeline Davis to write about butch and femme lesbians of post-World War II Buffalo, New York.[13] With the publication of their 1986 article, women for whom lust, not friendship, was paramount took center stage in lesbian history. Esther Newton's mid-eighties effort to rehabilitate Radclyffe Hall and her mannish lesbianism was critical to this shift as well.[14] Newton maintained that Hall, whose 1928 novel *The Well of Loneliness* remained for decades the best-known book about lesbianism, had taken up the medical discourse of homosexuality as gender inversion in large measure because she longed to escape the asexual model of Victorian romantic friendship. The inversion model at least explained to Hall her desire to take another woman. Other scholars have questioned the influence that these doctors had upon gay people. Jennifer Terry, George Chauncey, and Lisa Duggan have challenged the idea that medical professionals single-handedly invented the homosexual. In a provocative "against-the-grain" reading of psychiatric case histories, Terry revealed that homosexual research subjects often resisted their interrogators' pathologizing assumptions.[15] In his account of a homosexual scandal that rocked the Navy in World War I-era Newport, Rhode Island, Chauncey found that as late as the 1920s the medical discourse still played no significant role in the formation of working-class homosexual identities.[16] Drawing on Terry's against-the-grain approach, Duggan argued that the figure of the mannish lesbian had no single source. Rather it was created through mass circulation newspapers' lurid accounts of women's passionate relationships, which were then appropriated by doctors as "cases," and subsequently reworked by women themselves into "identities."[17]

During this period—roughly the 1970s and 1980s—considerable research was also being done on the history of male homosexuality. The leading historians of male homosexuality were deeply influenced by feminist critiques of gender and heterosexuality. However, the organization and visibility of male homosexual behavior and the existence of police and court records documenting it made for histories that were much more focused on sex than those produced by historians of lesbians. Just as historians of lesbians initially avoided butch and femme lesbians, historians of gay men were sometimes reluctant to explore the role of effeminacy in male homosexuality, not, however, because they were made uneasy by gay men's outlaw status, or, to be more accurate, the outlaw status of gay sex.

The evidence of male homosexual contacts dating back to the ancient Greeks raised very early on the question of whether acts are equivalent to identity. Following French theorist Michel Foucault, who had maintained that homosexuality, like heterosexuality, was a social invention, not the result of genes or hormones, many gay male historians argued that although men probably had sex with one another from time immemorial, homosexual identity—the idea that the act carries with it a particular type of personality or identity—is distinctly modern, emerging as recently as the nineteenth century. Classicist David Halperin, for one, argued that ancient Greek society, which many gay men had celebrated for its apparent acceptance of homosexuality, was really a culture where a "phallic sexuality of penetration and domination" that was age- and power-based held sway. The Greeks sanctioned sex between men and boys, citizens and noncitizens, he argued, but in no way condoned or even understood the idea of reciprocal erotic desire among males—the hallmark of modern homosexuality. Likewise, historian Randolph Trumbach argued that the 18th-century London subculture of effeminate sodomites should not be seen as some early version of modern homosexuality but rather as a fundamentally different sexual system in which effeminacy figured as much as homosexual desire in the making of identity. Although there were exceptions, historians of male homosexuality were often critical of the notion that gay history should be about searching history for replicas of ourselves, or the idea so popular in the gay and lesbian community that we've always existed in history, what John D'Emilio calls the myth of the "eternal homosexual."

The early nineties saw the publication of two landmark studies, George Chauncey's *Gay New York* and Elizabeth Kennedy and Madeline Davis's *Boots of Leather, Slippers of Gold*.[18] Chauncey's massive, encyclopedic book sets out to do for gay history what C. Vann Woodward's slim, but pathbreaking, 1955 book *The Strange Career of Jim Crow* did for the history of race in the South. Woodward argued that, contrary to public opinion, segregation, or Jim Crow, was not one of the South's "immutable folkways."[19] In fact, the "stiff conformity and fanatical rigidity" with which the South pursued segregation from the turn of the century through the early years of the civil rights movement did not occur immediately in the aftermath of Reconstruction, but took a good twenty years to cohere.[20] Similarly, Chauncey debunks the prevailing view that homophobia is a timeless feature of American society. He demolishes the so-called "Stonewall narrative," the standard story line which assumes that until the famous Stonewall uprising of 1969 gay men were lonely and self-loathing, isolated from one another and utterly invisible to heterosexuals. Instead, he finds that gay men of New York were more visible, more tolerated, and more integrated into society in the early years of the twentieth century than they were at mid-century. *Gay New York* uncovers the richness and vitality of homosexual life in the early twentieth century, but what makes this book truly dazzling to historians (if not always to the undergraduates who have to slog through all the detail) is the way in which Chauncey embeds gay history in American social history, everything from immigration and labor history to gender history and the history of popular culture.

Like other recent social histories, *Gay New York* also challenges the presumption that the middle class was more enlightened about sex than the working class. In fact, he proves that among much of the immigrant working class, men often "alternated between female and male partners without believing that interest in one precluded interest in the other," or that occasional sex with effeminate men branded one homosexual or bisexual. For men, in other words, gender normativity was not contingent upon exclusive heterosexuality. Chauncey maintains that the hetero-homosexual binarism with which we live today emerged within the middle class. Here his explanation for the shifting paradigm, the turn-of-the-century crisis in middle-class masculinity, has a certain deus-ex-machina quality to it. He never proves that concerns about the feminization and overcivilization of American middle-class men actually led those men to try to get a leg over working-class men by changing the rules of the game so that "normal" masculinity became contingent upon exclusive heterosexuality.

Chauncey clearly favors the older working-class model of sexuality, and students often rhapsodize about the fluidity of this sexual system that permits a man to be a man even when he is fucking a fairy. More discerning students sometimes wonder if Chauncey's own enthusiasm for this largely defunct sexual system may have led him to exaggerate the extent of working-class tolerance toward gay men.[21] Prevalence doesn't equal tolerance.[22] They also ask whether the active-passive model of sexuality is really any better than the hetero-homo binarism that supplanted it. After all, the only people permitted much latitude in the working-class paradigm were the "normal" men who didn't identify as fairies. For Chauncey, though, the emergence of the hetero-homo binarism is problematic because it leads to the ghettoization and invisibility of male homosexuals. However, the straight-gay dichotomy was also critical to the consolidation of homosexual identity and community, which, as others have noted, was, after all, a necessary precondition for homosexual activism.[23]

Just as Chauncey is enamored of the working-class fairies of gay New York, so Elizabeth Kennedy and Madeline Davis are taken with the tough, beer-drinking, barfly butches who dominate *Boots of Leather, Slippers of Gold*. But while Chauncey has big ambitions—to upend the standard understanding and periodization of gay history and to write gays into American social history—Kennedy and Davis set themselves the more modest goal of chronicling Buffalo's butch-femme bar culture. There's another striking difference. While *Gay New York* is chock full of stories about anonymous public sexual encounters and virtually silent on the topic of relationships, *Boots of Leather* concerns itself with lesbians' intimate relationships, while also documenting, in some cases, sexual practices. This reflects long-standing (and now eroding) differences in the sexual cultures of gay men and lesbians, but it also speaks to the evidence these scholars used. Chauncey relied on DA's case files, court records, the papers of state and city liquor licensing agencies, antivice commission reports, and to a much lesser extent, diaries, letters, and oral histories. By contrast, Kennedy and Davis based their study almost entirely on extensive oral histories with forty-five women, or "narrators," the majority of whom are white, working-class butches who entered the bar community in the 1950s. Students often complain that while Chauncey's study succeeds in mapping the "sexual topography" of gay New York, it fails to reveal very much about the individuals who made up this world.[24] Of course, this is typical of social history, which by relying on public records, rarely manages to convey the psychological complexity of those ordinary people whose lives it seeks to uncover. By contrast, Kennedy and Davis manage to get their narrators to reveal highly personal, even painful, parts of their lives. It makes for a riveting, often illuminating, read.

Kennedy and Davis argue that butch-femme culture was a way of organizing lesbian desire, making it visible. Perhaps even more crucially, butch-femme was about organizing a "stable culture of resistance," especially in the 1950s as the larger culture grew more repressive.[25] Butches protected and expanded lesbian space and asserted lesbian visibility. Kennedy and Davis also point to the ways in which butch-femme roles both mimed and transformed heterosexuality. Whereas heterosexuality was organized around male pleasure, butches were, if anything, in the traditionally female role, focused on giving their femmes pleasure. And while male privilege permeated heterosexual relationships, butches derived no socially sanctioned privileges from dressing like men. In fact, their masculine appearance often spelled chronic underemployment and unemployment, with the result that femmes were generally the more reliable breadwinners. Moreover, the everyday harassment of butch women meant that in some ways butches led more circumscribed lives than their femmes, who could "pass" as straight.

In their starched white shirts and men's pants, and with their slick-backed DAs, these women took real risks in announcing their "queerness" at a time when hyperdomesticity stigmatized anyone who wasn't married. Yet they were sometimes cruel, tyrannical, and violent. Story after story in *Boots of Leather* details the alcohol abuse, and the oppressive, sometimes violent, ways in which butches tried to control their femmes. There's a strange dissonance here between the narrators' sometimes chilling stories and the authors' upbeat evaluations of these relationships, the majority of which they argue were characterized by "caring and closeness."[26] They even judge the butch-femme sexual system "woman-centered and sex-positive" despite the extent of butch "untouchability."[27] Kennedy and Davis do acknowledge that the unwillingness of many butches to be made love to suggests an underlying ambivalence about their femaleness. They even note that the butch performance ethic could become burdensome to the butch and frustrating to the femme who could feel sexually disempowered by it. However, none of this affects their evaluation of the community, which remains curiously rosy. But what if this butch-femme culture that was so effective at declaring lesbian desire and building community was, in other respects, dysfunctional? What if the paranoia, possessiveness, and violence of butches inhered in this erotic system, which established butches as the true lesbians and femmes as their unreliable objects of desire, always in need of surveillance? Part of the problem may be that in *Boots of Leather* sexuality is primarily understood as subservient to community. Kennedy and Davis seem to favor a kind of functionalism that roots sexual customs in the preservation of the lesbian community, and not desire in all its disturbing and chaotic splendor.

Until recently, most work in gay and lesbian history has focused, in the manner of *Gay New York* and *Boots of Leather, Slippers of Gold*, on either gay men or lesbians. Gay men do turn up in Kennedy and Davis's study, but they are shadowy figures at best.[28] And Chauncey comes right out and declares that the differences in lesbian and gay history and the complexities of each make it "virtually impossible" to write a joint history that doesn't render one group's history an "appendage" to the other's.[29] Many factors came together to produce what has been from the beginning a very bifurcated field. Adrienne Rich spoke for many lesbian scholars when she argued in 1980 that lesbianism should be treated as a "profoundly female" experience. She cited numerous differences between the two groups, including the prevalence of ageism and anonymous sex among gay men and their defense of pederasty.[30] Of course, gay men's greater economic and political power, their access to the public sphere, and their sense of sexual entitlement have made their history in many respects strikingly different from that of lesbians. While historians of male homosexuality have been struggling to discover when desire for sex with other men became the basis of homosexual identity, historians of lesbians have asked when the desire for intimacy with other women became sexualized and a basis for lesbian identity.[31]

In the last ten years, though, gay and lesbian historians have shown more willingness to think about the ways that the two halves of this field are related. Critical to this shift were the feminist Sex Wars, which by emphasizing the centrality of sex to lesbianism, undermined much of the ideological insistence on the distinctiveness of lesbianism. If lesbians were motivated by lust, too, then might these groups share more common ground than previously supposed? Of course, the AIDS crisis and the activism it provoked also brought about stronger ties between lesbian and gay activists, which affected the scholarship as well. Two recent books, Martin Duberman's *Stonewall* and Esther Newton's *Cherry Grove, Fire Island*, reflect this shift.[32] The riots at the Stonewall Inn, a seedy, Mafia-owned dive in the heart of New York's Greenwich Village, have come to symbolize the birth of the modern gay rights movement. Duberman's approach—to include oral histories of two lesbians alongside those of three gay men and one transvestite—seems token. Neither Yvonne Flowers or Karla Jay were part of the Stonewall's scene, nor did they have much to do with the emerging gay liberation movement. In the end, their stories feel tangential, except insofar as they underscore the sexism of the gay movement. If Stonewall was *"the* emblematic event in modern lesbian and gay history," as Duberman asserts, we need to know more than we learn in this book about its consequences for lesbians.[33] Esther Newton's effort to write an inclusive history works better in large part because her book is about a bohemian community whose initial organizing principle was eccentricity rather than sexual identity. Newton's book is a brief for what she calls the Grove's "camp/theatrical" sensibility, which in its flamboyance and aversion to politics is worlds apart from the self-seriousness and "restraint" of the "egalitarian/authentic" sensibility—a mode she associates with the gay rights movement.[34] Newton's fondness for campy theatrical queers reflects in part her frustration with the gay and lesbian movement's sometimes prissy rejection of butches and drag queens. By focusing on fairies and butches, all these nineties books stand as a rebuke of sorts to the modern gay movement, which sometimes has shunned those on its margins, the stigma bearers.[35]

It's likely that future research will turn up more connections between gay men and lesbians, especially in the demimonde world where gay men mixed with female prostitutes, or as they were sometimes called "gay women." Although the term "gay" referred to their immorality and flamboyance rather than to their sexual identity, lesbianism was not unheard of among prostitutes, even in the early part of the twentieth century.[36] But gay men and lesbians socialized together outside red-light districts as well. Both *Boots of Leather, Slippers of Gold* and the wonderful Canadian film, *Forbidden Love*, suggest that upwardly mobile lesbians and gay men relied upon each other to get into the "right" bars and clubs and to ward off suspicions of sexual deviance, especially when the police were an issue. But relationships between gay men and women may have been less strategic, too. There is some evidence that lesbians, bisexuals, and gay men mixed easily in the beatnik enclaves of San Francisco's North Beach and on the Lower East Side of New York.[37] I also wonder about the extent of heterosexual experimentation in these communities, especially in the years before lesbians and gay men felt more pressure to define themselves as exclusively homosexual.[38]

If scholars do begin writing more inclusive histories it will probably be in part because of the meteoric rise of queer theory/studies within the academy, especially in the humanities where poststructuralism paved its way.[39] Queer theory calls into question the conditions by which binary oppositions (male/female, heterosexual/homosexual) are produced. It also claims to undermine all kinds of borders, not just those dividing lesbians from gay men, but those that separate queers from all manner of "deviants"—a point to which I will return. Indeed, if queer studies influences the direction of gay and lesbian history, it could throw open the field of historical inquiry to include virtually anyone whose sexuality troubles the "regimes of the normal."[40] Just as queer activism has tried, if somewhat fitfully, to build a politics based on affiliation rather than identity, so queer theory, which contests the idea of sexual identity as a stable and coherent category, has positioned itself as anti-identitarian. The point isn't to recover gay and lesbian history, according to queer studies, but instead to look at the process whereby heteronormativity and deviance are constructed and contested. (And in another important departure from gay and lesbian history, which focused on the recovery of gay experience, queer theory, following Foucault, is concerned with the discursive practices which it believes shape subjectivity and experience. It's through the study of cultural production and the sexual meanings inscribed within them that one can explore "real" lives and communities.) Queer theory doesn't require that its subjects be self-consciously gay; nor does it demand that their *primary* identification be gay, a requirement that often has peripheralized racial and ethnic minorities for whom sexual identity is usually not the sole defining characteristic. In fact, queer theory doesn't demand that its subjects be gay or lesbian at all, which is not surprising given that the father of queer theory, Foucault, maintained that "pleasure has no passport, no identification papers."[41]

The effort to move beyond the study of self-identified gays and lesbians is long overdue. The requirement that our subjects be "gay through and through"—Kennedy and Davis's chosen formula, and one that Kennedy admits skewed their study in favor of butches—is far too exclusionary.[42] It assumes a level of sexual absolutism or purity that rarely comes with the territory of sexuality. This queer turn away from coherent and fixed identity could encourage the inclusion of those who have been left out or have been on the margins of our histories: femmes, trade (heterosexually identified men who had sex with men, sometimes for money), female prostitutes, and probably the largest category of all: heterosexually married people who engage in queer sex and/or relationships.

Some queer theorists also challenge the focus on community that has characterized both gay and lesbian activism and history. Michael Warner argues that the paradigm of community works in relation to racial and ethnic groups, but fails to describe gays and lesbians whose history has so much to do with "noncommunity." For Warner, community is an especially inappropriate model because "nearly every lesbian or gay remembers being such before entering a collectively identified space."[43] Not only that, queers typically spend their childhoods in isolation, apart from community. This early alienation, this sense of not belonging, isn't a liability, in his view, but an advantage because it encourages a critical stance toward "the normalization of behavior."[44] Lesbian and gay scholars may want to rethink the centrality of community to their work, but not because Warner's critique is especially persuasive. His contention that gay history consists of noncommunity—read isolation—seems debatable in light of Chauncey's findings in *Gay New York*. Tellingly, gay men in the early part of the twentieth century didn't speak of *coming out of* the closet, but rather of *coming out into* homosexual society—a camp expression that referred, of course, to a debutante's coming-out party. In fact, the metaphor of the closet didn't even come into use until the 1960s.[45] Warner also assumes that there's a uniformity to queer experience—surprising in a leading exponent of queer theory, which is supposed to take difference as its starting point.[46] What of all those people, women in particular, who feel their queerness only later in life or who feel it only dimly or fleetingly in childhood? And does the awareness of queerness inevitably result in isolation? It seems likely that the isolation and alienation Warner associates with queerness is more typical of effeminate boys than tomboy girls.[47]

Whether in the political or academic arena, queerness involves a critique of normalization. Queerness is about claiming, not denying, the charge of perversion, and it means affiliating with others on the sexual fringe—transvestites and the transgendered, married men who have furtive homosexual sex in public restrooms, sex workers, and maybe even man-boy lovers.[48] According to queer theory, we shouldn't be distancing ourselves from those whose sexuality seems unknowable or unassimilable to our understanding of gayness; rather, we should be making them central to the project of queering history. Anyone who troubles, or queers, the project of gay and lesbian history should be embraced, even as unsavory a character as Harry Thaw, the turn-of-the-century celebrity murderer, s/m enthusiast and occasional lover of boys, whom Martha Umphrey calls a "swindler of lesbian/gay history—one who catches us off guard, then slips away."[49] I share Umphrey's desire to broaden the parameters of gay and lesbian history. However, I wonder if the new queer formulation won't bring about its own exclusions, or at the very least create a kind of hierarchy of perversion whereby the weirdest are anointed the queerest.[50] Even before the ascendance of queer theory, gay and lesbian historians were focusing on butches and fairies to the exclusion of most others. Queer theory's embrace of the non-normative could exacerbate this skewing of the field. A queered history can take as its subjects "sexual outlaws" and focus on "instability and scandal," as Umphrey has proposed, but we don't want to lose sight of more conventional gays and lesbians who on the surface appear to pose less of a challenge to regimes of the normal.[51]

Nor would we want a queer history that elided lesbianism. Yet much queer theory—such as Michael Warner's theorizing on queer childhood, which ascribes to lesbians experiences that seem more specific to men—purports to be inclusive, but is distressingly gender blind.[52] When queer theorists do acknowledge differences in the experiences of gay men and lesbians, they sometimes do so in a way that marginalizes women. For example, in her groundbreaking work on the representation of homosexual desire, Eve Sedgwick has focused exclusively on men because of the "relatively continuous relation of female homosocial and homosexual bonds," which she argues stands in contrast to the "radically discontinuous relation of male homosocial and homosexual bonds." Indeed, Sedgwick goes so far as to argue that desire between women is "of no great consequence; it is no source of conflict or contradiction."[53] As Teresa de Lauretis has pointed out, by implying that "sex and desire don't really matter or present problems for women" in the way that they do for men, Sedgwick ends up "denying lesbianism altogether."[54] Ironically, Sedgwick's argument for the continuity between female homosociality and homosexuality echoes the work of Adrienne Rich and other seventies revisionists, but in a way that reinforces the erasure of lesbianism. While I see much more conflict and contradiction in lesbianism than does Sedgwick, I do wonder if queer theory's concern with the non-normative doesn't unintentionally privilege the experiences of men, who historically have had much greater freedom than women to transgress society's sexual borderlines.

Although this privileging of the sexual fringe has not yet become problematic in historical studies, it has begun to bedevil the political arena, where queer politicos sometimes position themselves as the big nose-thumb, or fuck-off, to gay and lesbian activists of the 1970s and 1980s. As Donna Penn ruefully notes, the queer turn is producing a "problematic revisionism" whereby gay and lesbian *anything* is dismissed as "assimilationist, accommodationist, mainstream, conservative, and 'retro.'"[55] The repudiation of the conventional, or vanilla, and elevation of the non-normative or "bad," proved especially troubling at a 1997 meeting of Sex Panic, a group of queer scholars and activists who came together to oppose the closing of gay bathhouses and to mount a challenge to the alleged sexual conservatism of several prominent gay writers. In an odd display of fourth-grade insult-flinging, fliers for the meeting named Larry Kramer, Michelangelo Signorile, Gabriel Rotello, and Andrew Sullivan neoconservative "turdz." Sex Panic, whose members include queer theorists Michael Warner and Douglas Crimp, attacked as gay positive but sex negative this disparate group of writers who had been hectoring the gay male community to change its ways: to turn its back on sex clubs and bathhouses and to come out for monogamy and marriage.[56] Although Warner has said that support for "sexual culture" doesn't entail opposition to intimacy and monogamy, that's not the way it played out at the meeting. During the question-and-answer period, a member of the audience got up and declared that he was "what is known under Megan's Law as a sexually dangerous predator." He spoke of having been jailed for four years for having sex with underage boys and of now being shadowed by the police. The audience, according to journalist Caleb Crain, greeted him with a "stunned and respectful silence." Yet when another man nervously suggested that the gay community's "celebration of multipartner sex" made it harder for him to maintain a long-term monogamous relationship, the crowd interrupted and heckled him.[57]

How the pendulum swings! Twenty years ago Lillian Faderman was decrying lesbianism's "outlaw status," and today the pervert outlaw is all the rage—at least in queer circles. We saw the first glimpses of this during the feminist Sex Wars when nonkinky sex was sometimes disparaged as "vanilla." This turning of the tables, the reversal of the culture's hegemonic values, is typical of political movements, at least those rooted in identity politics. But, then, queer theory claims to have gone beyond identity politics and to be skeptical of efforts to invest sex with meaning, to encumber it with notions of authenticity and liberation. However, in the end, it seems that for all of us, even those dissatisfied with identity politics, meaning just sticks to sex. Not even the sophisticated arguments of queer theorists can undo that. I don't want to return to those days when lesbian historians were satisfied with romantic friendships and tried their best to make lesbianism respectable, even wholesome. However, all the recent efforts to "queer" homosexuality have made me wonder if we haven't lost sight of how unsettling heterosexuals often find "normal" gays. Maybe it's time to consider that as unsettling as straight Americans find our mannish women and effeminate men, that they may be as terrified by gays and lesbians who appear to be just like them.

9

"THOUSANDS OF MEN AND A FEW HUNDRED WOMEN": JANIS JOPLIN, SEXUAL AMBIGUITY, AND BOHEMIA

IN DISCUSSIONS OF JANIS JOPLIN'S sexuality, numbers always seem to come up as if they'll resolve once and for all that knotty question: What was she? On at least one occasion, when a Bay Area underground newspaper published an article claiming she was gay, Joplin herself deployed numbers to set the record straight. Joplin was backstage, drunk, and between sets at a San Diego gig when she heard the news. "You fly up there tomorrow," she yelled at the friend who'd shown her the offending article, "and tell this bitch that Janis has slept with thousands of men and a few hundred women."[1]

It's a great story that captures Joplin's irreverence, bravado, and fondness for hyperbole. Some would say it demonstrates her queerness, too. Joplin's sexual scorecard does tell us quite a lot about her feelings toward her own unruly desires. Joplin didn't deny she had slept with women. Rather, she emphasized the preponderance of her heterosexual home runs as if that would prove that she wasn't gay. Joplin made a point of trumpeting the Babe Ruthian dimensions of her heterosexual lust, especially to the press, even going so far as to have *Rolling Stone* notified of her one-night stand with football star Joe Namath. For much of her life, even before she was a celebrity, Joplin was involved in a relentless and frenzied pursuit of "cute guys."

Internalized homophobia may have been driving Joplin's much-publicized pursuit of men, but her interest in men was not simply a hypercorrection or a mere contrivance. Kim Chappell, who was lovers with both folksinger Joan Baez and Joplin's sometime lover Peggy Caserta, was a part of the Haight scene. Chappell, who is now an out lesbian, called herself bisexual then and slept with men as well as women. Today she describes her bisexuality as a "joke." However, when asked if Joplin's interest in men was faked as well, Chappell said, "God, I don't know. She sure did like guys."[2]

Joplin has a reputation as the sixties grooviest, most liberated chick—a woman who knew what she wanted and went after all of it, unencumbered by guilt or self-doubt. Of course, that's the reputation she wanted, the one she crafted. In *Queer Noises*, British rock critic John Gill proclaims Joplin "queer as fuck a quarter of a century before either the term or the political statement became fashionable." In his account, Joplin emerges a proud and pioneering queer without "any qualms about her lesbian feelings."[3] Gill's portrait is drawn from Ellis Amburn's lurid 1992 biography, *Pearl: The Obsessions and Passions of Janis Joplin*. From his line of questioning, it's clear that Amburn was hoping to prove that Joplin was really a lesbian. He finds some ammunition in Peggy Caserta's 1973 kiss-and-tell memoir, *Going Down with Janis*. Caserta's book opens with the memorable line, "I was stark naked, stoned out of my mind on heroin, and the girl lying between my legs giving me head was Janis Joplin." However, Caserta doesn't depict Joplin as exclusively lesbian.[4] In fact, her book features plenty of heterosexual sex and three-ways with men.

The idea that Joplin is a poster child of lesbianism or queerness is a nice fantasy, but that's all it is. Her great ambivalent retort about sleeping with thousands of guys and a few hundred women was never reported in the press. While many of her friends knew her sexuality was more complicated than her heterosexual facade suggested, her lesbian affairs went unreported until a year after her fatal OD, when *Village Voice* columnist and lesbian provocateur Jill Johnston claimed that the rock star had really been gay.[5]

Joplin wasn't heterosexual, but efforts to make her over into a lesbian or queer icon always miss the mark. Something always get airbrushed out of the picture. Marjorie Garber's portrait of the "very bisexual" Joplin is a case in point. She ascribes to Joplin a level of openness—even calculation—about her "bisexuality" that the singer never exhibited. Garber maintains that Joplin, like fellow rockers David Bowie and Mick Jagger, staged, or performed, her bisexuality, which she argues was an "important part of the mechanism of stardom" for all three performers.[6] But Joplin couldn't have been more different from glam rockers Bowie and Jagger. Onstage Joplin emphasized the authenticity of her feelings, while glitter boys Jagger and Bowie favored camp theatrics and provocative posing. Moreover, as anyone who has ever seen footage of Joplin in concert knows, she would have been hard-pressed to stage her bisexuality because she was surrounded by male musicians when she performed.[7] In truth, if Joplin was performing anything but a song onstage, it was heterosexuality.

This judgment may be hard for some to accept, particularly those who quite understandably have come to confuse Joplin with Melissa Etheridge, the rocker who has presented herself as Joplin's cleaned-up spiritual daughter. Etheridge not only performs Joplin songs in concert, until recently she was slated to play her in a Hollywood movie that her girlfriend, Julie Cypher, is producing. In her induction speech for the Texas-born singer at the 1995 Rock and Roll Hall of Fame ceremony, Etheridge wished Joplin were still alive, "making a comeback . . . being a women's-rights advocate or a gay-rights advocate, fighting against AIDS and intolerance."[8] Joplin may or may not have lent her name to those political struggles, but one thing's for sure: Joplin and Etheridge share little besides big voices and a certain ballsy self-presentation. In truth, Etheridge's temperament appears to be a lot sunnier and her sexuality considerably more straightforward than her idol's. Joplin was a sexual adventurer, for sure—the first woman at the University of Texas to go braless—but like many sixties rebels, she bore the scars of having grown up in the fifties. It troubled Joplin that she didn't want to marry, have kids, and be part of the house-with-the-white-picket-fence American dream. Sometimes she convinced herself she wanted nothing more than to settle down with a guy.

Of course, it's Joplin's remarkable rebelliousness, not her lifelong struggle with conventionality, that people remember. To many, Joplin's apparent sexual openness reveals not only how liberated she was, but how free the sixties were. However, at the very moment that the sexual revolution was apparently sweeping the country, merely holding hands or dancing together was risky business for gays and lesbians. Even in New York City, and as late as 1969, a man could be arrested for dancing with another man. Greenwich Village has long enjoyed a reputation as a gay mecca, but until 1969 the politically progressive *Village Voice* refused to carry ads that contained the word "gay."

Nor did the counterculture offer any real respite from the homophobia of mainstream America. The common perception is that the hippie counterculture of Haight-Ashbury broke virtually every sexual taboo, but it didn't.

Long-haired hippie men did pioneer an androgynous look that challenged traditional notions of masculinity, and the hippie rhetoric of free love did bring lots of gays to San Francisco. However, gays who came to the Bay Area expecting to find a queer-friendly environment quickly discovered the Haight wasn't what they had imagined. Indeed, when hippie entrepreneurs opened up a rock ballroom in the Haight they named it the Straight Theater as an in-joke to convey its hipness and, more important, to advertise that it was now a straight space, so that the gay men who were accustomed to coming there to watch porno flics would stay away.[9] "The homosexual thing was very separate, and it was taboo even in that scene," recalls Joplin's friend and band mate Dave Getz.[10] Joplin's lover Peggy Caserta agrees. "The hippies were straight kids," she insists.[11]

In fact, in this respect the counterculture of Haight-Ashbury stood in contrast to beatnik North Beach, which in many ways had been queer-inflected. But, then, the counterculture was a mass movement and as such shared more with the dominant culture than had the tiny Beat subculture of the fifties and early sixties. The Beats deliberately transgressed America's sexual (and racial) borders, and many of the best-known Beat writers, most notably Allen Ginsberg, wrote openly homoerotic work. Poet Diane Di Prima remembers going "to bed with whatever we went to bed with—male, female, whatever."[12] The Beats' sexual openness owed something to the fact that both bohemians and gays were underground, barely visible to straight America. Maria Damon notes that in bars like the San Remo in Greenwich Village and the Anxious Asp in North Beach, Beat and gay subcultures "overlapped in sometimes uneasy and sometimes mutually supportive proximity."[13] To Allen Ginsberg's friend Carl Soloman, the Beat world was so queer it almost felt like "you needed apostles of heterosexuality in those days."[14]

In the early-to-mid sixties, Joplin was very much a part of the fading beatnik scene of San Francisco's North Beach and New York's Lower East Side.[15] She had a relationship with an African-American lesbian for almost a year, and she counted among her friends many gay men and lesbians. Later, she lived in what one friend calls an "infamous gay rooming house of transvestites."[16] Even after beatnik North Beach was eclipsed by hippie Haight-Ashbury and she became America's first hippie pin-up chick, Joplin often described herself as an unreconstructed beatnik. And yet once her North Beach days were over, Joplin had little contact with the gay community, although she was intermittently involved with Peggy Caserta for two-and-a-half years.

PEOPLE OFTEN ASK if Joplin would have become a lesbian had she not OD'd in October 1970. Would gay liberation, by challenging the stigmatization of homosexuality, have permitted Joplin to "own" her lesbian feelings? Even Myra Friedman, who emphasized the predominance of Joplin's heterosexual relationships in her biography of the singer, has more recently suggested that Joplin might have "opted for a gay lifestyle" had she lived to feel the effects of gay liberation.[17] Anything is possible, of course, but the picture gets very fuzzy for me when I try to imagine Janis Joplin sitting through a Holly Near concert. Even if she had decided she was gay, it's a foregone conclusion that Joplin would have found Lesbian Nation, with all its diligent policing of desire, a pretty dreary place.

Rather than ask if Joplin would have come out in the seventies, perhaps we should ask what the world might have looked like had the counterculture appropriated more than the marijuana and Zen Buddhism of beatnik culture. What if hippie culture had been, like that of the Beats, more gay inflected? Would the gay and lesbian liberation movement have made membership contingent upon exclusive homosexuality had the new bohemia of the sixties been more gay friendly? And would Joplin's life have played out differently had the hippie scene not been so aggressively heterosexual and had the lesbian community not become more condemnatory of sex with men?

I was first prompted to ask these questions by novelist Edmund White's musings on Marjorie Garber's book about bisexuality, *Vice Versa*.[18] Writing some twenty-five years after Stonewall, White wonders whether he might have continued having relationships with both men and women had gay liberation not intervened and encouraged him to reinvent himself as exclusively homosexual. Declaring himself unambiguously gay was, he now thinks, his way of putting an end to his sexual ambivalence. Certainly Stonewall made the beatnik elevation of sexual fluidity and indeterminacy seem like an evasion, a cop-out. The idea that sex is neither right or wrong, but just *is*, didn't sit well with gay liberation's insistence that homosexuality was transformative, even liberatory, that "gay is good."[19]

When I started working on my biography of Janis Joplin I was so weary of the gay and lesbian community's preoccupation with consolidating and regulating sexual identity that I found it difficult not to romanticize the pre-gay-liberationist approach to sexuality. I still agree with Foucault that pleasure "passes from one individual to another," rather than being "secreted by identity," but five years of studying Joplin and the beatnik and hippie subcultures in which she moved have somewhat tempered my enthusiasm for those pre-Stonewall years.[20] While it's true that gay liberation closed down sexual possibilities for some, as Edmund White has suggested, the movement also opened up possibilities for others. For someone like Kim Chappell, whose bisexuality had been a fiction, Stonewall made possible greater sexual honesty.

Gay and lesbian liberation's faith in the stability and fixity of sexual identity feels shopworn today, however, the effort to label and fix identity has had its uses. After all, it's worth remembering poet Allen Ginsberg's comments upon surveying the partially cleaned up Stonewall Inn the weekend after the 1969 riot. "They've lost that wounded look that fags all had ten years ago," Ginsberg observed of the bar's patrons. The riots had transformed them, even made them "beautiful."[21] Gay liberation was transformative, double-edged though it was. As for Joplin, as appealing as her sexuality might appear, her fixation on finding one good man, and her relentless heterosexual boasting, suggest that she was no stranger to sexual confusion and shame. The very indeterminancy of Joplin's sexuality—that she was beyond straight or gay—seems the epitome of queerness today, but we shouldn't confuse her sexual fluidity with queer nonchalance.

10

GENDER DISOBEDIENCE, ACADEMIA, AND POPULAR CULTURE

DESPITE THE HYPE, GENDER-bending isn't an invention of the late twentieth century. People have been playing and messing with gender for years. Take the case of Murray Hall, a woman who passed as a man for twenty-five years and became a Tammany Hall power broker during the 1880s and '90s. Or Babe Bean, the "Trousered Puzzle," who served as a lieutenant during the Spanish-American War and lived most of her sixty-six years as a man. Stranger, still, is Lord Cornbury, the first colonial governor of New York, who came from England decked out as a woman and remained so for the duration of his term. Better known are the Native American *berdache*, men who lived as women and sometimes married men.

Now, however, more people seem to be crossing the line than ever before. And most curious of all, Americans can't seem to get enough of all this kinkiness. The Republicans may have captured Congress, but the transgendered seem to have hijacked the airwaves, or, at least the world of TV talk shows. These days, the transgendered are literally just a channel away.

Of course, the public's fascination with all this queerness may not signal a greater tolerance for gender ambiguity. After all, the studio audience on TV talk shows often functions as a kind of superego, reacting with such abhorrence that one thinks lions would be kinder. But not always. For instance, recently when a transgendered man (female-to-male, or FTM) explained that he had decided to forego phalloplasty because "you don't have to have a penis to be a man," the predominantly female audience went wild cheering him on. Queer nation, indeed!

For the last five years bending, subverting, or exploding gender have had a hold on the academic imagination as well. It wasn't always so trendy.

During the '6os and '70s the academic discourse on transsexuals (then the preferred term) was dominated by psychologists and sociologists who produced resolutely clinical books that were usually pathologizing in effect if not intent. It was, for example, simply an article of faith among sexologists that the problem lay with the transsexuals, transvestites, and drag queens they studied, not society.

Although sexologists monopolized the field, the '70s did witness the publication of two feminist books, anthropologist Esther Newton's 1972 jewel of an ethnography, *Mother Camp: Female Impersonation in America*[1] and Janice Raymond's *The Transsexual Empire*.[2] At a time when many feminists dismissed drag as woman-hating, Newton emphasized the way in which drag called into question the naturalness of gender roles. Newton's thinking about drag prefigured current postmodernist theorizing about it, but *Mother Camp* had little impact when it first appeared or when it was republished seven years later.

By contrast, Raymond's 1979 screed carried endorsements from three of feminism's then-reigning divas—Andrea Dworkin, Mary Daly, and Robin Morgan. *The Transsexual Empire* epitomizes the sort of paranoid feminism that passed for radical in the late seventies. Raymond advanced the truly bizarre idea that "all [MTF] transsexuals rape women's bodies by reducing the real female form to an artifact, appropriating this body for themselves." Worst of all, she claimed, were the MTF's who became lesbians in order to "become the man within the woman, and more, within the women's community." On the brink of Reagan's election, Raymond wrote as if the greatest threat facing feminists was MTF lesbians, not the right wing.

If transsexuals were the bogeyman for Raymond, many other feminists targeted pornography. As the feminist antiporn movement took shape, every sexual expression short of side-by-side, nothing-much-happening lesbian sex became fair game. Promiscuous and anonymous gay male sex, butch-femme, sadomasochism, drag, transsexualism, penetration (read: heterosexuality), and of course getting off on pornography—all were seen as symptoms of patriarchal conditioning, or in the lingo of the day false consciousness. In this climate thoughtful reappraisals of drag or anything else not focused relentlessly on the horror and danger of sexuality for women, were unlikely. So it went until 1982's Barnard conference on sexuality, which opened up the possibility, finally, that one could develop a complicated understanding of sexuality, one that didn't create hierarchies of good (feminist) and bad (patriarchal) sex.

Postmodern theorizing was not the driving force behind Barnard, but by 1982 po-mo was making inroads into many academic disciplines. If Barnard enabled a reconsideration of transvestitism and transsexualism, then the cultural capital enjoyed by poststructuralism provided the cachet. By the late '80s, anything gender-bending was on the way up the cultural escalator. Drag became the ideal vehicle for revealing the constructedness of gender, or what philosopher Judith Butler called its "performativity." No one was more responsible for putting drag on the academic map than Butler, whose *Gender Trouble*[3] was one of 1991's most hyped academic books. "In imitating gender," she contended, "drag implicitly reveals the imitative structure of gender itself—and its contingency." In contrast to many '70s feminists who had denounced butch-femme as hopelessly mimetic of heterosexuality, Butler suggested these roles simultaneously evoke and displace heterosexual conventions. But *Gender Trouble* really anointed drag as the prototypical example of gender performativity. The choice made sense given her conviction that "gender is an impersonation." Gender is performative, but it's not, according to Butler, reducible to style, as popularizers of her work often assume. One cannot, Butler has since argued, change one's gender at will. Rather "performativity is about repetition, very often with the repetition of oppressive and painful gender norms to force them to resignify. This is not freedom, but a question of how to work the trap that one is inevitably in."[4]

One reason feminist and po-mo scholars initially shied away from the transgendered community was its very embeddedness, some would say complicity, in the gender system. Although the transgendered denaturalize gender by pointing to the disjuncture between biological sex and gender identity, they have also confirmed naturalized notions of gender by posing the problem as the "wrong body." Psychological and sociological studies, and, until recently, even transsexual memoirs have emphasized the conventionality of transsexuals' thinking about gender.

In 1991's *Body Guards: The Cultural Politics of Gender Ambiguity*,[5] Sandy Stone argued that transsexuals' well-documented conventionality follows in large measure from the ideology of gender reassignment clinics. There doctors evaluated candidates for surgery on the basis of how well they "performed" the gender of choice. Stone pointed out that when the first candidates were evaluated, researchers were struck by how well their behavior corresponded with the criteria developed by Harry Benjamin, whose *The Transsexual Phenomenon* was the researchers' standard reference text. Several years passed before doctors discovered why their clients' profiles so closely matched Benjamin's. It turns out that transsexuals circulated dog-eared copies of Benjamin's book within their own communities. Pre-op transsexuals were "only too happy" to play by Benjamin's rules because there lay the path to surgery.

Sandy Stone and Kate Bornstein, both MTF lesbians, and, not coincidentally perhaps, po-mo academics, represent a new wave among the transgendered. Instead of craving acceptance as women, they *want* to live on the borderlands of gender, outside the familiar masculine/feminine binary. Bornstein, a self-described "former-man and not-quite woman" and author of last year's *Gender Outlaw*,[6] describes the transgendered person as a "trickster" whose performance of gender undermines the category itself. In *Vested Interests: Cross-Dressing and Cultural Anxiety*,[7] Marjorie Garber presents transsexualism as "one distinctly twentieth-century manifestation of cross-dressing." She attributes the cultural fascination with transsexualism to the "fear and desire of the borderline and of technology." In Garber's hands, cross-dressing becomes a way to explore the "category crisis"—the breakdown of "definitional distinction, a borderline that becomes permeable, that permits . . . border crossings from one apparently distinct category to another."

Predictably, I suppose, at the very moment poststructuralist and feminist scholars are embracing the meltdown of definitional distinctions and arguing for the very constructedness of such naturalized categories as gender, sexuality, and race, others in the academy are charting a very different course. If gender-bending is all the rage among many literary critics, film theorists, anthropologists, and historians, there has emerged among scientists and social scientists a parallel but opposing discourse, one which purports to establish that there are essential, and presumably intractable, differences between men and women, gays and straights, and blacks and whites. There's the search for a "gay gene," Simon Levay's hypothalamus research, Charles Murray and the late Richard Herrnstein's *The Bell Curve*,[8] and the recent claim about differences in male and female brain functioning. (The recent scientific finding that race has no biological basis is an important exception.) No single motive unites these researchers. Nor are all of them intent upon shoring up gender and sexual hierarchies, or the color line. But the current category crisis— which isn't so much the result of poststructuralism as it is the work of its twin, postmodernization (deindustrialization, the rise of multinationals, and new technologies)—makes this research fairly irresistible to those longing for a return to the old order. Of course, as technology further confounds gender differences (at work and in cyberspace, for example) the certainty of the body seems ever less recoverable.

In 1964, Mario Savio of the Berkeley Free Speech Movement, which helped jump-start the sixties of legend, urged his fellow students to stop the system by putting their bodies upon its gears and wheels, "upon all [its] apparatus." This was soon reduced to the exhortation, "put your body on the line." Bell-bottoms, tie dye, acid rock—all seem, sadly, more plausible today than the idea that individuals might be able to affect the course of history through collective action.

If today's po-mo intellectuals are preoccupied with the civil disobedience of the '90s—gender and sexual disobedience, especially as it's played out in popular culture—it's in large part because this is the only game in town given the collapse of the left, the pervasive perception of feminism and civil rights as "special interest groups," and the mass indifference to all things political. Although this protest is expressed in popular culture far more than on the barricades, it's not without some significance. Bikini-clad supermodel Cindi Crawford shaving a cross-dressed k.d. lang on the cover of *Vanity Fair*, the late Kurt Cobain French-kissing fellow band member Chris Novoselic before thousands of fans—these interventions confound the culture and will confound Republican efforts to re-Victorianize American society as well. Confounding gender can be subversive, but it doesn't signal some sort of post-gendered consciousness. After all, even "gender outlaw" Bornstein says she's "real glad" she opted for vaginoplasty. To paraphrase Marx, people may make gender, but they are most surely not free to make it any way they want. But in screwing up the great machinery of sex and gender, these efforts to "work the trap" of gender—these protests that are written on the body—at least expand the realm of possibility.

PART 3

TURN THE BEAT AROUND

I have always loved popular music, but I didn't begin writing about it until the mid-nineties when I was researching Janis Joplin's life and doing a lot of freelance writing. As a sixties historian I had already come to feel that most histories of that period had given short shrift to popular culture, which was in part how I'd come to write about Joplin. My cultural turn corresponded to the rise of cultural studies, an interdisciplinary field that began making waves in American universities in the late 1980s. The idea that popular culture can be transgressive and empowering—a key proposition in much of this work—has proven especially appealing in this period when mass-based political protest has sometimes seemed a thing of the past. I was influenced by a number of cultural studies theorists, including Eric Lott and George Lipsitz, whose work I discuss in "White Faces, Black Masks," a piece that was published in the *Village Voice* in 1994. Much of the work in this field, however, elevates culture at the expense of everything else, particularly politics. Thus, the popularity of Cole Porter's music is said to prove the queerness of American culture in the 1930s, despite the fact that ample research has shown that it was anything but a swell time for gays. This privileging of cultural politics has raised hackles inside the academy, but even the *New Yorker*'s Adam Gopnik has groused, "Cultural politics aren't politics." I wouldn't go quite that far, but the idea that slain rapper Tupac Shakur "is the closest thing to a revolutionary we have had," as one hip-hop writer recently claimed, is a sad commentary on the current confusion between politics and culture.

In the end my writing was probably as influenced by the music sections of the *Village Voice* and the *L.A. Weekly* as all those hefty cultural studies readers that were de rigueur in the nineties. In 1994 the *L.A.*

Weekly published "Ball of Confusion," my first effort to make sense of the disco wars of the late seventies. Both my thinking and the world of popular music had changed too much to reprint that essay here, so last year I wrote a much more substantial article, "Shaky Ground: Popular Music in the Disco Years," for this collection.

This section also includes interviews with Joni Mitchell, John Paul Hammond, and Lenny Kravitz. It was sheer fan enthusiasm that made me want to interview Joni Mitchell. When I learned she was coming out with a CD in late 1994 I thought she might be more amenable than usual to doing an interview, which turned out to be right. "The Soul of a Martian: A Conversation with Joni Mitchell" originally appeared in the *L.A. Weekly* under a different title. In the intervening years, Mitchell has found herself in "the right place," getting all kinds of awards and kudos. She nabbed a Grammy for 1994's *Turbulent Indigo*, was elected to the Rock and Roll Hall of Fame in 1996, and received strong reviews for *Both Sides Now*, her recent collection of standards.

Bluesman John Paul Hammond interested me because his approach to the blues was so different from Janis Joplin's. He plays faithful renditions of the blues whereas Joplin was intent on using the songs to tell her own story. The son of a legendary music producer, Hammond has a fascinating history, which I relate in "The Refuge of the Lions' Den," a piece that was published in the *L.A. Weekly* in 1995. I have never been wild about Lenny Kravitz's music, so when *MTV Online* asked me to write a feature piece about him I hesitated before accepting the assignment. However, Kravitz had a lot to say about race and rock music and his childhood years. As different as these musicians are, their stories help illuminate how individual lived experience both confounds one's culture and history and partakes of it. Think of Joni Mitchell, who resists and succumbs to the conventions of good-girl femininity. Or Lenny Kravitz, whose music subverts the idea that music can be racially categorized and yet, when accused of being insufficiently "black," resorts to those very categories. Or John Paul Hammond, whose music challenges the idea that only downtrodden African-Americans can play the blues, but only by taking on, facsimile style, the voice and playing style of the blues masters.

11

"SHaKY Ground":
POPULar MUSIC In THE DISCO YearS

Beat is getting stronger
Music's getting longer too.
Sly and the Family Stone,
"Dance to the Music," 1968

WHEN SLY AND THE FAMILY STONE hit the stage at Woodstock few could resist their call to "dance to the music." The band was so pumped up, especially its leader Sly Stone. With his bushy Afro, white space-cowboy jumpsuit, and huge aviator glasses, Sly "kicked *ass*," in the words of rock impresario Bill Graham.[1] It was a killer performance reminiscent of Otis Redding's triumph at Monterey Pop just two years earlier in 1967. Neither festival had managed to attract more than a few black artists, and of them only Otis and Sly had a substantial following among young blacks. But Otis's music was straight-ahead Southern soul, while Sly's sound was "a whole new thing," as he liked to say. "I Want to Take You Higher," for example, had echoes of James Brown and Booker T. and the MGs, but it also owed a debt to Jimi Hendrix, free-form jazz, and San Francisco acid rock. "You can't figure out the bag I'm in," he boasted in "Everyday People," a song that, like most of the band's singles, soared to number one on both the R&B and pop charts.[2] "You really don't know which way he's taking it," said singer Jerry Butler, who marveled at the way Sly mixed it up—"black, white, electric, and unamplified."[3]

Sly's funky music sounded thrillingly bent, edgy, and at first even a little ragged. He did it all with a wink and a nod, a mischievousness conveyed by none of the other leading soul men of the day. And though he was playful, Sly wasn't clownish. If the sarcasm of "Thank You (Falettinme Be Mice Elf Agin)" sailed right past most white listeners, there was no missing the meaning of "Don't Call Me Nigger, Whitey" or that of his hit single "Stand," in which Sly admonished his audience for "sitting much too long." Along with Curtis Mayfield and James Brown, Sly helped make possible more overtly political soul music such as Stevie Wonder's "Living for the City" and Marvin Gaye's "What's Going On."[4] Sly was R&B's first auteur, the one whose chart-topping success, with albums, not just singles, allowed Wonder and Gaye to take control of their music.

Sly not only rewrote the rules of soul music, he made almost anything seem possible. And as the sixties came to a close, the fantasy of limitless possibility was nearly as irresistible as his music. A lot had happened since the Summer of Love when Otis had wowed the white crowd at Monterey, not the least of which was a growing pessimism about realizing the dream of black and white together. But Sly's hybridity, coupled with the infectious optimism of his music, suggested we were a family, not opposing tribes, a perception underscored by the band itself, a multiracial group in which the women actually played their instruments rather than just singing back-up. Other sixties artists—Janis Joplin and Jimi Hendrix, for example—confounded easy generalizations about "black" and "white" music, but Sly was the one artist whose recombinant music appealed equally to blacks and whites. Hendrix was "too way out" for most blacks, as funk maestro George Clinton observed, but Sly managed to "bridge the gap between Jimi and the Temptations."[5]

Yet a decade after Sly played Woodstock, the color line in popular music had reemerged and felt nearly as solid as the days before Chuck Berry and Little Richard broke through it.[6] When Prince, whose own experiments in musical miscegenation owed so much to Sly's, opened for the Rolling Stones in 1981 at the Los Angeles Coliseum, the audience taunted him with racist slurs and threw garbage at him and his band. What made this especially curious is that the Stones had always toured with black musicians—everyone from B.B. King and Stevie Wonder to Ike and Tina Turner—without incident.[7]

So how did we get from the late '60s when the white rock community embraced Sly's funky music to the late '70s and early '80s when a significant portion of the white rock audience turned its back on virtually all contemporary R&B? How did rock and roll, which had broken the color line in '50s popular music, come to shore it up again? Many factors contributed to rock's racial retrenchment, but nothing polarized popular music more than the incredible disco tsunami of the 1970s. With its plush orchestration, extended instrumental breaks, throwaway lyrics, and that instantly recognizable 4/4 thump, disco music was both immensely popular and deeply despised, and it changed the racial realities of American popular music in the '70s and '80s.

Skirmishes broke out everywhere, but especially on the dance floor, around the juke box and the radio, and wherever people came together to party.[8] Of course, if disco had remained a minority taste it never would have inspired such a vicious backlash. But disco's Blob-like takeover of popular music was unprecedented. Within four years disco went from being an underground secret to a mass (marketed) phenomenon. And after the runaway success of 1977's *Saturday Night Fever*, disco was ubiquitous, inescapable.[9] The film's soundtrack remained the most successful record in the history of pop music until 1983 when Michael Jackson's *Thriller* dethroned it. By 1978, 40 percent of all singles and albums on Billboard's Hot 100 were disco tunes.[10] The following year, two hundred radio stations nationwide had adopted an all-disco format, including two 24-hour stations in Los Angeles.[11] At disco's peak, there were twenty thousand discos across America, generating six billion dollars annually.[12] And they were everywhere, including just about every cheesy motel with a bar and a mirror ball. Suddenly all sorts of improbable people from the Rolling Stones to Ethel Merman were trying to cash in on the disco craze, and everything from Beethoven's *Fifth* to the theme from *Star Wars* was getting disco-ized. What little cachet disco once had, it lost. By 1979 there was no escaping the backlash. A year later disco crashed. Record labels scrambled to dump their disco divisions, and radio stations switched to other formats. The Grammy Award category for Best Disco Recording, which was hastily established for the 1979 ceremony (and won by Gloria Gaynor's "I Will Survive"), was junked after only one year.[13]

Discophobia proved remarkably durable, remaining a feature of our cultural landscape until the mid-nineties. As late as 1993, the Bee Gees, a band on the skids until disco made them superstars, said that they would like to dress up their monster disco hit "Stayin' Alive" in a "white suit and gold chains, and set it on fire."[14] Disco artists or those whose work drew on the maligned genre could count on being disparaged by music reviewers and rockers alike. For years, Madonna was scorned by critics, who considered her nothing more than a "little disco tart," as she put it.[15] In the early '90s urban contemporary stations that played R&B and hip-hop sometimes programmed disco . . . as an April Fool's Day joke.

Disco quietly enacted its revenge; it didn't die, it was renamed "dance music," and over the years it has spawned house, techno, industrial, trance, and subgenres of those. The biggest-selling music among white teens today isn't rock, but rap, a genre that wouldn't have existed without disco, which pioneered outsized beats and the splintering and remaking of songs. With the resurgence of dance tracks, even classic disco has been rehabilitated. Since the mid-'90s urban contemporary stations have taken to programming disco oldies all the time, not as a once-a-year prank. Even some rockers who bashed disco now claim a fondness for it. Johnny Lydon (aka Rotten) former-ly of the punk group the Sex Pistols, recently admitted that he had always loved disco.[16] "Once mocked for being shallow and synthetic," disco, notes rock critic Jon Pareles, "has turned into roots music."[17] Indeed, compared to the chart-topping teeny-bop dance music of the Backstreet Boys, 'N Sync, and Britney Spears—much of it masterminded by black producers, songwriters, and managers—seventies disco sounds almost lo-tech, even un-processed.[18]

Nevertheless, it's taken twenty years for people to grow nostalgic about disco. So why is it that, long after disco was declared dead, it remained the great embarrassment of post-World War II popular culture? Cultural critic Walter Hughes asks a somewhat different question, "Why did [disco's] scat-tered intellectual champions arise so much more slowly than with other pop idioms associated with dancing, sex, and African Americans—jazz, rock and roll, reggae, rap?" Some would say the music was so patently awful that its trashing requires no further explanation. But the intensity and persistence of discophobia suggests that it was motivated by something more than the music itself. After all, for every execrable disco tune like "Fly, Robin, Fly," there was an equally wretched rock hit like "We Are the Champions." Hugh-es contends that homophobia is the reason disco remained for so long lodged at the bottom of our cultural escalator. Certainly disco flourished in the gay community and was inseparable from the growing visibility of gay men in urban areas. And, as Hughes points out, the criticisms of disco and the gay male urban subculture that arose coterminously with it were almost inter-changeable. Disco was "mindless," "repetitive," "synthetic," and "commer-cial," and the gay men who danced to it were "trivial," "indistinguishable," "unnatural," and "decadent."

Antigay prejudice played a critical role in discophobia, but so did race. Indeed, by the end of the seventies disco had come to be seen by many white rock 'n' roll'ers as "an ugly amalgam of gay and black music."[19] There was an undeniably racist quality to the attacks on disco, as rock critic Lester Bangs discovered. Detroit-born Bangs was no fan of disco, but he was nonetheless dismayed to discover that to much of New York's punk hipoisie—the staff of *Punk* magazine and the inner circle of musicians at CBGB's—classic '6os soul, even Otis Redding's music, was "disco nigger shit."[20] Disco brought out the racism of mainstream rock 'n' roll'ers, too. When *Rolling Stone* capitulated to pressure from advertisers and reluctantly featured disco, once in 1975 and again in 1979, the magazine received "decidedly racist" mail from angry readers, even though its coverage was "halfhearted" at best.[21] Rock deejays bashed disco, and their stations routinely sponsored popular "Disco Sucks" campaigns. The most spectacular incident of discophobia occurred in July 1979 when a Chicago rock radio station sponsored a "Disco Sucks" night before a baseball game at Comiskey Park, a white enclave in the middle of a black ghetto. As deejay Steve Dahl detonated a ton of disco records in center field, thousands of white teenagers rushed the field, causing such pandemonium that the Chicago White Sox had to forfeit the game to the Detroit Tigers.[22]

Today disco has become everybody's music, but in the late '7os disco was associated with racial and sexual minorities—outsiders to the world of '7os rock. Explaining *Rolling Stone*'s hostility to disco, one critic there admitted that "it was something that existed outside of the rock & roll population that we belonged to personally. . . . It was a different audience, blacks and gays and women."[23] (The idea that women, plenty of whom considered themselves rock 'n' roll insiders, could be dismissed as part of this "different audience" underscores just how unself-consciously sexist rock 'n' roll was until recently.) White rockers' antagonism toward disco mirrored the anger and alienation many white leftists felt as the Movement of the sixties unraveled and splintered into many movements—black power, gay rights, and feminism. Just as many white lefty men felt themselves shoved to the sidelines by women, ethnic minorities, and gays, many rock fans believed disco was taking over, possibly even supplanting, rock.

To a great extent, the backlash against disco was specific to the '7os, and, as others have argued, reflected white male anxieties about displacement—both economic and cultural. Disco's popularity coincided with stagflation—a peculiar and unprecedented combination of stagnation and inflation—and deindustrialization, a process that had begun decades earlier but wasn't fully felt until the '70s when whole areas of the Northeast and Midwest turned rust belt. The economic downturn happened against a backdrop of affirmative action and school busing—civil rights measures that provoked sometimes fierce white resistance, especially among working-class whites, who saw themselves on the frontlines of change and feared being surpassed by upwardly mobile blacks. Feminism and gay liberation also threatened to turn the world upside down in the '70s. The early success of the Equal Rights Amendment, the Supreme Court decision legalizing abortion, and the refusal of gays to stay in the closet sparked the growth of an insurgent conservative movement. By the mid-seventies, feminists and gays could claim important victories (including the election of a number of openly gay officials such as Harvey Milk), but the ERA was dead, abortion was besieged, Anita Bryant was spearheading an antigay movement in Dade County, Florida, and the Briggs initiative, which prohibited gays and lesbians from teaching in public schools, was on the ballot in California.

Despite these setbacks the fear of displacement was acute, and it could cut across ideological lines. Even politically progressive heterosexual white men who deplored the resurgence of conservatism sometimes harbored ambivalent feelings about the new movements—women's and gay liberation and Black Power—which had challenged their hegemony in the larger Movement of the 1960s. Having felt shoved to the sidelines once before, they were not ready to roll over and let disco edge out their music, at least not without a fight.

But it wasn't always crude racism, sexism, or homophobia that fueled the disco backlash. After all, black musicians, critics, and audiences were divided about the merits of disco. And plenty of gays preferred rock 'n' roll or opera to disco. For that matter, many disco-bashing rock critics had been friendly to R&B in the '60s and would embrace rap in the '80s. Although disco did provoke a racist response, the racial politics of disco aren't easily untangled. Disco grew out of R&B, and its leading stars were African American, but it refused many of the qualities of classic soul music, so much so that some listeners thought the new music sounded "white," a perception fueled by the number of white artists who jumped on the disco bandwagon in 1979.[24] In fact, disco's popularity with pop listeners owed a great deal to the way it mainstreamed blackness by rendering artists' color incidental, almost irrelevant. Disco's apparent racelessness allowed it to cross over with the white pop audience, but it alienated many white devotees of the blues and classic R&B. "What happened to the soul?" asked Rolling Stone Keith Richards, who deplored all the high-tech button-pushing in R&B.[25]

In some ways, the history of '70s R&B is a tale of white expectations of black soulfulness and African Americans' refusal. Telling the story of disco and discophobia requires looking at the way rock music was constructed by promoters, radio programmers, and those ideological gatekeepers, the critics. It involves exploring the evolution of soul music and the complicated racial and sexual politics that surround it. It also requires returning to the '60s because, Sly Stone's success notwithstanding, R&B and rock were already diverging by the late '60s.

TOP 40 AM RADIO offered no hint of this growing racial divide. Top 40 was committed to playing the hits, and by 1967 its deejays moved easily between artists as diverse as the Supremes, Bob Dylan, Aretha Franklin, the Beatles, and the Beach Boys. But when rock moved onto the FM band, there emerged a very different style and philosophy. FM had been the home of classical music and educational programming. That began to change in 1967 when San Francisco's KMPX started broadcasting what came to be called progressive free-form rock. Within two years most decent-sized cities had a tiny station broadcasting the same sort of eclectic music mix. The pioneers of FM free-form radio saw themselves as creating a liberated space where deejays would follow their own personal aesthetic rather than a tight playlist driven by the station's bottom line. They were fiercely anti-commercial; if Top 40 played it, they wouldn't. As a result, free-form deejays played the records of black artists like Miles Davis and Muddy Waters but ignored popular R&B songs, particularly the Motown hits that were such staples of AM radio.[26]

The exclusion of most popular soul artists was not motivated by racism; in fact, most of the people who worked at these early free-form radio stations were antiestablishment.[27] It's just that, like almost everyone in the developing rock community, they believed their music should be treated as an art form, not mere product. Sixties rockers from Bob Dylan and Jimi Hendrix to Janis Joplin and the Doors saw themselves as serious artists, not peddlers of teeny-bop pop. The notion that rock is art also guided the programming of the electric ballrooms, which featured veteran bluesmen like B. B. King and rock 'n' roll pioneers like Chuck Berry, but rarely showcased contemporary soul artists. It didn't matter that black performers like King and Berry saw themselves as entertainers; among young whites who frequented the ballrooms they had the status of, well, roots musicians.[28] What promoters and radio programmers of the '50s and early '60s had believed was R&B's biggest handicap among white teens—its rawness or "blackness"—became its selling point in the late '60s among hip rock audiences, who began to look down upon most "commercial" black music.

By the early '70s, rock and R&B audiences were moving even farther apart. With rock musicians jettisoning the catchy, two-and-a-half-minute pop song in favor of something more improvisational and ambitious—and some would say pompous and self-indulgent—rock and R&B shared less common ground musically. Led Zeppelin's "Stairway to Heaven" couldn't be easily reconciled with the music of Al Green or the Stylistics. And radio programmers and booking agents made no effort to bring these audiences together. Crowds at the Fillmore had at least been exposed to black musicians, even if they were performers whose fan base was now mostly white. But when rock deserted the ballrooms for the more profitable arenas and stadiums, black and white acts rarely even played the same bill, save at Rolling Stone concerts.

The situation worsened with radio, too. By the mid-'70s, radio consultants fixated on the bottom line were transforming free-form radio into adult-oriented rock, a format geared to "narrowcasting" rather than broadcasting. AOR targeted white males between the ages of thirteen and twenty-five by playing nothing but hard rock: Journey, Reo Speedwagon, the Who, and lots of Led Zeppelin. AOR, or "classic rock" as it's now called, subscribed to such a narrow definition of rock that it made '60s AM radio seem positively multicultural. In fact, critic Ken Tucker claimed that AOR guidelines represented nothing short of "institutionalized racism and sexism."[29]

AOR playlists helped shape peoples' understanding of what constituted rock music, and it served up the worst sort of revisionist history. When San Francisco FM station KSFX ran a special eight-day program in 1981 chronicling rock's history from 1965 to 1980, only three of the almost two hundred segments concerned the work of black performers, or actually just one,

Jimi Hendrix.[30] Nor was black radio, which avoided playing anything that sounded like rock, any better than AOR. Top 40, now on the FM band, continued playing a mix of soul and rock, but AOR and the new Adult Contemporary format, which featured soft rock, had eaten into Top 40's market share, and it was no longer the dominant force it had been. Racial segmenting of the airwaves had a profound effect on listening tastes—white and black. In this context Jimi Hendrix's blues-inspired music became so linked to white rock that to a gay black waiter at the disco where I worked his songs were simply "white trash music." AOR listeners would never know that black rock was not an oxymoron, that Nona Hendryx and Parliament-Funkadelic rocked with the best of them.[31] The apartheid policy of rock promoters and radio programmers affected black performers, some of whom, like future disco hitmakers Bernard Edwards and Nile Rogers, simply gave up trying to break into rock and went back to playing R&B.

Rock criticism, like free-form radio and the electric ballrooms, was a distinctly '60s invention. Although *Rolling Stone* used a more inclusive definition of rock music than AOR radio, the paper's coverage of female and black performers left a lot to be desired. The first time *Rolling Stone* featured women was a cover story on groupies. Although the paper lavished attention on Hendrix, whose music was quite recognizably rock, it gave even Sly Stone and Stevie Wonder short shrift. It did publish long and loving features on Little Richard and Chuck Berry, but as roots musicians. As one angry letter writer observed, black musicians were more likely to turn up in the obituaries than anywhere else in *Rolling Stone*. Typical was the magazine's treatment of bluesman Arthur Crudup, who'd written and recorded "It's Alright, Mama" the song that would launch Elvis's career. When Crudup died, *Rolling Stone* ran an obituary. The caption under his picture actually read, "He never expected anything good. That's all right, Mama"[32]

Rolling Stone's privileging of white rock reflected the lily-white composition of its mostly twenty-something staff. From its founding in 1967 through the 1980s, the paper employed no black writers. The paper's treatment of black performers also owed a lot to the rock-equals-art mantra, which held great sway with rock critics, many of whom felt that soul music, by virtue of its commercialism, fell far short of that standard.[33] All too often, critics treated black musicians like dinosaurs, "precursors who, having taught the white men all they know, must gradually recede into the distance."[34] *Rolling Stone*'s senior editor Ralph Gleason didn't want black musicians to lumber off into the distance; he wanted them to emulate the new hippie bands of Haight-Ashbury. As early as 1967, he chastised "Negro performers from James Brown to . . . the Four Tops" for being "on an Ed Sullivan trip, striving as hard as they can to get on that stage and become part of the American success story, while the white rock performers are motivated to escape from the stereotype."[35] Gleason advised black musicians to come to the Fillmore where they might learn the new hip style from groups like the Jefferson Airplane.

Not everyone at *Rolling Stone* was ready to consign black music to the dustbin of history. In its early years, the paper's writers included a number of R&B aficionados who wrote with great passion about the music. However, the ease with which many of these same critics passed judgment on which R&B records were authentically "black" and which weren't is startling.[36] Stax and Atlantic artists like Aretha Franklin, Otis Redding, and Sam and Dave usually passed muster, but Motown acts often flunked the test. Time and again, *Rolling Stone* condemned the Detroit company for producing formulaic, assembly-line black pop for white people.[37] Motown's records were "Tom travesties," snickered one writer, and its artists were "locked into their plastic nightclub performing style."[38]

No Motown group came in for more criticism than the Supremes. *Rolling Stone*'s highly influential and famously cranky critic Jon Landau declared that the group was "totally committed to show business values and lost their soul long ago."[39] By contrast, Stax artist Otis Redding was the quintessential soul man, whose singing, Landau wrote, was "direct," "simple," and "unintellectual."[40] Otis's "understanding of music was not something he could put on or take off, depending on chart trends," wrote Landau, approvingly. "He was truly a 'folk' artist."[41] Landau's understanding of R&B echoed Norman Mailer's patronizing view of jazz as the expression of feeling, "the music of orgasm," uninformed by intellect.[42] What Landau and other critics seemed to value most about soul music was its apparent resistance to musical trends. It was familiar: raw, intuitive, expressive, and sexual—perhaps just like the people who made it. But black musicians, like other black people in the '60s, weren't standing still. And as the decade wore on white rock critics didn't always like what they heard.

Don't forget the Motor City
Dancing in the street

Laura Nyro with Labelle, "Dancing in the Street,"
1971, produced by Gamble and Huff
(originally recorded by Martha and the Vandellas
for Motown Records, 1964)

ACTUALLY, BLACK PEOPLE WEREN'T standing still in 1959 either, the year that Berry Gordy founded Motown Records. Indeed, the critical disparagement of Motown stemmed in large part from Gordy's deliberate efforts to make black music the "Sound of Young America," something unthinkable just a few years earlier. Although the "crossover concept" was part of R&B from the very beginning, independent R&B record companies in the postwar years nonetheless assumed that their core audience would be black.[43] What set Gordy apart was his conviction that he could make music that would finally obliterate the color line by appealing equally to white and black teenagers. Gordy didn't think that having his tunes covered by white artists was the most he could hope for. Motown records would be pop hits in their own right, just as his acts would penetrate the better white clubs rather than be restricted to the chitlin circuit. Gordy's refusal to be confined to the black market was, as Gerald Early argues, the "really revolutionary thing" about Motown.[44]

To many rock critics, though, Gordy's crossover strategy was reactionary: it contributed to the denaturing or bleaching of black music. Typical is *Rolling Stone* writer Peter Guralnick's view of Motown as "so much more popular, so much more socially acceptable, so much more arranged and predictable, so much more white."[45] In fact, he excluded Motown from his landmark book, *Sweet Soul Music*, on precisely these grounds. Yet to millions of African Americans, Motown was soul music as surely as Atlantic or Stax.[46] And though white rock critics hailed Atlantic Records as the real stuff, the company's founder, Ahmet Ertegun, has described his label's sound as "urbanized, watered-down versions of real blues." Atlantic's R&B approximated "authentic blues," according to Ertegun, but it was "cleaner, less rough and perforce more sophisticated," which made it an easier sell to white teens.[47] Ertegun may have been tailoring the sound for white consumption, but until the mid-sixties Atlantic artists remained far more popular among blacks.

In truth, blacks' musical tastes have always been elastic enough to encompass crossover artists like Nat "King" Cole, the Mills Brothers, or Sam

Cooke. As far back as the early twentieth century, black musicians who played in juke joints and nightclubs had to mix blues with ragtime and hokum because black audiences preferred variety.[48] But the idea that African Americans are a monolith, united in taste and behavior, is a potent one, for whites and blacks alike. "Varieties of speech, rhythm, diction, accent, taste, and style are fine for white people," as cultural critic Stanley Crouch has pointed out, "but there must be a psychological and spiritual tub of tar a Negro should sit in each morning before facing the day."[49] This idea proved especially seductive in the late '60s when black power promoted precisely this sort of racial essentialism.

Motown wasn't more white than Stax Records, but it was more pop—a category of music that it turns out was never truly white. African-American songwriters played such an important role in early twentieth-century popular music that Irving Berlin once felt it necessary to point out that not all of Tin Pan Alley's composers and lyricists were black. As blues historian Francis Davis points out, standards like "Pretty Baby," "I'm Just Wild About Harry," and "Some of These Days," seem "raceless" to us now in part because their writers "no doubt strove to leave race out of them," but they were all written by African Americans.[50] Even the blues, which white preservationists like folklorist Alan Lomax promoted as a kind of folk music immune to market forces, was a form of pop.[51]

Popular music—rock, R&B, pop, and even the blues—is so much the product of musical miscegenation that there's no such thing as music which is truly "white" or "black." That said, this isn't the perception of most listeners, critics, radio programmers, and record company executives. A gospel moan or wail, or singing "ax" instead of "ask," tag a record as black.[52] In the early years of Motown when Gordy was trying to conquer white America, there was a limit to how much "blackness" Gordy would allow. Hyperconscious about black representation and white reception, Gordy and his two sisters instituted an artist development program. Female singers were sent to the Motown charm school where they learned how to walk, sit, fix their hair, and wear white gloves and long gowns on stage; male performers were put through their paces, too. Given many whites' racial prejudice or just deep ignorance about African Americans, it made sense for Gordy to prioritize artist makeovers. The Supremes and the Temptations were often young whites' first encounter with black culture. Even admiring whites sometimes harbored attitudes about blacks that were distressingly Maileresque.[53] Up against entrenched racial attitudes about blacks as a simple, spontaneous people lacking restraint and polish, Gordy worked against stereotype, sometimes to a maddening degree.

Gordy's sensitivity to white sensibilities could be problematic. As late as 1966, the year "black power" began edging out "we shall overcome," he came close to nixing Stevie Wonder's cover of Bob Dylan's "Blowin' in the Wind" because he feared the song was too controversial.[54] He promoted the tiny-voiced Diana Ross over fellow Supreme Florence Ballard, who had the "pipes," because Ross had the "poise" and a pop voice to match.[55] And he sweetened the music. In the early years, he also showcased female singers, calculating that they would encounter less white resistance than male singers. Strategically, this may have been the proper course to follow. After all, just two years before Motown's founding, black rock 'n' roller Frankie Lymon had set off a scandal when he danced with a white girl on Alan Freed's TV show.

Although one wishes Gordy had been less attuned to white tastes, the blanket dismissal of Motown as too "white" rested on certain assumptions, particularly the idea that blacks "remain unaffected," as Ralph Ellison put it, "by the social structures, national manners" or the "the complex give and take of acculturation."[56] Accordingly, most white rock critics assumed soul artists received their musical education in church, preferred gritty soul to white pop, and only recorded the standards under duress or because they were sell-outs. Yet this didn't describe Motown's artists, most of whom received their musical education in the Detroit public schools.[57] Nor did the Supremes record the standards because they were "foisted" on them by Motown. Rather, says Supreme Mary Wilson, the group's "roots were in American music—everything from rock to show tunes—and always had been."[58] Wilson's own influences included the McGuire Sisters, Patti Page and Doris Day. And she was hardly alone. Marvin Gaye longed to sing like Frank Sinatra and Smokey Robinson claimed black jazz-pop singer Sarah Vaughan as a critical influence. These artists weren't less black for liking pop music or "corrupted" because "they didn't sound like Aretha Franklin or Otis Redding."[59] Rather, their embrace of pop and their desire to cross over reflected their sense of themselves as fully American. Like many other African Americans growing up in the '50s during the Second Reconstruction they weren't sitting at the back of the bus. Or as Stevie Wonder put it, "When you say I'm a black musician . . . that's putting me in a particular box and saying . . . *stay* . . . *right* . . . *where* . . . *you* . . . *are!*"[60] At Motown artists laid their claim to the American Dream; in the process they changed American music and culture.

Hey Nineteen, that's 'Retha Franklin
She don't remember the Queen of Soul
Steely Dan, "Hey Nineteen," 1980

BY THE LATE '60S, MORE AND MORE R&B artists were struggling to break past the constraints—musical and economic—of soul music. Otis Redding aspired to assume the mantle of his friend Sam Cooke, the great gospel-turned-pop singer. At the time of his fatal plane crash, though, Otis had never penetrated the pop Top 10. Guitarist Steve Cropper, with whom Otis wrote the posthumously released 1968 hit "(Sitting on) the Dock of the Bay," admitted that they had set out to make a pop record. "You can't just keep doing R and B songs like 'Mr. Pitiful,'" he said, "because it's only going to cater to a certain amount of people."[61] Aretha Franklin had always struggled to transcend the limits of rhythm and blues. After all, it was she who demanded that "Over the Rainbow" be included in her 1960 session with Columbia Records. But when the popularity of Southern soul started to wane in 1969, "Lady Soul" tried to reposition herself as a "mainstream pop/jazz singer" while at the same time playing up her new Afrocentric style. "Thus in 1971," wrote one white critic, "we were confronted with an enigmatic new Aretha, wearing her natural hair and African clothes, singing tunes like "This Girl's in Love with You" and "Call Me" backed by a large orchestra."[62] To some critics, Aretha's move to a slick pop-soul was further evidence of what critic Guralnick called her distressingly "middlebrow" taste.[63]

Aretha was hardly the only artist trying to break past hardcore, funky soul music. She did it by covering songs like Simon and Garfunkel's "Bridge over Troubled Water," and pop-oriented material, but her singing remained fiery, passionate. However, her labelmates at Atlantic Records, Roberta Flack and Donny Hathaway, helped advance a laid-back, minimalist, jazzy black pop. So did Bill Withers, whose brooding 1971 hit "Ain't No Sunshine," was produced by ex-Stax player Booker T. Jones. However, no one was as smooth as Al Green. On songs like the slinky "Here I Am (Come and Take Me)," Green, in his plaintive, aching falsetto, conveyed romantic yearning like few other singers. Green was one of many falsetto vocalists whose records dominated the charts in this period. In fact, so much creamy, cool soul music featured falsetto singers like Eddie Kendricks of the Temptations and Phillipé Wynne of the Spinners that critic Jon Landau dubbed it "sissy soul." And it's true that these singers sounded tentative, pleading, and yielding by contrast to the full-throttle masculinity of the sixties' leading soul men—James Brown, Otis Redding, Wilson Pickett, Johnnie Taylor and Eddie Floyd.

Much of the new suave soul was coming out of Philadelphia, where songwriters Kenneth Gamble and Leon Huff began producing artists in 1966. The duo's work with Jerry Butler, who'd first made a name for himself in the '50s with Curtis Mayfield in the Impressions, would become a prototype for the new cool soul.[64] But Gamble and Huff are best known for Billy Paul's "Me and Mrs. Jones" and their work with the O'Jays ("I Love Music"), Harold Melvin and the Blue Notes featuring Teddy Pendergrass ("The Love I Lost"), and their house band, MFSB, whose massive hit "TSOP (The Sound of Philadelphia)" became the theme song for the TV show Soul Train and an early disco hit.[65] When Gamble and Huff teamed up with producer Thom Bell and established Philadelphia International Records they set out to build a Motown-like empire.[66] PIR would become the dominant force in black music through the seventies. During the disco years, while Motown stumbled, PIR prospered.

PIR was always a purveyor of smooth soul, but this wasn't true of Stax Records, the epicenter of down-home Southern soul music. In 1969 Stax pioneered a whole new kind of soul when it released Isaac Hayes's offbeat album Hot Buttered Soul. Hayes had written and produced Sam and Dave's biggest hits with his collaborator David Porter. However, Hayes's own album sounded nothing like "Soul Man" or "Hold On! I'm a Comin.'" Nor did the record's cover, which featured a strange top-down shot of the artist, look anything like the cover art of other R&B albums. Hayes didn't strike the usual soul-man pose, smiling winningly at the camera. In fact, his face was barely visible. What stood out instead was Hayes's shiny bald head, cool shades, and the imposing gold chains draped around his neck. "I suppose bald was as black as you could get," he later said. "We did it as a joke, but everyone liked it 'cause it was different and it was out front."[67] Hayes set out to be different and break the mold, and Hot Buttered Soul had a weird, almost experimental feel to it. This wasn't a calculated crossover move, and Stax was surprised when the album hit number four on the pop album charts. With its schlocky, over-the-top arrangements and super-long cuts (only four on the album), *Hot Buttered Soul* was cool, languid bedroom music. His twelve-minute cover of Dionne Warwick's "Walk on By," which Hayes embellished with psychedelic guitar shadings, spaced-out sound effects, and innumerable false fade-outs, sounded like music waiting for a movie. In 1971, Hayes scored the music for the blaxploitation movie *Shaft*, and his theme song for it hit the top of the pop charts and won an Oscar. Instantly recognizable with its tireless four/four hi-hats and irresistible wah-wah guitar, "The Theme from *Shaft*" edged soul music closer to disco.

Hayes's solo efforts sounded like a refusal of Stax's gritty, raw brand of soul music and they prefigured the lush music of disco's big man, Barry White. The singer who most influenced Hayes was Sam Cooke, the original cool soul man. "He was sophisticated," Hayes later explained, and "that's what we wanted."[68] Hayes was just one of many soul artists who bridled at the idea that the color of his skin meant he should sound recognizably "black." If be-bop was black jazz musicians' response to the perennial problem of white appropriation, or theft, as Thelonious Monk claimed ("we're going to create something they can't steal because they can't play it."[69]), perhaps this silky, polished soul was in some way about denying white America's expectation that soul music was about the "hard" life, music that had all "the authenticity of collard greens boiling on the stove," as *Time* magazine put it.[70] Just as many blacks had abandoned the blues because it was so redolent of trouble and bad times, so many now embraced music that broke with the idea that soul must sound earthy and primitive.

Maybe the ascendance of soft soul reflected black musicians' annoyance with the white rock community's knee-jerk veneration of veteran black bluesmen and soul men, the grittier the better. One thing's for sure, many white rock critics were mystified or disdainful of this new lite soul, which they judged "too artificial."[71] "What happened to the days when black music was black and not this mush of vacuous Muzak and pretentious drivel?" sneered Britain's *New Musical Express*.[72] If the new sweet soul was wildly popular with pop audiences, the white rock audience, tuned into the hard rock of AOR or the singer-songwriter music of Adult Contemporary radio, was oblivious to it.

By 1980, most teenagers, like the nineteen-year-old in the Steely Dan song, probably wouldn't have recognized the music of Aretha Franklin.

People movin' out, people movin' in
Why? Because of the color of their skin
Run, run, run, but you sure can't hide
"Ball of Confusion," The Temptations, 1970

AT THE SAME TIME THAT SOUL music was becoming creamier and cooler, it was also beginning to reflect the new black consciousness.[73] This was a strange moment in R&B because no one really knew how far the envelope could be pushed before whites turned off or how far it needed to be pushed to remain "relevant" to black fans. Ironically, the political imperative was felt at the very moment when the opportunities for inclusion in the musical mainstream had never been more plentiful. After all, by 1969 lots of soul artists were playing Vegas and R&B hits routinely made the pop Top 10. So just as black artists were reaping the benefits of crossover like never before, they encountered friends, family, and politicos who expected them to stay "real," be "black."[74] Even living large became suspect. Joe Billingslea, formerly of the Contours, captures the "funny crossfire" in which Motown artists found themselves by the late '60s. "Here's a bunch of black kids going flat-out after the American Dream. The nice house, the clothes, the car. Just what everybody else has always gone for. But with what was going on, the riots, the Vietnam mess, it was the *down* side of the dream. And so just when some cat gets enough to afford the Continental—bang—it's not *cool* to drive it, disrespectful to the movement or whatever."[75]

The apparently contradictory pressure of making music for all Americans or music geared to other blacks, crossing over or being "black," was a conundrum for some African-American musicians.[76] After all, James Brown had found himself locked out of the pop Top 10 after he cut "Say It Loud, I'm Black and I'm Proud" in 1968.[77] However, in this period tectonic shifts seemed to occur in a matter of months and what seemed radical quickly became merely reasonable. By 1970, a full four years after black power began eclipsing integration, record companies began to grasp that there was a lucrative market for music that reflected the new black consciousness.

Motown tested the water in the summer of 1970 with the Temptations' "Ball of Confusion," which topped the black charts and just missed duplicating that success on the pop charts. "Ball of Confusion" opened with an indictment of white flight, but it quickly devolved into a cover-all-the-markets number in which the Temps recited a laundry list of issues and events, everything from rising "unemployment" and "tax deductions" to "the Beatles' new record." The song tried to be relevant to African Americans, but without alienating whites, for whom the psychedelic guitar break was presumably intended. While "Ball" was still in the Top 10, Motown released Edwin Starr's "War," an unequivocally antiwar anthem whose opening line went, "War, what is it good for? Absolutely nothing." Starr's song hit number one on the pop charts, and was only slightly less popular with black listeners. Six months later, Motown put out Marvin Gaye's "What's Going On," the first in his extraordinary aural triptych that included "Inner City Blues," and "Mercy Mercy Me (The Ecology)." Throughout most of 1971, Gaye's music was so popular it was just a spin away on the radio dial, but, then, his tone was plaintive, even perplexed, never angry. With the Undisputed Truth's "Smiling Faces Sometimes," R&B became edgier, with lines like, "Beware of the pat on the back/It just might hold you back," which took aim at duplicitous white liberals.

Motown's "Smiling Faces" was one of the big hits of the summer of 1971, and it represented a watershed moment: black power had finally entered the Top 10. However, Sly Stone's long-awaited *There's a Riot Goin' On*, which was released during 1971's holiday season, set a new standard for uncompromised honesty. Sly had promised that this LP would be his "most optimistic of all," but there wasn't a glimmer of hopefulness anywhere on it.[78] Songs that on the surface seemed perky and upbeat were disconcertingly bleak upon further listening.[79] The first single, "Family Affair," which had a bubbly, syncopated rhythm track and a catchy refrain, shot up the charts to number one. But its subject matter was heavy, and its source apparently personal: families and the damage they cause. One child "grows up to be somebody that just loves to learn," Sly sings, the other child grows up to be "somebody you just love to burn." Newlyweds try to stay faithful, but love may not be enough. "You can't leave cause your heart's there, but you can't stay cause you've been somewhere else." Throughout, Sly moaned, shrieked, mumbled, growled, and slurred his words as though he were on the verge of nodding out, which he may have been. By this point, Sly was routinely missing gigs and his mischievousness had acquired a nasty edge—the result, many figured, of drugs.[80] Sly had his personal demons, but he sounds so weary on this album that one wonders if the effort to make music that appealed equally to whites and blacks hadn't become too great a burden.

Riot drew raves from those rock critics who were still engaged with R&B.[81] But they agreed the album was "no fun." With *Riot*, Greil Marcus wrote, Sly's "old politics had turned into death, his exuberance into dope, and his old music into a soundtrack for a world that didn't exist." Despite the album's darkness, it quickly jumped to the top spot on both the R&B and pop charts, most likely because of its great dance grooves.[82] Critic Dave Marsh maintained that Sly's white fans were put off by the album. "The white counterculture," he wrote, "responded with all the racism that a decade of consciousness-raising hadn't stamped out. White kids may have danced to Sly's new music, but they weren't happy with it."[83] *Riot* was unmistakably antiestablishment, but it didn't speak to whites. There were no cheery songs extolling the brotherhood of man. Sly even made fun of his popular hit "Thank You (Falettinme Be Mice Elf Agin)," with the excruciatingly stretched-out, slowed-down, bass-heavy "Thank You for Talkin' to Me Africa." Finally he gave the song a sound to match the haunting lyrics of the original.

Sly could still summon pop hooks easily enough, but with *Riot* he went deeper into the funk. With its portentous bass and sometimes enervated beats, *Riot* seemed to be suggesting that soul music in its most "chipper, choreographed, commercial form" was passé.[84] Likewise, Sly's voice, more cartoonish than ever, seemed a refusal of the romantic soul man tradition.[85] Yet, *Riot*'s use of the synthesizer and the drum machine—one of its earliest uses ever—anticipated disco, the perkiest music of all. Certainly "Family Affair" was a rhythmic influence on two early disco hits, George McRae's "Rock Your Baby" and the Hues Corporation's "Rock the Boat." Sly's music had a raw, almost haphazard quality at odds with the lockstep predictability of disco, but, as others have noted, rhythmically his music nonetheless prefigured disco.[86] Some producers and musicians took *Riot*'s dance grooves to help create disco, others—Stevie Wonder, the Isley Brothers, War, Rufus, and George Clinton's Parliament-Funkadelic crew—carried on Sly's work of smashing the boundaries between soul, rock, and pop music.

Riot's influence on R&B wasn't simply musical, though. In the year and a half after its release, it was as though the floodgates of black disillusionment and despair had opened up. The summer of 1972 saw the release of Curtis Mayfield's soundtrack for the blaxploitation film, *Superfly*. Both the mordant "Freddie's Dead" and "Superfly" deliberately undercut the movie's celebration of the living-large gangsta and were radio staples well into 1973. Before the year was out Mayfield's songs were joined by a remarkable group of singles: the O'Jays' "Back Stabbers," Marvin Gaye's "Trouble Man," War's "Slippin' into Darkness," Stevie Wonder's "Superstition," and the Temptation's protodisco "Papa Was a Rollin' Stone" with its haunting last line, "and when he died, all he left us was alone." Several months later, Wonder released his epic "Living for the City." This was music of "worry," ruthlessly honest music that looked fearlessly at the problems within black communities.[87] In contrast to earlier message music like Curtis Mayfield's "We're a Winner" or James Brown's "I'm Black and I'm Proud," these songs aren't feel-good anthems of racial pride. More often than not the trouble in these songs lies inside the community, as in "Slippin' into Darkness," where "the brothers never say their names." In the end, this music feels inseparable from African Americans' growing apprehension that the black movement had lost its momentum (not to mention its leaders) and white America its will to change.[88]

Curiously, although this music dealt with racism, it dominated the pop charts. It was "an uneasy and exciting conjunction," thought critic Dave Marsh, who wondered if white audiences would continue to support "mature" black pop.[89] However, white listeners' tolerance for troubled music about black America wasn't tested again in the '70s. Sly took off two years before cutting *Fresh*, the highlight of which was his improbable cover of Doris Day's "Que Sera, Sera,"[90] He continued to have moderate success through 1975, after which point his career took a nose dive, but he never cut an album like *Riot* again. And Marvin Gaye followed "Trouble Man" with the slinky, make-out hit "Let's Get It On." R&B shifted gears as the brooding, foreboding music of the early '70s gave way to cheery party music without any apparent political meaning. As R&B made the disco turn, sympathetic white critics were dismayed by the way that everything—melody, lyrics, singer, and players—was now subsumed by the beat.[91]

Reflecting on the turn away from socially engaged R&B, Greil Marcus noted that most of it had been made by producers whose commitment was to hit-making. Instead of making music that made history, they simply "drifted into accommodation."[92] Marcus saw parallels between the change in R&B and the about-face of the Black Panther Party, which in 1972 became involved in electoral politics and began working with black churches.[93] The retreat into disco and more glossy black pop reflected, he thought, what happens when "something like the truth is out."[94] While the truth, complicated and messy as it was, undoubtedly was a casualty of the disco turn, it's not clear that accommodation was driving this shift. Maybe disco was about dissembling or camouflage, or maybe it represented an effort to move beyond the despair of the early seventies. Nile Rodgers has said that the music he made with the popular disco group Chic was his effort to provide a sense of hopefulness. To Rodgers, who had been involved in the Black Panther Party, there was a political utility and a political message in upbeat songs like the dance floor favorite, "We Are Family."[95]

If there's a cure for this, I don't want it
If there's a remedy, I'll run from it.
Diana Ross, "Love Hangover," 1976

BEFORE THERE WAS DISCO, THERE were discotheques. The national dance craze spawned by Chubby Checker's 1960 hit "The Twist" made New York discotheques like the Peppermint Lounge famous during the early '60s. But with the arrival of psychedelia in the mid-'60s discotheques began to seem hopelessly square. A new kind of free-form, anything-goes dancing took root in hip rock ballrooms like the Avalon and the Fillmore in San Francisco. Some speculate that the early '70s shift from acid to downers put an end to the dancing, but hippie ballrooms also began closing in the wake of Woodstock. After 1969's huge outdoor festival, the move to more profitable arenas was on. Rock music, or a lot of it, also became more arty and pretentious, and less danceable.

However, the rise of stadium rock had no effect on the nightlife habits of blacks, gays, and Latinos, who had never been much interested in the hippie ballrooms, which were, after all, overwhelmingly white and heterosexual. At private parties and clubs and in neighborhood bars they made Motown and post-Motown soul their soundtrack. People called it "party music," and *Rolling Stone*'s R&B critic Vince Aletti wrote about it as early as the fall of 1972. Early disco culture was an underground scene, one that record companies couldn't have cared less about and made no effort to exploit. Deejays developed their own independent network for publicity and record distribution (in the form of record pools) without help from large record companies. It was an engineer, Tom Moulton, who came up with the idea of providing club deejays with long-playing, twelve-inch singles that were specially mixed with extended instrumental breaks for smoother segues.

Most of the leading creators of early disco, from Gamble and Huff to Motown's Norman Whitfield and Van ("The Hustle") McCoy had worked for years as songwriters and producers of soul music. At first, disco was practically indistinguishable from R&B.[96] One of the first disco hits, 1974's "Love's Theme," by Barry White's Love Unlimited Orchestra could have been mistaken for an Isaac Hayes song. That summer's big dance music hits, "Rock Your Baby" and "Rock the Boat," sounded like lots of other slick, sweet early '70s soul. In fact, early disco, from George McRae's "Rock Your Baby" to the Jackson 5's "Dancing Machine" to "Do It ('Til You're Satisfied)" by the B.T. Express was much slower than later disco and lacked disco's signature 4/4 thump. Over time, of course, disco did become "disco," which is to say it evolved into something much more formulaic. Even so, disco was not monolithic. There was melodic R&B-flavored disco, funk that defied the 4/4 beat, and the hyperstylized, synthesized Eurodisco of Swiss-Italian producer Giorgio Moroder. In many discos, especially those that catered to African Americans, Donna Summer and Gloria Gaynor were routinely mixed with funk, from Cameo to Parliament-Funkadelic. But if there were deep connections between R&B and disco, the new dance music did severely limit the opportunities for a vocalist to stretch out and improvise. Some singers, particularly those in Chic, sang in a clipped, almost flat fashion. Singers were prisoners of the beat or they were dispensed with altogether in instrumental tracks. When a song had words, the lyrics were often inconsequential and self-referential, as in "shake your booty," "put your body in it," or "get down tonight."

Disco came to be associated with the glitterati of Studio 54, but its origins were working-class, as anyone who listened to the lyrics could tell. One piece of evidence, as journalist Andrew Kopkind pointed out, was the regularity with which "weekend" turned up in disco tunes. "Working-class kids toil all week and wait for their one big shot at fun, escape, and dreams on the weekend," wrote Kopkind. "Quite the other way with rock culture," he notes. "Hippies hang out all week and can't tell Saturday night from Tuesday afternoon."[97] Disco's fantasy of the good life, of upward mobility, betrayed its working-class roots just as rock's bohemian fantasy of downward mobility betrayed its middle-class roots.

If going to the disco was a way that working-class blacks and Latinos could reclaim the body as an "instrument of pleasure rather than an instrument of labor," then for gays it was a way to assert an identity often hidden during the day. "The nighttime [became] the right time."[98] Or, to be more accurate, in the wake of 1969's Stonewall riot (where gays fought the police and many believe gay liberation was born), the nighttime finally became the right time for gays, too. Until Stonewall many gay bars hadn't even permitted same-sex dancing. At one popular gay male bar on Fire Island employees monitored the dance floor by shining a flashlight into the eyes of anyone engaging in "illegal behavior," defined as two men even facing each other as they danced.

With gay liberation gay men in big cities were suddenly visible. "I was shocked by how much the city had changed," recalls writer Edmund White of his return to New York in 1970. "Where before there had been a few gay boys hanging out on a stoop along Christopher Street, now there were armies of men marching in every direction off Sheridan Square." White had been gone only six months, but in his absence a cultural revolution had swept Manhattan. Homosexuals, even once-shy white gays, radiated a new-found boldness and daring. Decked out in snug micro shorts and T-shirts, they moved through Sheridan Square "shouting and waving and surging into the traffic" as if the streets were theirs. "Is this a holiday or what?" was White's amazed, amused reaction. Key to the revolution were the new gay discos, which White writes had all of a sudden "sprung up like magic mushrooms." "Out of the closets and into the streets" may have been the rallying cry of the newly emergent gay liberation movement, but in the '70s discos and bathhouses, not politics, were arguably the adhesive in the gay male community. Not since the pansy craze of the Roaring Twenties when the homosexual subculture was so vibrant that gays spoke of "coming out" *into* gay society, had gay male culture been so public.

Some say that the first commercial disco was Fire Island's Ice Palace, which opened in the summer of 1970, just one year after the Stonewall riot.[99] But others maintain that the ur-disco was the Loft, a private gay club in Manhattan, which opened Valentine's Day, 1970, in the home of David Mancuso. What is certain is that within months Manhattan boasted many gay discos including the Tenth Floor, 12 West, Aux Puces, and the Sanctuary. It's no accident that the first discos began cropping up so soon after Stonewall. After years of being hassled by management and arrested during police raids, gays refused to act straight and refused to stop dancing. Dancers, accustomed to juke boxes that left them stranded awkwardly on the dance floor waiting for the next song—a most unwelcome return to reality— could now dance all night long without interruption. Deejays made that possible by mixing records together so that the music never stopped, and in especially expert hands, even sounded seamless. That was the point. No more being interrupted by raids or hostile bartenders, or by straights looking for a freak show, or by something as simple as a song ending. In gay discos "the throbbing lights, the engulfing sound, the heightened energy, and the hyperbolic heat" created the impression, wrote one journalist, "that the world is enclosed in this hall, that there is only *now*, in this place and time."[100] Gay discos were liberated space in the '70s, a time, writes *Village Voice* columnist Richard Goldstein, of a "psychic Intifada: a sloughing off of centuries of shame and a venting of pent-up desire."[101] In those days, it wasn't unusual for gay clubbers to stay out dancing until noon the next day. If there was a "cure" for disco fever or for homosexuality, gays were having none of it. They were staying in the now, chanting along with Diana Ross, "Don't call the doctor, don't call my momma, don't call the preacher, I don't need it."

Most observers believed that the new dance music was at odds with the ethos of the sixties. Critics thought disco a perfect expression of the shallow, coked-up, narcissistic seventies—the much maligned Me Decade. Journalist Andrew Kopkind had a more complicated reaction to disco. He conceded that many found disco narcissistic, but he pointed out that others believed a disco dance floor offered greater possibility for connectedness than a rock concert. He cited the example of a heterosexual female friend, a rocker-turned-disco-lover, who felt that "there did get to be a point of no return" in rock culture. "The '60s was so solitary, so solipsistic, so narcissistic," she mused, "look at the way people danced." By contrast, on a disco

dance floor "you get high with someone else."[102] To Kopkind, a sixties veteran who became an ambivalent convert to the new music, the '60s were
"braless, lumpy, heavy, rough and romantic," whereas disco seemed "styl-
ish, sleek, smooth, contrived, and controlled." But beneath its sleek stylishness, Kopkind saw in disco a welcome challenge to the white, male, middle-class, heterosexual character of rock culture.

Disco spoke to those not included in sixties rock culture: minorities,
gays, women. Although there was a lot of "high-marketplace maneuvering
that brought disco onto the pop scene," as literary critic Houston Baker put
it, disco began as music "from below," offering cheap, all-night entertainment.[103] Disco's roots were in racially and ethnically mixed gay clubs and
bars, not Studio 54 or corporate backrooms.[104] Manhattan's first disco, the
Loft, was both "inter-racial," and "pan-sexual." According to Andrew
Holleran, much of whose novel, *Dancer from the Dance*, takes place at 12
West, a "strange democracy" prevailed at New York's gay discos, where the
"only ticket of admission was physical beauty—and not even that sometimes."[105] Vince Aletti, the first rock journalist to cover disco, maintains the
new music was "driven by an underground idea of unity."[106] Cultural critic
Walter Hughes goes considerably further, arguing that disco celebrated the
bad black girl, and encouraged gay men to "identify with rather than lust
after (much less despise) the 'bad girl.'" According to Hughes, disco's black
divas offered the white gay male a dare he found "particularly provoking":
the possibility of trying on the "supposedly degraded subject position" of
the black woman.[107]

There were transcendent moments when the music dissolved all sorts of
social hierarchies and the spirit of the "beloved community" seemed to en-
velop the dance floor. On a crowded, sweaty dance floor certain songs—
"Ain't No Stoppin' Us Now," "I'm Coming Out," "There But For the Grace of
God" and "We Are Family"—created a feeling of solidarity that felt political.
But the revisionist view that discos were edenic sites of egalitarianism
where white gay men were "tempted to occupy the position of the racial and
sexual other" is no truer than than the caricatured view of discos as exclusionary haunts of the rich.[108] Some discos, such as the Loft or the legendary
Paradise Garage, where black deejay Larry Levan presided over the floor,
were inclusive—at least of gay men. But at many gay discos unity didn't extend to people of color, or to women, even (perhaps especially) lesbians.

The feminist and gay press in the '70s carried numerous stories about gays of color and women coming up against discriminatory door policies. Gay deejays who weren't white or male found that jobs at the better-paying gay discos eluded them. And owners and managers sometimes tried to manipulate the music. The managers at the gay disco where I worked in the late '70s asked me on several occasions to "switch" the music from the "blacker" funk that I favored to "whiter" sounding disco. But if discos were not always models of racial and gender equality, there was considerable mixing in them, far more than at '70s rock concerts.

To rock critics and fans, however, disco was not about unity or community. Disco was mindless, monochromatic, repetitive, mechanistic, and soulless.[109] "Muzak that made you want to move," judged one critic.[110] Soul music was already on a collision course with rock; but disco elaborated all that the critics disliked about current R&B. For starters, disco reduced the role of rock's signature instrument, the guitar, to a percussive instrument. The subordination of the guitar to the Almighty Beat seemed to arouse real anxiety in hardcore rockers. In disco the assaultive, phallic work of the lead guitar was taken over by the whomping beat. At rock concerts the music reverberated noisily in one's eardrums, but discos cranked the bass up so high that the beat penetrated, literally rocked, one's entire body.[111] A disco with a good sound system "was akin to an audio orgasmatron," recalls dance music aficionado Frank Owens, "that worked on erogenous zones you never knew you had."[112] Guys at discos not only had zero opportunity to play air guitar, they found themselves assaulted, violated by the beat. In the process, "conventional constructions of masculine selfhood" were upended.[113] *Saturday Night Fever* tried to masculinize disco dancing by casting hunky John Travolta as a woman-chasing dance floor wiz, but the strategy didn't entirely succeed.[114]

For straight, white, male rock 'n' roll'ers accustomed to barely moving on a dance floor, disco, which required some attention to form and style, could be truly daunting. But, then, boys and men have often been portrayed as dance-floor shy. In fact, one of the first big disco hits, 1975's "Shame, Shame, Shame" by Shirley and Company, whose chorus went "Shame on you/if you can't dance too," mocked men's uneasiness on the dance floor. Discos didn't just indulge women's apparently greater passion for dancing, however. Discos played music, much of it sung by women, about love, or to be more precise, about love-making. In fact, in *Rolling Stone*'s history of rock music, critic Ken Tucker ventures that discophobia arose in part because "the implicit sexuality of the disco experience—the building, peaking and climaxing of the music," made teenaged rock 'n' roll'ers, who were more often than not sexually inexperienced, nervous. They preferred rock, which "dealt with sex as anticipation and neurotic fantasy." In his view, disco had greater appeal to a slightly older, more sexually experienced audience.[115] Yet plenty of thirty-something rockers hated disco, and not for lack of sexual experience.

The resistance to disco probably had more to do with the way in which the music foregrounded female desire. "Lady Marmalade," with its soaring "more, more, more" climax, Gloria Gaynor's "Honey Bee," which included the line, "I'm your honey bee, come on and sting me," and Evelyn Champagne King's memorable "Shame," were songs about women's lust. And then there was Donna Summer's one-of-a-kind hit "Love To Love You Baby." Summer's song, which featured much orgasmic moaning, was over 17 minutes long, as if to say, this isn't going to be any two-and-a-half-minute number. Of course, the radical women's movement had made the revolutionizing of heterosexuality among its central goals. In her affectionate send-up of the early women's liberation movement, novelist Alix Kates Shulman has one of her characters demand "three hours minimum" for sex. Women were changing the terms of sex, and disco, far more than rock, reflected this cultural shift. In a 1993 interview Barry White argued that the disco " '70s was approached as if it was a woman being romanced and made love to."[116] White notwithstanding, disco tapped into heterosexual men's anxiety about women's sexuality, and what Walter Hughes calls the "supposedly unmappable progressions, limitless multiplicity, and mysterious triggers" of the female orgasm.

Of course, disco's loudest detractors didn't attack disco on the grounds that it promoted women's sexual assertiveness. To them, disco's facelessness, formulaic sound, and unabashed commercialism flew in the face of rock's ten-year-old struggle to recast itself as serious music with artistic merit. Rock had succeeded in elevating the performer to an auteur and in enshrining the album as an art form. Disco came along and shifted the spotlight away from the performers to the producers, DJ's, and dancers. It also "rediscovered the single and then inflated it back up to 12-inch proportions."[117] To many in the rock community disco felt like the return of bubblegum, a perception helped by the fact the disco's ascendance was aided and abetted by the king of '6os bubblegum, Neil Bogart, founder of the leading disco label Casablanca Records. Nor did it help disco's standing among rock critics that in the States disco, not punk, had managed to attract working-class kids.[118]

Disco had its detractors within the world of R&B, too. James Brown cut a disco single, "Too Funky in Here," but said he hated the music. Although Curtis Mayfield's music helped pave the way for disco, he claimed disco left him "flat wondering what the hell to do and even how to do it" because it was so "monotonous."[119] George Clinton decried disco for plunging dance music into "the blahs." African-American music critic Nelson George went farther, arguing that disco killed R&B.[120] George blamed everyone from celebrity deejay Frankie Crocker of New York superstation WBLS to "beige" crossover artists like George Benson and club deejays, the true "movers and shakers" of disco, who whitened the music because they were often gay and their taste "pseudosophisticated."[121] He also targeted insidious relationships between putatively independent, black-owned companies like Gamble and Huff's Philadelphia International Records and major companies like CBS, which he claimed dumped R&B in favor of crossover music. In the end, George saved his fury for upwardly mobile, assimilationist blacks. Having gained a foothold in a more integrated America, bourgeois blacks struggled to live as though they were colorless. Consuming crossover became part of the great beige way.[122]

George blamed crossover for the death of R&B, yet he also vilified disco for ruining the crossover possibilities of black artists. It turns out that, in George's view, there was good and bad crossover. When artists like Sly and the Family Stone and Isaac Hayes ruled the airwaves "crossover really worked" because "blackness still fascinated whites and inspired Afro-Americans. . . ." But soon, he argued, the airwaves were flooded with bad crossover by disco artists like Barry White and Donna Summer. George is right that after the disco bubble burst all black music was tarred with its brush.[123] Nowhere were the effects of discophobia more apparent than at MTV, which began broadcasting in 1981. In its first eighteen months, the station broadcast 750 videos, of which fewer than two dozen featured black artists, even including racially mixed bands like the English Beat.[124] It took

Michael Jackson's 1982 runaway hit "Thriller" to break the color barrier at MTV.[125] Incredible as it seems today, the network agreed to play videos from Jackson's album only after Columbia Records threatened to pull all of its artists' videos from the station if it continued snubbing Jackson.[126]

George faulted disco for both bleaching and feminizing R&B. Disco's stars were women, and the exceptions—Barry White, Sylvester, and the Village People—were hardly soul men in the tradition of James Brown. After all, the corpulent White sang of "playing your game"—the ladies' game. Queeny Sylvester, with his piercing falsetto, was openly gay, and the Village People, whose act was a send-up of the new gay hypermasculinity, were understood to be gay by many people, if not the Navy officials who permitted the group to film its "In the Navy" video on one of their ships. R&B's masculinity deficit didn't immediately improve with disco's demise, according to George. Michael Jackson and Prince may have made wonderful music in the '80s, but they also "ran fast and far from blackness and conventional images of male sexuality."[127] To George's relief, with the emergence of rap "solidly masculine black male acts" took center stage.[128] George is not alone in thinking that real soul men aren't sissies. Black literary scholar Houston Baker has justified the homophobia and misogyny in rap on the grounds that disco had displaced "funky black music" and any number of black, male R&B acts.[129] That hip-hop culture involved a "reassertion of manhood rights . . . was a natural thing."[130] In this schema, where authentic "blackness" is macho, women are reduced to bit players and black gays are cast out as "souls on ice," unassimilable to "blackness." This particular criticism of disco's gender dynamics echoed writer Ishmael Reed's attacks on Toni Morrison and Alice Walker. The success of black women writers, like disco's elevation of the diva, implied a symbolic castration of the black arts through the displacement of "real" black men.

Since the days of blackface minstrelsy, black masculinity has driven whites' fascination with "blackness." And by the mid-'70s "blackness" had pretty much ceased fascinating white America. Disco hastened its demise. The classy disco style and the tamed masculinity that seemed to accompany it was guaranteed to deflect the admiring gaze of rebellious white kids and bohemians. African-American performers, whether they were wearing white tuxedos or red, bell-bottomed jumpsuits held no cachet. Nor did identifying with and being knowledgeable about contemporary popular black culture any longer confer a badge of hipness upon whites. Rockers looking for marginality could and sometimes did turn to other kinds of music—reggae, punk, new wave. What put disco beyond the pale for many rockers and some blacks—its promotion of upward mobility and a softer masculinity, the prominence of women, and the lack of racial otherness—reassured white Middle Americans. The fact that there were only a few disco personalities—and pretty shallow ones at that—may reveal that love of the music didn't extend to its performers. People didn't buy disco records because they were intrigued by its performers; the music's popularity was almost in spite of its mostly black creators.[131]

Now I know what to do
No more sellin' me to you
Sly Stone, "I Don't Know (Satisfaction)," 1973

RAP FIRST PENETRATED THE AIRWAVES in 1979 and it brought macho back to black music. In contrast to disco, rap, at least what made it to the airwaves, was pretty much guys-only territory at first.[132] From the very start, the celebration of masculinity was a key part of rap. Hip-hop culture "was built to worship urban black maleness: the way we speak, walk, dance, dress, think," according to rap writer Touré.[133] In other ways, too, rap developed a very different sensibility from disco. For rappers and their fans, "realness" has been everything, whereas disco's allure was that it offered an escape from the real. And in contrast to disco, which diminished the artist, hip-hop made the rapper a larger-than-life personality. But rap also grew up alongside disco and had a more ambivalent relationship to it than many writers imagine. After all, disco provided the backing tracks for most early rap. The record that first put hip-hop on the map was the Sugar Hill Gang's 1979 hit "Rapper's Delight," which adapted the rhythm track from Chic's disco hit "Good Times." Although rappers looked more "street" than disco artists, most white rockers and critics considered rap indistinguishable from disco—vapid party music—yet another instance of black music gone astray.

Most rock critics didn't begin taking rap seriously until 1982 when Grandmaster Flash and the Furious Five cut "The Message," a chilling song of black anger and despair. "The Message" proved that hip-hop could be about something besides partying or boasting about one's rhymes or sexual prowess, and it transformed rap music. It opened up a space for others like Public Enemy to use the music to explore the state of black America, in much the way that Sly's *Riot* had done a decade earlier.[134] "The Message" was a huge hit within black communities, but it had a negligible effect on white listening patterns. That didn't begin to change until Run-D.M.C., three middle-class kids from Hollis, Queens, who decked themselves out in hats, gold chains, and untied Adidas sneakers, hit the scene. Later they donned leather jackets, which as one former executive at their rap record company says, made them "cool for black people," and "rock & roll for white people."[135] In fact, the group and its record company, which was owned by Run's older brother, Russell Simmons, and his white partner Rick Rubin, always seemed to have had their eye on crossing over to the rock crowd.[136]

Run-D.M.C. were middle-class kids with insider connections, but they looked "street," and they rapped about the "hard times" of ghetto life.[137] They also developed a distinctive sound—a tense, sparse rap with big fat beats that rocked as hard as anything on MTV. Even so, the racial divide in popular music was so entrenched that the group failed to make the pop charts despite hitting the R&B Top 25 seven times in two years. They finally hit number four on the pop charts in 1986 when they collaborated with the rock band Aerosmith and recut the latter's 1976 hit "Walk This Way." Later that year, *Rolling Stone* put Run-D.M.C. on its cover, the first time the magazine had ever done a cover story on rap. The next breakthrough came a year later when for the first time a hip-hop album hit the top spot on the pop chart. Given America's racial politics, it's not surprising that the album, *Licensed to Ill*, was by a white group, the Beastie Boys.[138] In contrast to Vanilla Ice, a flash-in-the-pan white rapper who strained to be "street," the Beastie Boys were all-irony-all-the-time, though few noticed at first. Despite their differences, the Beastie Boys and Vanilla Ice provided the initial crossover push for rap. In 1988, MTV, which had been at best lukewarm to rap, launched *Yo! MTV Raps*. "The inner cities weren't even wired for cable when the show took off," notes sociologist Fred McDonald. "It was the white kids," he says, "who showed the music executives that they would buy that sound."[139]

White rappers helped put hip-hop over in suburbia, but by the early '90s, black rappers had captured the imagination of young whites who were too young to remember the disco wars or that time when black music was too unhip to admit to liking. It was the gangsta rap of Schooly D, Ice T, NWA, and Snoop Doggy Dogg that really captivated white teenage boys, the critical demographic group that the rock industry had always taken for granted.[140] In fact, the more hard-edged and "street" rap became, the more appealing it became to wannabe white kids. For almost a decade now, a period that corresponds to gangsta's ascendancy, rap has outsold rock among white teens. And eight years after its debut, *Yo! MTV Raps* had become the channel's most popular show.[141] A full seventy percent of all rap is sold to whites, mostly young people.[142] Today, rap "is like a birthright, something white kids grow up listening to."[143]

It's no secret that rap, particularly of the gangsta variety, has been especially popular with white boys. It's probably no accident that gangsta rap's popularity in the suburbs was coterminous with the rise of alternative rock. As one critic observed, '90s rock was filled with "testosterone-challenged" guys—cross-dressers, self-proclaimed "losers,"and sensitive mope rockers. "Boys," he wrote, "apart from gangsta rappers, bless them—whine about their confusion, especially over (sigh) success."[144] For alienated white boys who feel angry—about school cliques, the college-entrance rat race, the breakdown of traditional masculinity, the ever-growing assertiveness of women, gays, and maybe even minorities—gangsta rap more than meets the rage quotient. While disco offered sexual and racial minorities an escape from racism and homophobia, gangsta rap, with its hyper-real stories of drug dealing, drive-bys, bitches and hoes, has seduced white kids eager for an alternative to their vanilla suburbs and entranced by the outsize masculinity of their idols.

In the last ten years we've seen the return of Norman Mailer's White Negro in the form of "wiggers," white boys so infatuated with the hardcore fantasy of blackness that they adopt the jargon and the sartorial tastes of their hip-hop heroes.[145] Some observers believe that this new multicultural hip-hop generation can help lead us out of the morass of racism. "These white kids aren't the same white kids," says one veteran member of the hip-hop nation.[146] Wigger-turned-performance artist Danny Hoch points out that the cross-racial popularity of rap has given kids across the color line a common set of cultural referents. In fact, today's cross-racial culture represents a remarkable turnaround from the cultural apartheid of much of the '80s. One wigger who has written about his relationship to rap, Billy Wimsatt (aka Upski), believes that hip-hop allowed him to repudiate his white privilege. Wimsatt says he jumped out of his container "like spilled milk" and began hanging out with blacks as well as whites.[147] However, for the most part the hegemony of hip-hop culture has not led to greater contact between whites and blacks. In time it may, but residential segregation is a formidable barrier. Moreover, white boys' fascination and identification with "blackness" seems to be built upon distance. Even Danny Hoch admits that most wiggers don't really want to contend with what it means to be black in America.[148]

To some African Americans, the problem isn't the shallowness of white identification, but the substance of that identification. Is gangsta rap popular with white kids because it peddles the same old nefarious stereotypes? Hip-hop writer Kevin Powell worries that "white people are sitting back and saying let's watch the niggas wave guns in videos and talk [shit] and grab their crotches and amuse us. It's almost as if we have become the minstrels of the 1990s."[149] Henry Louis Gates has also condemned the way some rap has "fallen back on fantasies of the street." Gates blames this on middle class blacks who feel guilty about their financial success and their "inability to put forth a culture of their own."[150] It's a provocative argument, since most white people wrongly assume that rap is solely the creation of underclass blacks.[151]

Black intellectuals have been debating this issue of black self-representation for years, especially since the days of the Harlem Renaissance when Young Turk writers like Zora Neale Hurston turned their backs on the idea that they were obligated to provide positive images of African Americans and instead wrote fearlessly and honestly about black life. Some thought these writers were reinforcing racial stereotypes. Richard Wright even claimed that Hurston's now classic novel *Their Eyes Were Watching God* was in the "minstrel" tradition.[152] Poet Langston Hughes, one of the leading lights of the Harlem Renaissance, was no stranger to these debates. Speaking at the First World Festival of Negro Arts in 1966, Hughes argued that black writers who were indifferent to "whether they straddle the fence of color or not, are usually the best writers, attempting at least to let their art leap the barriers of color, poverty, or whatever other roadblocks to artistic truth there may be." But he emphasized the unique position of black artists, who face the dilemma of "which set of readers to please—the white or the black, or both at once?"[153]

Negotiating race is always treacherous for black performers, as the man who wrote "Thank You (Falettinme Be Mice Elf Agin)" understood. For a time, Sly managed to appeal to both blacks and whites, but he clearly came to feel that he was walking a tightrope. And then there's the example of Jimi Hendrix. Today Hendrix lives on as a race-bending guitar god, but when he played Monterey Pop in 1967 some critics attributed his success with young whites to his willingness to "tailor a caricature" for his white audience by humping his amplifier, "jacking his guitar around his midsection," and "grunting and groaning on the brink of sham orgasm."[154] Hendrix dropped the act, but the conundrum of self-presentation continued to haunt him. By 1969 Hendrix was walking his own tightrope as his white handlers urged him to drop his black sidemen and get "the cute English guys back," and black acquaintances criticized him for "selling out to whitey."[155] This problem of representation and reception hasn't gone away. If disco made race seem a little too incidental, then rap often reified race. Male rappers managed to make themselves the object of fascination once again, but often by confirming white America's image of them as "a kind of walking phallic symbol," to borrow James Baldwin's phrase.[156]

But as we enter the new millennium, there are signs that we are moving beyond the impoverished possibilities that have so long constrained black artists. Gangsta rap no longer rules the airwaves and rap has become, in the words of Roxanne Shanté, truly "co-ed."[157] Although there's plenty of misogyny and gay-bashing in today's rap, some artists are cutting sassy feminist tracks and tackling homophobia.[158] Within the hip-hop community some have challenged the notion of authentic blackness. Cultural critic Tricia Rose has criticized the idea that there is such a thing as "authentic rap" on the grounds that it not only misapprehends rap but also "silences women rappers and consumers."[159] Even Chuck D., whose group Public Enemy is known for its black nationalist raps, has cautioned against judging rappers on the basis of their apparent "blackness." "You can't stop where [hip-hop] goes," he's chided those trying to patrol rap's racial borders.[160] Indeed, Public Enemy, which has a substantial white following, wants to fashion itself a cult band: a black version of the Grateful Dead no less. Maybe in the years ahead black artists finally will be able to speak to both black and white audiences without making compromises or betraying themselves.[161] Bring the Noise!

12

WHITE FACES, BLACK MASKS

TED DANSON NOTWITHSTANDING, it's been about sixty years since white men blackened their faces, donned oversized, ragged "Negro" costumes, and sang, danced, and burlesqued as blackface minstrels. But blackface minstrelsy, the most popular form of entertainment in nineteenth-century America, is more than a curious relic. As Eric Lott suggests in his dazzling new book, *Love and Theft: Blackface Minstrelsy and the American Working Class*,[1] its traces are everywhere: "Every time you hear an expansive white man drop into his version of black English, you are in the presence of blackface's unconscious return." And what is rock 'n' roll if not white men trying on the accents of "blackness"? One can hear blackface minstrelsy's "wink at the counterfeit alongside a nod toward 'blackness'" in Elvis's recounting of what occurred when he first began getting airplay: "You could hear folks around town saying 'Is he? Is he?' and I'm going 'Am I? Am I?'" With his dyed, pomaded hair, loud threads, black moves, white skin, and hybrid sound, Elvis was nothing if not racially ambiguous. While he owed much of his popularity to his race-bending, some whites, as Greil Marcus noted, found him "too complicated . . . you couldn't tell what he might be slipping over."[2]

Were white rock 'n' roll'ers' appropriations of black style a form of cultural plundering or a courageous violation of America's color line? Was it theft or love? In *The Death of Rhythm and Blues*, Nelson George, who calls Elvis a "mediocre interpretive artist,"[3] weighs in with a judgment only

---

This essay was previously published in the Village Voice, February 15, 1994.

slightly more generous than Public Enemy's. But most historians of rock have followed Greil Marcus whose 1975 essay, "Elvis Presliad" argued that Elvis's significance lay in his "nerve to cross the borders he'd been raised to respect."[4] Like Marcus, most writers emphasize the syncretism of American culture (and the resulting difficulty of labeling music black or white). They stress the challenge that race-bending white rockers posed to the American color line. George Lipsitz,[5] for example, contends that white, middle-class kids' embrace of rock 'n' roll in the fifties represented a rejection of the segregated suburbs and a yearning for the heterogeneity of the industrial city. With the ascendance of cultural studies, a field eager to find subversion everywhere, there's been a proliferation of upbeat, against-the-grain readings of rock 'n' roll with the result that the most provocative work on rock has failed to explore the ambivalence and complexity that informed these border crossings.

For Lipsitz, Johnny Otis embodies the progressive impulse of early rock 'n' roll. In contrast to Elvis, whose race bending was all about the wink and the nod, Otis not only crossed the border but courageously stayed on the other side. Fronting one of the most successful rock 'n' roll bands on the West Coast, Otis racked up fifteen Top 40 R&B hits between 1950 and 1952. He discovered and produced Little Esther Phillips, Big Mama Thornton, Little Willie John, and Three Tons of Fun. In the '50s he had shows on three L.A. television stations and promoted rock dances. These mixed dances were such an affront to L.A.'s color line that local authorities forced Otis to move them to nearby El Monte.

As his memoir *Upside Your Head!: Rhythm and Blues on Central Avenue*[6] demonstrates, Otis was an important (and largely unheralded) pioneer of rock 'n' roll. But what makes Otis so compelling to anyone arguing for rock's subversive power is his renunciation of whiteness. Born Johnny Veliotes, Otis was the son of Greek immigrants who lived in a predominantly African-American neighborhood in Berkeley, California. His visits to "sanctified" black churches and exposure to the black community convinced him, he said elsewhere in an interview, that black culture was "richer and more fulfilling and more natural." Indeed, black culture "captured" him. He married a black woman, settled in the black community and began to identify himself as black. He also became a tireless fighter in the struggle against racial discrimination. Although no one went as far (and with such

integrity) as Johnny Otis, many early white rock 'n' roll performers, producers, songwriters, and DJ's "went black," as it were. It may have been the
Beats who caught Norman Mailer's attention in his 1957 essay "The White
Negro," but Otis and Elvis many other rockers made the racial Maginot Line
more porous than Jack Kerouac and Neal Cassady ever would.

As Lipsitz explains in his incisive introduction to *Upside Your Head!*,
Otis's understanding of race is more cultural than biological. In contrast to
the White Negro jazzman, Mezz Mezzrow, Otis doesn't believe that exposure
to the black community darkened his skin and "burred" his hair. Rather, he
defines himself as "Black by persuasion." Lipsitz assures us that Otis un-
derstands there are "some dimensions of the African-American experience
he cannot feel," and that he has had the "theoretical option of living as
'white.'" Curiously, Otis doesn't acknowledge this or explore his complicated racial identity anywhere in *Upside Your Head!*. While his wonderful evo-
cations of L.A.'s rock 'n' roll world and the eighty-odd pictures documenting it make the book required reading for anyone interested in rock's
history, it sheds little light on this particular question. We're left wondering
what his willed blackness really meant for him. Those who want to see in
Otis's life an affirmation of poststructuralist theorizing about identities as
"labile sites of contestation and negotiation" will be disappointed by this
book. For Otis doesn't so much defy racial categories as revalue and reify
"blackness." He denounces white musicians who try to play "black" music
as "copycats" who invariably get it "Bassackwards." He complains that
today's black performers are "pathetically bland" by comparison to those of
his generation. In the end, Otis's declension narrative enshrines a particular kind of "blackness," one whose authenticity is implicitly understood.

No one could charge scholars of blackface minstrelsy with ignoring its
underside. Most recent work on the subject has characterized it as yet another instance of racial domination. In *Love and Theft*, Lott complicates the
picture considerably by showing that blackface performance involved "the
dialectical flickering of racial insult and racial envy, moments of domination and moments of liberation, counterfeit and currency . . . all constituting a peculiarly American structure of feeling." Lott argues blackface signaled "panic, anxiety, terror, and pleasure" more than "absolute white
power and control." While most writers have emphasized performers' contempt for black culture, Lott claims their contempt often masked their real

interest in "blackness." Blackface minstrels did, after all, engage and inhabit "blackness," if only to cross back over into "whiteness."

And in the industrializing, antebellum North where blackface developed, the distance between "whiteness" and "blackness" was not always so
vast. Lott contends the overlapping racial and class codes of blackface reveal
the extent to which Northern blacks and working-class whites shared a
common culture. Early blackface minstrelsy made tentative connections
between the brutality of the shop floor and the plantation, and often articulated class difference by using the "insurrectionary resonances" of black
culture. But if interracial contact could promote solidarity of sorts across
the racial divide it could also generate anxiety among working-class whites.
Lott argues that capitalist consolidation and class stratification further un-
settled Northern white working-class men's precarious racial identity. By
the 1840s blackface "substitute[d] racial hostility for class struggle" as
white working-class unity was achieved "over the bodies of black people."

Or, the bodies of black *men*. For, as Lott shows, "blacking up" also involved a "manly mimicry" of black men, who exist as a hypersexualized caricature in the white imagination. Lott suggests that we can see the contours
of masculine whiteness taking shape in blackface performers' "clumsy
courtship of black men." This fascination with blackness is, Lott argues, inseparable from industrial capitalism's new moral order, which required ab-
stemiousness from the white working class. Ambivalent about their own desire, whites imagined the Other had stolen it. Fantasies about blacks'
"special, excessive enjoyment" allowed the pleasure to return, nowhere
more so than in blackface where white workingmen both "take their enjoyment and disavow it."

In complicating blackface, Lott never loses sight of its devastating consequences for blacks, especially black performers trying to "repossess the
means of cultural representation." When blacks began performing blackface they were unable to break from established minstrel types because they
had to meet the ideological imperatives of the minstrel show. These minstrel types proved enormously resilient, so much so that Johnny Otis recalls
hearing older black musicians talk about having had to blacken up and engage in "overt Uncle Tomming." Although black musicians are no longer required to darken up as the light-skinned Billie Holiday was when she played
Detroit in the 1930s with the all-black Basie band, they are nonetheless ex-

pected to be recognizably "black." Black artists who defy the tests of "blackness"—that they embody sensuality, spontaneity, and gritty soulfulness—may achieve superstardom, but they often find their racial crossings leave them open to charges of self-loathing and selling-out. Race-bending white musicians, by contrast, are hailed for their brave transgressions.

In this remarkable book Lott maps white masculinity, explicates the interconnectedness of race, gender, and class, and provokes us to consider the ways in which love and theft still inform cultural commerce across the color line. While the music and the styles have changed since Otis "went black" fifty years ago, recent developments in rap point to whites' continuing fascination with black masculinity. Lott's commitment to connecting the cultural and the political, and to exploring rather than castigating the structure of feeling behind blackface, make *Love and Theft* a model for how to study popular culture.

13

THE REFUGE OF THE LIONS' DEN:

AN INTERVIEW WITH JOHN PAUL HAMMOND

I N THE ANNALS OF ROCK 'N' ROLL, 1965 stands as a watershed, the year Bob Dylan went electric at the Newport Folk Festival, infuriating hardcore folkies and inspiring countless others to plug in. Dylan's electric turn brought about a sea change in popular music, but, in truth, he was a step behind John Paul Hammond. By 1965, the college student-turned-blues musician had already cut one electric album, 1964's *Big City Blues*, and recorded another, *So Many Roads*, with the Hawks, a Canadian group later famous as the Band. In fact, it was Hammond, not Dylan, who brought the Hawks to America. And it was Hammond who in 1966 discovered Jimi Hendrix in the dumpy Café Wha! playing songs from *So Many Roads*. Hammond brought Hendrix to the "up-market" Café Au Go Go, where Hendrix backed him up and "stole the show." The rest was history . . . for Hendrix.

Stardom has eluded Hammond, but over the last thirty years he's been in the thick of things, playing with Hendrix, John Lee Hooker, Michael Bloomfield, and the Band. Although Hammond seemed poised to break out in the late '60s and early '70s, it never happened. In 1973, he formed a supergroup, Triumvirate, with Mike Bloomfield and Dr. John. "But," Hammond recalls, "three days into the tour, Clive Davis was fired, Columbia became the target of an FBI drugola investigation, and every project the company had was frozen. So the album never got any promotion, the tour was cancelled. I said, 'Forget it,' and I returned to solo performing. I had my hopes

---

This essay was first published in somewhat different form in the *L.A. Weekly*, August 18, 1995.

so high." Speaking like a bluesman, Hammond reflects, "You have to take a loss as a lesson."

When he was starting out, Hammond, like most other young white folk and blues artists, played acoustic guitar. After leaving Antioch College in 1962, he traveled to Florida, where John Hammond Sr., the legendary Columbia Records producer, claims his son acquired a pair of "blind man's glasses and a tin cup, and took to the streets to play the blues." According to his father, Hammond felt that "only by disguising himself would he be allowed to enter black taverns." Hammond denies he ever tried to pass himself off as blind or that he carried a tin cup, but he does admit he bought a pair of big, round, sunglasses that he thought were "pretty cool." He soon became friends with a local harp player who took Hammond to a "juke joint where I guess they thought I was cute. After I played, I passed around my hat."

Hammond officially began his career in Los Angeles, not back east or in the midwest. "It was a whole new world and I was going to be a new person. I was going to be a blues singer." Not incidentally, L.A. was also "as far away from home as possible." His first gigs were at the Ash Grove, L.A.'s legendary boho coffeehouse. Hammond loved Ed Pearl's Melrose Avenue coffeehouse and returned there often, including one memorable visit in 1965. After closing out his set with Robert Johnson's "Terraplane Blues," Hammond walked backstage, where the middle-aged headliner growled at him, "Come here and sit down. Where the fuck did you learn to play that?" He wasn't the first to wonder how a white boy like Hammond came to sound like Robert Johnson reincarnated, but Howlin' Wolf was surely the most physically imposing person to have ever posed the question. After Hammond explained he'd taught himself the song by listening to the record, Wolf demanded he play it again for him "right now." Afterward, Hammond remembers, Wolf said, "Man, that's evil."

We can't know whether the evil lay in Hammond's playing or the whole package. But Wolf seems to have been more ecumenical than proprietary when it came to that vexed question of who can play the blues. Wolf made a point of telling people that his mentor, the early bluesman Charley Patton, was part Indian, and he always claimed white country singer Jimmie Rodgers as an influence. "I wanted to yodel [like Rodgers] in the worst way," he explained, "and all I could do was make a howl." Wolf may not have seen the blues as the exclusive preserve of African Americans, but, then, it's also true that in 1965 the idea of whites playing the blues was still largely hypo-thetical. After all, besides Hammond, there were only a handful of white guys—most notably, Mike Bloomfield and Paul Butterfield in Chicago, Eric Von Schmidt in Cambridge, John Fahey on the West Coast, Johnny Winter in Texas, and John Koerner, Tony Glover, and Dave Ray in Minneapolis—play-ing the blues. Newport changed all that, sparking the blues revival of the '60s. After Dylan, the most controversial act at Newport '65 was the Paul Butterfield Blues Band whose electric set precipitated a ludicrous wrestling match between blues-purist and musicologist Alan Lomax and Albert Grossman, who managed both Paul Butterfield and Bob Dylan. To Lomax, everything about the Butterfield Band—from their amps to their (mostly) blue eyes—was an affront. Above all, he hated what he thought they signi-fied: the commercial viability and artistic debasement of the blues.

Like other white players, Hammond encountered resistance from blues purists. He laughs at Koerner, Glover, and Ray's retort: "Who says we can't sing good blues because we're on the wrong end of the Mississippi?" But thinking back on those years, Hammond marvels at his luck. Pop Staples took him aside after one of his first nights at the Ash Grove and said, "Man, I don't know where you learn this stuff, but don't ever stop doing it." Ham-mond admits, "I'm so fortunate I didn't get my feelings hurt badly, because I was so sensitive at that point, so uptight about playing. And I walked into the lion's den, in a way, by playing the blues. I didn't say I was a folk singer; I said, 'I'm a *blues* singer.'" Hammond wasn't like his friend Michael Bloomfield, who was apparently fearless about getting up onstage and jam-ming with his idols Muddy Waters and Howlin' Wolf.

Of course, Bloomfield hadn't grown up with John Hammond Sr. as his father and Benny Goodman as his uncle. During his many years at Colum-bia, Hammond Sr. signed Billie Holiday, Count Basie, Lester Young, Aretha Franklin, Bob Dylan (best known around Columbia after his signing as "Hammond's folly") and Bruce Springsteen. Hammond Sr. was a music maven who must have owned hundreds of records, but he rarely played any for his son. And Benny Goodman, whom Hammond describes as "very standoffish," only showed up once to hear his nephew play, and left without saying a word. So the Wolf's world may have been the lion's den, but it was there, far from home, that Hammond came to "feel like somebody."

14

"PLAY THAT FUNKY MUSIC":
AN INTERVIEW WITH LENNY KRAVITZ

"**I** WANTED TO BE A SESSION PLAYER. I never wanted to do this." Lenny Kravitz a reluctant star? A thwarted studio musician? Maybe it's the grueling interview schedule for his new album "Circus" that provokes the thirty-year-old Kravitz into saying something so absurd. Or maybe it's the nose-ring he broke getting out of bed this morning. But the idea that this opinionated, headstrong, shoot-from-the-hip musician ever aspired to be a sideman is preposterous. After all, this is the guy whose 1993 hit "Are You Gonna Go My Way" opens with the boast that he's "the chosen" one who's "come to save the day." With his Luddite views about recording and his fondness for vintage instruments and sounds, Kravitz isn't likely to go anyone else's way.

Beginning in 1987 when he was signed by Virgin, Kravitz garnered a lot of press, in part because of his high-profile marriage to actress Lisa Bonet. But if the tabloids found him newsworthy, the rock press skewered Kravitz for wearing his musical influences (Jimi Hendrix, Sly Stone, the Beatles and Curtis Mayfield, among others) on his sleeve. Dubbed "retro," he was dismissed as more "recreative" than creative. His work often sounds as if he had ransacked classic rock and soul of the sixties and early seventies, but what interests me about Kravitz is his rejection of the racial borders of popular music. Kravitz's refusal to knuckle under and produce predictably "black" music is something he shares with a growing number of African-American artists, including Basehead, the recently reformed Fishbone and the now-defunct Living Colour. In their indifference to the musical color

---

This interview first appeared in *MTV Online*, September 1995.

line, these musicians are truly the products of integration. As one self-described black rocker put it, "Hendrix, the Doors, the Yardbirds, that's part of my culture too . . . We're products of integrated schools and integrated neighborhoods." Kravitz may have listened to Motown and the artists of Gamble and Huff's Philadelphia International Records, but he also listened to the Beatles and Led Zeppelin, not to mention Jimi Hendrix, the obvious prototype for artists looking to mix it up. Kravitz's genre-busting has something to do with his background. His mother, actress Roxie Roker, who played Helen on the seventies hit series "The Jeffersons," is Bahamian and his father, TV producer Sy Kravitz, is Jewish. He grew up first in New York City and then in Los Angeles, where he attended Beverly Hills High.

Kravitz's ecumenical approach has attracted a predominantly white audience—a situation that stems in large part from today's rigid radio formats. He may have many more white than black fans, but Kravitz bristles at the idea that his music is "white." Like other race rebels, Kravitz inhabits a kind of racial twilight zone. Black musicians, however, often find their excursions across the color line criticized, not praised, and attributed to crass commercialism, or worse, internalized racism. Perhaps because he's sensitive to the charge that he's insufficiently "black," Kravitz seemed determined in our interview to establish his roots in black music and culture. Kravitz didn't engage in any homeboy posturing, but from the musical heroes he listed to the L.A. soul food restaurant where we lunched, he seemed to be saying, "this is my home, too." With his print shirt (uncharacteristically buttoned up), tight leather pants, huge white-rimmed sunglasses, and trademark dreads, Kravitz may look a bit like a "pimp from the planet Rasta" but he's far from flaky.

AE: You spent your childhood on both the tony Upper East Side and funky Bed-Stuy in Brooklyn. How did you come to inhabit such divergent worlds?

LK: My grandfather and grandmother lived in Bed-Stuy and when my mom got married she moved to the upper East Side with her husband. At first I spent the majority of my time in Brooklyn with my grandparents while my parents worked during the week. I'd see my parents every day, though, because they'd come to Brooklyn for dinner. And during the weekends when they were off I'd go with them. I went to preschool in Brooklyn, but once I started first grade I lived in Manhattan during the week and went to Brooklyn on the weekends.

AE: One of the most striking aspects of your work is your disregard of musical boundaries.

LK: Yeah, I've taken so much shit for that. It's ridiculous.

AE: I would imagine that your indifference to musical borders has quite a lot to do with your childhood.

LK: Of course. I mean I had such variety in my life. It was like different colors, different religions, different people, different neighborhoods. I saw it all. And I heard it all. My parents and my grandfather took me to everything from a rock concert to, say, James Brown at the Apollo in '69 when I was five years old. We would go see opera, ballet, symphonies, and jazz. We used to go see Duke Ellington a lot and Miles Davis. So instead of keeping me at home they took me out a lot. Also to the theater because my mom was in theater. She was in the Negro Ensemble Company. She used to do poetry and Theater in the Park and lots of off-Broadway stuff. Being around all these artists and musicians like Sarah Vaughan and Miles Davis was incredibly important.

I didn't realize what I was seeing when I saw it, but somehow it all ended up in my subconscious. I absorbed it.

AE: You've said that at a certain point your exposure to this artistic community ended. Did it coincide with your move to L.A.?

LK: Yeah, it began to end then. Producer Norman Lear saw my mom on Broadway in "The River Niger" and asked her to come to L.A. and then we all ended up out here. I was eleven and I felt really out of it in L.A. Growing up in New York, I'd been walking the streets since I was six years old. I walked to school. Kids in New York take the bus. Then we moved here and, God, I couldn't go anywhere unless someone drove me. There was nobody playing out on the streets. I couldn't walk anywhere. It was so strange. But also it was the lack of theater out here. It wasn't like New York where you get the *Village Voice* and you find a play and you go see it. So it was the end of that.

AE: Your music owes quite a lot to the sixties. What do you find so appealing about that period?

LK: I'd probably say the freedom. I mean the freedom of expression. There were always colorful people around playing instruments, doing theater. My mom dressed really cool, lots of way-out clothes. People ask me why I dress the way I dress. They thought I was trying to do a "sixties" thing. But what I was really trying to do was my mother 'coz she had all this cool stuff, you know, the great hats and jackets and furs—the fashions of that time. When you're young you don't know what's in or out, all I knew was that's how my mom dressed. I liked the way she looked, I thought she was incredible. When she'd go out I used to play in her clothes. I'd try on her boots and her coats and act like I was a musician, the whole thing.

AE: Any musician in particular?

LK: The Jackson 5, completely. That was the group I was really into when I was young.

AE: Speaking of the Jackson 5, I hear echoes of early seventies soul in your music.

LK: That's my favorite era of soul music—the early seventies. Such beautiful free music. Such a groove. All the Motown stuff, Al Green, Curtis Mayfield, Aretha Franklin, and Gamble and Huff.

AE: What do you think happened? Why do you believe the quality of the music deteriorated?

LK: Technology. People like Aretha and Gladys Knight, who I adore, making these weird records because they feel they gotta keep up when they've already surpassed any limit. See, it's all enmeshed with radio now and they program the listeners. It's a big brainwasher. And with MTV, if you're older now and you're not what they say is attractive, you ain't gonna be on it, unless you're Tony Bennett. But that's not just MTV, that's media in general.

AE: Back to the sixties, it was a time when the color line was breached, perhaps most of all, musically. But it wasn't just white kids turning on to black music, was it? There were lots of black kids listening to white music as well.

LK: Yeah, back then you look at the music charts. The Top 10: The Supremes, the Temptations, the Beatles, Bob Dylan, Peter, Paul and Mary, Simon and Garfunkel. It was this mixture. Now we got the black chart, we got the white chart, and on and on.

AE: There was almost a meltdown of musical categories then.

LK: But you also had the phenomenon of black guys playing music,

and no black people really showing up. Like Hendrix. I have that problem now. I wouldn't say it's a problem, but I find it odd.

AE: When asked about this a year ago you were quoted saying your
music is white.

LK: No, my music isn't white at all! To begin with I have a soulful
voice. It's that people have been brainwashed. You have white kids
growing up not knowing the history and thinking they invented rock
and roll. I've come across people who've said things like, "You're black,
nigger, why are you playing our music?" I mean, white musicians in the
sixties did amazing things with black music. But the fact of the matter
is that black people did invent it.

And then you have black people . . . We're throwing our own music
away. I don't know why it is but you go to a blues concert or a jazz concert
I see mostly white people. It's our music, how come we don't support it?
We seem to always support what's hip at the time. Believe it or not, there
was a funk festival at the Coliseum a few weeks ago with the Gap Band,
Chaka Khan, Bootsy, Zapp and Roger Troutman, the Bar-Kays—all these
incredible people. And you'd think the way rap is right now where all
they're doing is sampling all this music, that all the kids who are into rap
would show up. But the place was empty. No one showed up. It holds
97,000 and there might have been 5,000 people there.

AE: So, even funk, which is all over the airwaves in the form of sam-
ples, is being abandoned. Or the artists are. In *The Death of Rhythm and
Blues*, critic Nelson George contends that black people have left behind
these older musical genres—a fact he bemoans—in part because "black
music is in constant flight from the status quo." Blacks' musical restlessness, he argues, places a premium on the innovative and new.

LK: What's new about it? Rap ain't new. My grandfather can tell you
about people back then doin' the rhyming.

AE: You've been in the vanguard of the low-tech move with your use
of vintage instruments and low-tech, analog recording. You even own
the Beatle board—the original mixing console used by the Beatles to
record a number of their albums. Yet most people attribute the low-
tech trend to grunge.

LK: Yeah, but you know what? A lot of the music you would think is
grunge is really recorded more slick than you think. The guitars are

loud and distorted, but they don't do it the way we do it. And they all sound the same—all those records. They all use the same gear and model after each other.

AE: San Francisco engineer Fred Catero, who's worked with Bob Dylan, Janis Joplin, Laura Nyro, and Santana, recently said that "forty years ago music was 'created' by musicians playing in real time in the studio. Today most recordings are 'manufactured' with the help of the engineer, allowing many performers who previously wouldn't have stood a chance in the studio to turn out incredibly impressive albums."

LK: These kids today could not handle the players back then. When you think about Motown, for example, you had to play good, you had to sing good, you had write good, you had to perform good. People had to be so polished and professional. Now you get some kid who can barely squeal out a sound and knows a chord or two and he can be a big, huge star. But nothing grooves like a human being who has the groove. James Brown is the prime example. That band locked. Funky—tight, but loose. Some bands play so tight they're like anal, they're weird. But not James Brown—those guys were on fire. And a computer can't do that. It has no soul.

15

"THE SOUL OF A MARTIAN":
A CONVERSATION WITH JONI MITCHELL

*B*OTH OF US ARE APPREHENSIVE.
I wonder, what if she's aloof and bored? Or worse, a Scientologist? This isn't some abstract worry, mind you. Joni Mitchell and I are doing this interview at the Manor Hotel, which is part of the behemoth Church of Scientology Celebrity Center on the corner of Franklin and Bronson in Hollywood. The hotel is open to the public, but the first floor is a virtual shrine to L. Ron Hubbard. First you pass a museumlike display of the Great Man's study, and then you enter the lobby, where a small baby-grand piano churns out schlocky ballads as if it were serenading the nearby bust of L. Ron. "Why are we here?" I want to ask her. Instead, I wait and ask her publicist, who assures me the photographer chose the site. When I see Mitchell a week later, she laughs, "I heard you were checking up on me to see if I'm a Scientologist."

After we're introduced, her smile fades into something else—worry, maybe. But her apprehension evaporates as soon as she begins to feel she's "going to get a fair shake," as she later puts it. I've brought four pages of questions, and after about an hour and one page, I worry out loud, "I'm going to wear you out." "No way, I'm a talker," she insists. And what a talker! Disarmingly honest, Mitchell speaks quickly and precisely, all the while chain-smoking and looking directly at you. The interview seems to energize her. As I'm getting ready to leave and making small talk with her manager and publicist, Mitchell bounds down the stairs, squeezes my shoulder, and tells them to send the (mythical) next journalist up. Later, she told me she'd gone to bed that night remembering stories she'd begun

This essay was previously published as "Thirty Years with a Portable Lover" in the *L.A. Weekly*, November 25, 1994.

but hadn't finished. I went to bed thinking maybe I should write a biography of Joni Mitchell.

"MY MUSIC IS NOT DESIGNED to grab instantly. It's designed to wear for a lifetime, to hold up like a fine cloth. If you're in the right place, these records are waiting to go off in your life, you know. But if you're in the wrong space, which, luck of the draw, for the last twenty years I seem to have had reviewers in the wrong space . . . and I've been trashed for *too* long. The final insult is to watch my imitators elevated while I'm still being trashed. So if I don't get my just dues soon, I'm going into hermitdom. Fuck you all. [*laughing*] I'm going to take up my brushes. I don't care."

Joni Mitchell, the queen of rock twenty years ago, can afford to laugh because she knows hermitdom is not in the cards for her. The critical and commercial black hole she entered in the late '70s when she moved from pop into what she calls the "forest of jazz," is behind her. Even if she now prefers painting to music, as she claims, the buzz won't let her put down her guitar. After years of bad press, the musician whose mid-to-late '70s experiments with jazz and world music anticipated those of Sting, Peter Gabriel, and Paul Simon, is finally beginning to get her due.

The elegantly minimal *Turbulent Indigo*, her new release on Warner Reprise, has been getting good notices. KCRW deejay Chis Douridas helped lay the foundation, giving the disc lots of airplay. Suddenly, Mitchell, who told me, "If it's hip it's too late for me," finds herself, well, hip. Everyone from the usually crusty Chrissie Hynde ("We *want* you, Joni") to the acid-tongued Sandra Bernhard ("Joni's awesome") is invoking her name. And after years of omission from the by-now obligatory "Women in Rock" articles, Mitchell is now appearing alongside the more predictable, even canonical, figures—Patti, Chrissie, Joan, and Janis. Although a weak back (the result of childhood polio—the same epidemic that hit fellow Canadian Neil Young), the expense of staging a tour (she made less than her roadies on the last one), and negative press have kept her off the road since 1983, Mitchell says she is now "itching" to perform again.

The turnaround began several years ago when artists as varied as Prince, Jimmy Page, and Seal began citing Mitchell as an important influence. Younger female singer-songwriters such as Tracy Chapman, Sinéad O'Connor and Tori Amos began paying homage to Mitchell around the same time.

With 1991's wistful *Night Ride Home* the critical drubbing began to let up—after a very long sixteen years.

In spite of, or perhaps because of, the critical abuse, Mitchell has a healthy ego regarding her work. Friend David Crosby was exaggerating when he (affectionately) called Mitchell "about as modest as Mussolini," but it's true that she exhibits none of the modesty or self-effacement that marks many female performers. She believes her music has a place in music history, which is why she bristles when critics liken the new generation of female singer-songwriters to her. "When they start saying these girls are like me, you know, you gotta get an education." She calls herself a "composer in the small, modern form," and is quick to point out that, unlike most musicians, she's made fourteen albums (including her debut effort, which David Crosby "pretended" to produce) without a producer. "People assume Henry Lewy, my engineer, was my producer, but it's not true." Mitchell's sense of herself, her refusal to submit to the critical disparagement of her late '70s/early '80s records, doesn't sit well with all reviewers. After noting her dismissal of some critics as "jackasses" and "idiots," the *Los Angeles Times*'s Robert Hilburn recently observed, "Mitchell's outbursts are likely to be followed by disarming giggles—as if she's surprised and amused at her own bratty language."

Although she's not bratty, and doesn't giggle, Mitchell is opinionated, and she cracks up a lot. She doesn't behave like a celebrity. Indeed, Mitchell may be a diva about her work, but there's no haughtiness in her demeanor. When asked if she's listened to Hole or L7, she replies, "No, should I? I mean, if they're good I should." She'll tell you she has more "armor" now than she did in the early '70s, when, as she told *Rolling Stone*, "I felt like a cellophane wrapper on a pack of cigarettes." But she acknowledges still having "sensitive pockets." In contrast to so many musicians, she cares less about her self-presentation than her music. She is an artist who never compromised, whose creative restlessness took her places the critics and fans refused to go, and she never gave up.

SOMETHING IS BOTHERING MITCHELL TONIGHT. Her parents have let her know she's "disgraced them in front of all of Canada" during her recent appearance on Much Music, Canada's music-video channel. Mitchell never set out to offend them. In fact, in 1979 she admitted to one interviewer that she has sometimes been less than completely candid with the press to protect her very "old-fashioned and moral" parents. Mitchell joked, "I keep saying, Momma, Amy Vanderbilt *killed* herself. That should have been a tip-off that we're into a new era." That she was still struggling with these issues when she was thirty-six isn't so surprising. Watching Joni Mitchell, now fifty-one years old, grappling with parental disapproval is both wonderful and terrifying.

Before the show, the producers gave Mitchell some sake to warm up her vocal cords and control her jitters. "I entered the room with a pretty glowy and goofy spirit. It began so lightly that to gear down into the spirit to sing these tragedies that I write was pretty tricky stuff." During a phone-in segment, after her first set, an earnest young woman asked if she was "proud to be a Canadian." Mitchell, who divides her time between L.A. and British Columbia, didn't give an easy answer. She spoke of her "annoyance" with "borderlines"—"clogged arteries," she called them— and jokingly termed herself "bi-national." After expressing her affection for Canada, she said she preferred warmer climates. "The cold [Canadian] winters and Scottish and Irish blood [not coincidentally, perhaps, her mother's ethnicity] create an emotionally withholding people." Mitchell was trying to convey the complexity of her feelings. "I feel I've been damaged by the culture I came from, yet I love it so much." She closed the show with "Happiness Is the Best Face Lift," a new song inspired by an argument with her mother about the propriety of her "shacking up" with her lover in her home town. Before singing it, though, she said, "Momma, if you're listening tonight, I love you so much."

It was a tender performance that revealed Mitchell's warmth, vulnerability, thoughtfulness, and humor. Although the show generated no negative response, even from Canadian nationalists, her parents were ashamed to see their daughter smoking and singing songs with an occasional curse word. The taping was an occasion Mitchell should have been proud of, but instead of reveling in her success Mitchell seems unable to shake the parental rebuke.

"I'm almost tempted to give them the opportunity to disown me. Yeah, it's too stressful. The last thing I want to do is bring them disgrace, but to fully be myself in the world, apparently that's the effect." Speaking of her performance, she says, "I'm an iconoclast by nature, but in the process I also deglamorize myself. I've always tried to do that so I can walk around."

Mitchell's decision to recount this incident (in slightly different versions twice during the interview) was perhaps another way of deglamorizing herself. After all, what could be more leveling than the disclosure that she too gets reprimanded by her parents?

But the story is significant in other ways. It was, after all, the suggestion that she was somehow too American that "pushed her button." Mitchell has made a career of assailing various borderlines—the borders separating jazz, rock, and pop, and, more tentatively, those dividing black from white, and male from female. And there was something else in the story—the connection between integrity and exile. For Mitchell, being herself involves being disowned, orphaned, and exiled. It's not accidental that "Joni (After Van Gogh)," the self-portrait that graces *Turbulent Indigo*, appropriates Van Gogh's famous self-portrait, substituting Mitchell's face. Mitchell has her sanity, several homes, both ears, and a record label, but, like Van Gogh, she's found her work passed over in favor of "the nice and the normal." But if being "orphaned" was "hurtful," she admits, "it was also, in a certain way, freeing." Nor has it interfered with her sense of humor. On Much Music, Mitchell announced that a "mini-ear" would, "like a Cracker Jack prize," fall out of the first 10,000 copies of her new CD.

BORN ROBERTA JOAN ANDERSON, Mitchell grew up in Saskatoon, a small, dry Canadian prairie town founded by the Ontario Methodist Colonization Society in the late nineteenth century. As a teenager, Mitchell developed a passion for painting, rock 'n' roll, jitterbugging, and all-around carousing. Although John Lennon once chided her for being "overeducated," Mitchell not only flunked the twelfth grade; she never even finished her first year of art school. She only began playing music because the art school she attended was "a joke." In Canada, as in Britain, art school often functioned as a holding tank for those deemed academically ungifted. "We were stuck between cafeteria cooking and auto mechanics. The attitude was 'they're kind of dim, so let's give them a trade.'"

One of rock 'n' roll's many art-school émigrés (Lennon, Richards, Davies, Townshend, Clapton, Page, and Bowie), she began performing in folk clubs by 1964, after progressing from a $36 baritone ukulele to the guitar, with the help of a Pete Seeger instruction record. The guitar, she claims, transformed her into "an introvert." Formerly a "good-time Charlie," she suddenly had "this portable lover, and I was all curled up around it in the corner at parties. Putting two chords together was, like, oh my God! The thrill of hearing a three-chord progression in the beginning cannot be matched." The one guitarist who she says influenced her was Elizabeth Cotten ("Freight Train"), but "I couldn't master her style of picking. My left hand is impaired from polio, and my left thumb works in an odd way, so I simplified the left hand with open tuning, which makes the guitar much more orchestral."

The other big influence was a folk singer she'd originally dismissed as a Woody Guthrie clone. But when she heard Bob Dylan's "Positively Fourth Street," it hit her—poetry and music could be combined. "I'd never heard anger expressed in a song. And I thought, This means it's wide open, you can write about anything. It was brilliant." She imitates Dylan's contemptuous, nasal style, but speeds it up, "You've got alotta nerve to say you are my friend." Mitchell points out they also share a similar approach to songwriting. "Dylan's songs are theatrical, and my songs are theatrical. But most songs are made for singers to sing, not actors to act. You almost have to throw away your singing to concentrate [on giving] the words their right reading. There's no room for vibrato or singers' tricks."

Virtually all the white North American rock stars of the late '6os started out as folkies, and Mitchell was no exception. "Folk music was so easy I was a professional in six months." Mitchell's songwriting distinguished her from others in those days when "the folk world was divided into two camps. There were the Gibson players, who were usually young Jewish kids, singing black blues. And there were the Martin players who were usually WASP-y and singing English ballads." When she was first starting out she sang in a very high soprano because she was "mimicking" female folk singers like Joan Baez. But "it felt unnatural, and eventually became stressful."

After moving to Toronto in 1964, she met and married the American folk singer Chuck Mitchell, with whom she performed. Their marriage collapsed in 1966, not long after they'd relocated to Detroit. She continued performing in boho folk clubs as a solo, and moved to New York, where she became known to other folk singers like Judy Collins and Tom Rush, who began covering her songs. Mitchell was making about $15 a night, which, she notes, was "pretty good pin money in those days." To hear her describe those times, it's clear she enjoyed mixing with the audience, even if she didn't always share their assessment of her work. "You'd go out and eat with people who'd say things like 'Gee, you're as good as Peter, Paul and Mary, and you don't even have a record deal.'"

By the mid-'60s, in the wake of Dylan's electric turn and the next-new-thing, folk rock, "Nobody wanted to hire a folk singer. Folk music was dead." Serving as her own manager, she turned down "slave labor" deals with Elektra and Vanguard. Even after she acquired a manager, Elliot Roberts, who in 1967 got her a contract with Reprise, she still assumed she might have to return to selling women's clothing—a job she'd held as a teen. Her Reprise contract was, she claims, "a terrible deal. But most deals for first-time artists are terrible. It's like sharecropping, because everything is billed back to you. It's amazing how much money I *have* made given how bad the deals have been."

Mitchell moved to L.A., where boyfriend David ("The Byrd That Got Away") Crosby staged impromptu performances before his famous friends. Peter Fonda recalls Crosby stopping by one afternoon with Mitchell. After borrowing Fonda's 12-string guitar, "she detunes the fucker and then plays 13 or 14 songs, warbling like the best thing I'd ever heard in my life." Asked if she was nervous about performing before the likes of Fonda, she says, "Yeah, I was round-shouldered shy. But it had nothing to do with them being famous. I was intimidated by them because they were *people*." Through the efforts of Crosby and deejay B. Mitchell Reid, people in L.A. knew of her before her first album was even released in March 1968. Although Mitchell was developing her own unique style on her first three albums, she was still somewhat in the shadows of those covering her songs.

All that changed with her fourth album. 1971's *Blue*, a painfully honest post-mortem of the giddy highs and devastating lows of romantic love, was a critical and commercial success. "At that period of my life, I had no personal defenses . . . There's hardly a dishonest note in the vocals," which is why *Blue* remains one of the great breakup albums of all time. *For the Roses*, her follow-up, took aim at the music industry, but was centrally, as always, about the travails of love. It, too, was lavishly praised.

AMID ALL THE ACCOLADES, about the only sour note was John Lennon's admonishment, "Why do you let other people have your hits for you? You want a hit, don't you? Put some fiddles on it." As Mitchell noted years later, "He said this about *Court and Spark*, mind you." The jazzy, rocking 1974 album was a huge success. If there was the usual angst and self-doubt, there was also greater compositional complexity and more humor. *Court and Spark* topped the *Village Voice* critics' poll and yielded two Top 40 singles. The *Voice*'s hypercritical Robert Christgau rated her the "best singer-songwriter there is right now." From 1971's *Blue* through 1974's live *Miles of Aisles*, Mitchell experienced the Roar.

And, then, she says, "because I suddenly had commercial success, it was time to get my ass, period. And that's what happens to artists, period." She maintains she would have been creamed even had she continued working the same ground. Mitchell is probably right that her run was up, but she also made a decision, as she admits, to move on. There's a telling moment on 1974's *Miles of Aisles* when an exasperated Mitchell delivers a good-humored retort to fans shouting out their requests. "No one ever said to Van Gogh, 'Paint a *Starry Night* again, man.'" Mitchell was letting fans know she wouldn't become "a human jukebox." In fact, by 1975 she had tired of fans' expectations that she "weep and suffer for them for the rest of my life. I had that grand theme for a long time: Where is my mate? Where is my mate? Where is my mate? I got rid of that one." She now thinks, "There was a morbidity to the public attention. The only saving grace was it was very well put. It wasn't just maudlin introspection, but it was a catalyst to a lot that was really maudlin. That's why the singer-songwriter [genre] was finally exhausted."

Mitchell claims she originally became a "confessional poet" because "I thought 'You'd better know who you're applauding up here.' It was a compulsion to be honest with my audience." But by the mid-'70s, Mitchell's audience had grown far beyond anything she could have imagined when she was still contemplating a sales career as her "ace in the hole." Baring her soul no longer narrowed the gap between performer and audience; it was, after all, the source of her celebrity. Moreover, from the beginning, Mitchell's confessional songwriting fostered speculation about the identity of the boyfriends behind all this romantic angst. In 1971, *Rolling Stone* proclaimed her the "Old Lady of the Year," and published a diagram revealing which of her songs were about which of her famous boyfriends. Mitchell was so angered by the sexist, tabloid-like treatment she refused the magazine interviews for eight years. "There were people on that list I was never with," she says, still irritated and hurt.

So on her follow-up to *Court and Spark*, 1975's *The Hissing of Summer Lawns*, Mitchell banished the "brokenhearted waif" of earlier albums. Although the record reached No. 4 on the charts, fans and critics alike seemed to feel betrayed by *Hissing*, a dystopian view of suburbia rendered in the sounds of cool jazz. "Self-conscious artiness," wrote Ariel Swartley in *Rolling Stone*. Mitchell believed the backlash had a lot to do with her decision to write "social description as opposed to personal confession. People thought suddenly that I was secure in my success, that I was being a snot and was attacking them." The photograph—a very L.A. shot of a long-legged, glamorous Mitchell relaxing in a swimming pool—didn't help.

Hissing was Mitchell's "demand for liberty," and in it she crashed through the borderlines of pop and countercultural hip. In "The Boho Dance" ("Nothing is capsulized in me/on either side of town/The streets were never really mine/Not mine these glamour gowns") the former "Woodstock girl" challenged the orthodoxy of the counterculture, which condemned her new sartorial stylishness because it fell "outside the hippie uniform of rock 'n' roll." There were no signs of the terminally unhappy hippie girl anywhere on this album, and, given the public's fascination with tortured and depressed artists, especially female artists (Plath, Sexton, Holiday. Joplin, etc.), this was problematic.

While her next effort, the lush road album, *Hejira*, represented a return to the personal, it was hardly a pop move. Although some critics, such as Swartley, understood that it was about the "motion of the music," which was as "hypnotic" as the highways she sang about, others, such as *The Voices*'s Perry Meisel, were contemptuous ("Mitchell lacks any real understanding of what her work is and how it behaves"). *Hejira* marked the beginning of her very fruitful four-album association with bassist Jaco Pastorius. "I was already," she says, "forming pretty strong opinions about what the bottom end of the music should be doing." Mitchell believed "the bass should not only anchor the music, by playing the root, but wander up into the melody register," a style with which Pastorius was already experimenting. "Here was a guy playing the way I dreamed of. He was a godsend." *Don Juan's Reckless Daughter*, the (sort of) collaborative *Mingus*, and the live *Shadows and Light* solidified Mitchell's status as "a person without a country. I was considered an expatriate from pop music." Critics tagged her a pretentious dabbler who had abandoned all semblance of melody.

Jazz purists took aim as well. Although Mitchell says it was Mingus who approached her about collaborating, she believes she was perceived by some as a "white chick," and, worse, an "opportunist who'd come to exploit Charles." Ironically, Mitchell "was not a fan." John Guerin, her drummer and boyfriend, was incredulous when Mitchell told him of Mingus's overture to her. " 'You unconscious motherfucker. You don't even *like* his music. Why didn't he come for me?'" Mitchell maintains her music from this period was "not like jazz. Only the great jazz musicians could play it. A lot of the lesser jazz musicians were annoyed by it too because it wasn't like jazz." This refusal to subordinate her vision (and it is a vision—"I paint with notes") to the strictures of any genre infuriated some critics, who saw it as hubris.

In 1982, she left Elektra for her old friend David Geffen's new label. But the '80s proved equally inhospitable as 1982's *Wild Things Run Fast* was dismissed as "I Love Larry songs." (During the recording she became involved with bassist Larry Klein, whom she later married). If the political *Dog Eat Dog* of '85 was "adolescent," 1988's *Chalk Mark in the Rain Storm* was "overproduced." Mitchell still bristles at the suggestion that Klein had "interior decorated me out of my music." *Chalk Mark* was, she explains, "a sonic experiment in multiples. On most of the album, every guitar part was either 12 or 16 times one guitar. I was seeing how much I could add." The nadir occurred in 1990 when Geffen briefly dropped *Wild Things Run Fast* and *Dog Eat Dog* from its catalogue.

Compared to Mitchell's '80s albums, both *Night Ride Home* and *Turbulent Indigo* sound scaled back, which befits albums that find Mitchell confronting the sobering realities of middle age. Although Mitchell has said *Turbulent Indigo* is about a quest for justice, it also deals with the finiteness of life and love. (She and Klein broke up the day before they began recording the album.) These are wonderfully warm and intimate albums, but it would be a shame if the hoopla over them overshadows her more experimental work. *The Hissing of Summer Lawns*, *Hejira*, and parts of her double-LP, *Don Juan's Reckless Daughter*, remain as compelling as *Blue* or *Court and Spark*. In the late '70s Mitchell dared to paint big, and the remarkable chordal movement of her music is still astonishing.

Mitchell may soon release an album of covers, something she was contractually prevented from doing in the past. She'd like to cover songs by Cole Porter, Frankie Lymon, Edith Piaf, Chuck Berry, Noel Coward, and

Billie Holiday, among others. As for a box set, she groans, "Oh, God, I don't really want to do it. It will kill my catalogue. I'm going to have to take two songs from each album. (This assumes a three-CD set of 30 songs. Mitchell will do no more than 10 songs per CD because, she says, the artist is paid for only 10 songs even if there are more.) "What two do I take from *Court and Spark*? How would I reduce my entire repertoire down to thirty songs? And they want outtakes, too. I don't know how I'm going to do it."

"I SEE LIKE AN ALIEN. I don't have the soul of a white woman. I have the soul of a [*pauses*] Martian [*laughing*], because I wander through this world as if I'm not of it, which is I suppose the perspective of an artist in the first place—the alien outlook."

Sometimes Mitchell hasn't always even looked like a white woman. In 1977, she decided to go to the photo session for *Don Juan's Reckless Daughter* with "a trick up my sleeve." Mitchell says this particular photographer "got good pictures," but could be brutal as he struggled to "undo [your] psychology." So, after her fourth costume change, she emerged as a black man. Clueless as to her identity, people on the shoot came up to her and said, "Can I help you?" The cover of *Don Juan* is that shot.

This was more than a trick, though. Mitchell's exile from the land of pop may explain why she feels a kinship with African-American artists whom racism has relegated to the periphery. To her, the real geniuses of the twentieth century are Robert Johnson, Charlie "Bird" Parker, Jimi Hendrix, and her own musical love, Miles Davis. Mitchell talks passionately about the injustices suffered by black musicians. "I find it offensive to see certain white artists praised and called geniuses when the person they're emulating went to the grave poor and hardly recognized. Look at Bird, you know. You hear a lot of white saxophonists being called geniuses, and you say, 'No, man, they're not the genius, Bird was the genius. He was the one that started it.' I hurt for Bird. I hurt for all the great ones who were never fully appreciated."

Mitchell also feels black musicians have been more willing than their white counterparts to credit her. "Sting won't admit [my influence] to this day. He will to me, but not to the press," she laughs. Jimi Hendrix was, she says, among those who have appreciated her. "There was a night in Ottawa where Jimi knelt at my feet at the bottom of a very short stage and taped the whole show with a big, cumbersome reel-to-reel. We were both freshly signed to Reprise. He had finished a show at the Capital Theater at 10:30 and he came to see my show. He came up and introduced himself to me: 'Hi, I'm Jimi Hendrix. Can I tape your show?' Jimi was a unique guitarist, and I was a unique guitarist. Everyone else was derivative of something. There are never that many originals, and usually they recognize each other."

There was Mingus, too, though Mitchell admits it's "kind of a mystery" why he sent for her. She suspects it had something to do *Don Juan*—both the photos of her cross-dressed as a black man and her composition "Paprika Plains." But as well as they got on, they were, she explains, musically an "odd match. He loved cacophony, and I don't really." Since *Don Juan*, Mitchell has also worked with Wayne Shorter, whom she names "the greatest living jazz musician." Shorter allows Mitchell to edit his sax work when he plays on her albums. "He knows I'm not going to make his performance schizophrenic." Mitchell reports that when he finishes playing, Shorter (who is a fellow painter—thus, Mitchell claims, their rapport) "turns to me and says, 'I'm leaving now, you sculpt.'"

Yet Mitchell is one of the few white rock singers who hasn't copped a black vocal style. "Yeah, the universal rock 'n' roll dialect is southern black," she observes. "It's as affected as opera. Hardly anyone sings in their real voice." And, worse, "once white people started playing rock 'n' roll, the roll—the joy that [characterized] the tail end of the Swing Era—went out of it." Mitchell believes some black musicians are drawn to her work because "I write like a black poet. I frequently write from a black perspective."

In these days of hyperawareness about who can speak for whom, Mitchell's conviction that she writes like a black poet is, at best, unfashionable. Everyone knows, or so we think, a white woman is a white woman, is a white woman, is a white woman. More to the point, there is no single, monolithic black perspective. Yet I understand the desire to breach the boundaries of race and gender. I can see why Mitchell considers the praise of an unnamed black piano player to be the "greatest compliment" she ever received. " 'Joni,' he said, 'I love your music. You make raceless, genderless music.' "

"I HATE TO SEE CHICKS PERFORM," Bob Dylan told *Rolling Stone*. "*Hate* it . . . because they whore themselves."

"Even someone like Joni Mitchell?" asked interviewer Kurt Loder.

"Well, no," Dylan replied. "But then, Joni Mitchell is almost like a man [*Laughs*]. I mean, I love Joni, too. But Joni's got a strange sense of rhythm that's all her own, and she lives on that timetable. Joni Mitchell is in her own world all by herself, so she has a right to keep any rhythm she wants. She's allowed to tell you what time it is."

Three years ago, when Mitchell was asked if she was offended by Dylan's remark, she said, "In a way he's right. Music has become burlesque over the last few years." Today, she says, "It's interesting that even for Bobby a certain amount of accomplishment makes you an honorary male even if you don't act like a male. We *are* living in a male world here." Unlike some women rockers, Mitchell freely admits that it's not exactly a level playing field out there. In the early '70s, Reprise ran an ad campaign built around the following copy: "Joni Mitchell Takes Forever," "Joni Mitchell is 90% Virgin," and "Joni Mitchell Finally Comes Across." "That's what happens," she maintains, "when you don't show your tits." Worst of all was the *Rolling Stone* diagram. "I was horrified to see my own generation turn on me like that. I would have expected it from the one before. I thought, 'Oh my God! This whole thing is a ruse. There is no freedom for women. The madonna-whore thing is never going to disappear.'"

Although Mitchell admits that she's sometimes found that male musicians have a hard time taking instruction from a woman, for the most part music has offered her a refuge from the conventions of gender. In fact, when I ask her why she became interested in music, she tells me a long, revealing story about her childhood.

"It started in childhood. Play should be fun, that's what it's about, right? Okay, I try to play with the girls. All their games are nurses, tea parties, and dress-up. Sometimes we don't have clothes to dress up in, so we do imaginary dress. I'd say, 'I'm wearing a gold lamé dress, and I'm Ginger Rogers, and I'm descending a long staircase.' 'No, you're not, I am.' So even on the level of imaginary play, there was a lot of irrational competition.

"So then I try to play with the boys. The boys play Roy Rogers and war. Roy Rogers is the one that invents all the activities and chooses the site. They choose a new Roy every day. So I say, 'Let me be Roy.' They say, 'You can't 'cause you're a girl.' So Christmas comes and my parents say, 'So, what do you want.' I say, 'I want a Roy Rogers shirt and a Roy Rogers hat.' 'Oh dear,' says my mother. There's a big conference with my father. 'The girl

wants a Roy Rogers shirt.' This is very bad. My father says, 'Let her have it.'
So come spring when you get all your woolly layers off, here I stand in my red
Roy Rogers shirt, says 'Roy' right on it. And my red Roy Rogers hat, says
'Roy' right on it. And I've got all these places . . . I know this ravine that
would be just great . . . And I say to the boys, 'Let me be Roy.' 'You can't.'
'Why not? ' 'You're a girl.' 'But, look, it says, Roy Rogers right here!' 'That
means you're Dale Evans.' 'Why?' 'Because you're wearing Roy's clothes.'
'Well, what does Dale do?' 'She stays home and cooks.'

"So now I find a piano prodigy, a young boy who can play very, very sophisticated classical music, and his friend who was studying voice. They
were both baby classical musicians. Because I was exposed to a lot of classical music, I began to dream I could play the piano. A desire to compose woke
up in me at about the age of eight. They were artists. And there was no role-
playing, so play was able to happen. Had that play not existed, it would have
changed my destiny."

For Mitchell and many other female rock 'n' rollers, music exists beyond
the familiar territory of gender, a kind of liberated zone. This is why she so
resents being categorized as a "female singer songwriter" who writes
"women's songs." And it's why she wastes no time in explaining she's no
feminist, even as she is acknowledging male dominance. It's not simply that
feminism is "too radical" or "divisional," or that she's "never found a herd
she could raise her fist in the air with." Perhaps more to the point, feminism seems to grant too much power to gender. It involves returning to the
ghetto, that stifling world of girls playing dress-up. Mitchell isn't alone in
this. Most women rockers see feminism reinscribing the very category
they're trying to escape.

But if feminism, by necessity, involves mobilizing women on the basis
of their gender, it's often to refuse the very category of woman. As cool as
many women rockers are to feminism, their new-found prominence would
be unthinkable without it. Feminism has transformed the ground upon
which we all walk. Of course, it does no good to condemn female musicians
for the distance they often put between themselves and feminism. After all,
Mitchell has addressed the hypocrisy of the Catholic Church, the sexual
abuse of girls, and the battering of women on her last two releases. And she
doesn't hesitate to say that the adjudication of her work is the one area
where she feels gender has worked against her. "Were I a male I think it

would have been different. The critics didn't lump Dylan in with others" they way they invariably have with her, she points out. Angry about one critic's dismissal of her mid-'80s work as "cranky," she says, "Dylan is far crankier than me, you know. Do they call Dylan cranky for making social commentary? It's like an angry man is an angry man, and an angry woman is a bitch."

"AND WHAT ABOUT JONI? Why is everybody forgetting about Joni?" Chrissie Hynde asked *Rolling Stone* recently. "Hell, she's a fuckin' excellent guitar player, excellent. I don't know any guitar players, any of the real greats, who don't rate Joni Mitchell up there with the best of them. . . . We want you, Joni. Get out there. Put down your paintbrush for five minutes, please."

Why had everyone forgotten about Joni? Even the Rock and Roll Hall of Fame recently passed her over for its 10th annual inductions. After all, in contrast to most women singers of the '60s and '70s, Mitchell played the guitar and the piano, and wrote her own material. Moreover, no one better captured the dilemma facing women in the wake of feminism's revival: how to reconcile the desire for connectedness and intimacy with the equally compelling desire for freedom and autonomy. While I don't think Mitchell's serial monogamy ("I've had the equivalent of about five marriages") or her apparent childlessness ("Is my maternity to amount to a lot of black plastic?" she once asked before she was united with her daughter, whom she gave up for adoption when she was an infant) should afford her special entry into the feminist-inspired annals of women-in-rock, you might imagine that for some it might have.

But Mitchell's problem is that she's never been a bad girl. She was never bawdy, tough, or obviously androgynous. Her one experiment in bending gender and race went largely unnoticed, and, in any case, was never part of her self-presentation. Although she believes a "good piece of art should be androgynous," her androgyny is revealed in her lyrics, the way she sometimes writes from the perspective of a man ("Free Man in Paris" or "The Sire of Sorrow"). Finally, the music for which she is best known reveals a vulnerability at odds with the angry riot-grrrl pose that's been so in vogue. Janis bared her soul, too, but then she was the rowdy bad girl of the '60s. It's a shame because Mitchell often avoided casting herself as the wimpy girl eager to glom onto a guy ("You said, 'I'm as constant as a northern star.'/

And I said, 'Constantly in the darkness/Where's that at?/If you want me I'll be in the bar.'").

Reflecting on her exclusion from the ranks of the great "mothers" of rock, Mitchell observes, "Because it's a man's business some women have the mistaken idea they have to do what men do. Whereas, why can't you make strong music without losing your femininity? I mean, I think it's silly when a woman plays the guitar like it's a big cock. I think it's silly when men play the guitar like a big cock. The guy who was the best at it was Jimi Hendrix. And he confided to me that he couldn't stand it anymore."

One moment Mitchell is talking about being one of the guys and making genderless music, and the next she's extolling the naturalness of gender. Mitchell emphasizes, "I was always one of the boys," but then quickly adds, "I didn't lose my femininity." The story she then tells, however, reveals that she sometimes did "lose" her femininity. "If I got too rough, I'd embarrass the boys because they respected me. Although I was one of the boys, they gave me a line out of their respect for me. On occasion I'd get caught up in the spirit of their rough language, and you'd see, you'd embarrass them." In other words, it wasn't that Mitchell had an unerring sense of where the line lay, but that her male friends would let her know when she'd ventured too far into their territory.

It is ironic, given Mitchell's disdain for borderlines, that she, of all people, should talk of obeying the line between femininity and masculinity. But, ironic or not, she's in good company. Women today find themselves at some moments wanting to explode the very category of gender, and at others returning to its familiar shelter. And we all have trouble locating the line delineating the feminine from the unladylike. What's too coarse, too sexy, too bitchy, or too ambitious? Although Mitchell never transgressed the line of feminine respectability the way the more celebrated bad girls of rock did, she did cross it. Indeed, the critics' trouble with Mitchell isn't just that she's a woman. It's also that she hasn't behaved enough like a woman. She ranks herself right up there with Hendrix, talks of her place in the history of music, and, most important of all, has earned that place with the boldness and originality of her work. In challenging the equation of greatness with maleness, Mitchell is, unbeknownst to herself and all the young trouble girls of rock, the baddest of them all.

notes

Chapter 1. Hope and Hype in Sixties Haight-Ashbury

1. Joan Didion, "Slouching Towards Bethlehem," in *Slouching Towards Bethlehem* (New York: Dell, 1968), 122.

2. Tom Wolfe, *The Electric Kool Aid Acid Test* (New York: Bantam, 1969); Didion, *Slouching*. The most effective and affecting account of the Haight from an insider is Peter Coyote's memoir, *Sleeping Where I Fall* (New York: Counterpoint, 1998), which focuses on the Diggers. Also useful is *Rolling Stone* reporter Charles Perry's *The Haight-Ashbury: A History* (New York: Random House, 1984). Interesting but far from reliable is Emmett Grogan's *Ringolevio: A Life Played for Keeps* (New York: Citadel Press, 1990), another account of life in the Diggers from the man Peter Coyote called a "life star" as opposed to a "life actor." A thoughtful and skeptical account is political radical Warren Hinckle's "A Social History of the Hippies," *Ramparts*, March 1967, reprinted in Gerald Howard, ed., *The Sixties: The Art, Attitudes, Politics, and Media of Our Most Explosive Decade* (New York: Pocket Books, 1982). For a compelling fictional account, see Jennifer Egan, *The Invisible Circus* (New York: Picador, 1995).

3. Carol Brightman, *Sweet Chaos: The Grateful Dead's American Adventure* (New York: Simon & Schuster, 1998), 120.

4. This essay draws on oral histories I conducted with over a hundred veterans of Haight-Ashbury for my book, *Scars of Sweet Paradise: The Life and Times of Janis Joplin* (New York: Metropolitan Books, 1999).

5. For an account that treats the San Francisco rock explosion as a story of lost innocence, see Joel Selvin's informative book, *Summer of Love* (New York: Penguin, 1994).

6. Michael Schumacher, *Dharma Lion* (New York: St. Martin's Press, 1992), 339.
7. Brightman, *Sweet Chaos*, 223.
8. I will be using Beat and beatnik somewhat interchangeably here because to many, including the wannabe beatnik kids who moved to North Beach in pursuit of the Beats, the two seem to have not been particularly distinct. Of course, to mainstream America, the Beats were beatniks, a term said to have been coined in the aftermath of Russia's Sputnik launch by San Francisco newspaper columnist Herb Caen, who thought that Beats were "far-out" like Sputnik. See Dennis McNally, *Desolate Angel: Jack Kerouac, The Beat Generation and America* (New York: Delta, 1979), 253. Beats were quickly caricatured as "beatniks," with Maynord Krebs of the *Dobie Gillis* show being America's best-known bearded boho. However, it's recently been claimed that African-American Beat writer Bob Kaufman, not Caen, coined the term beatnik. See Mona Lisa Saloy, "Black Beats and Black Issues," in Lisa Phillips, ed., *Beat Culture and the New America, 1950–1965* (New York: Whitney Museum of Art, 1996), 163.
9. Author's interview with Peggy Caserta.
10. Todd Gitlin, *The Sixties: Years of Hope, Days of Rage* (New York: Bantam, 1987), 242.
11. Author's interview with Bob Seidemann.
12. Wolfe, *Electric Kool Aid*, 121.
13. Quoted in Gitlin, *The Sixties*, 9.
14. Bill Graham and Robert Greenfield, *Bill Graham Presents: My Life Inside Rock and Out* (New York: Doubleday, 1992), 184. Coyote writes about the free food distribution in his memoir. Digger Peter Berg was already familiar with some of the literature on post-scarcity society. At some point, the Diggers called on the people of the Haight to "sew the rags of surplus into tepees." See Gitlin, *The Sixties*, 223.
15. Digger leaflet quoted in Perry, *Haight-Ashbury*, 97.
16. The phrase "anonymous good guys" was Didion's, but this was most decidedly not her view of the group: Didion, *Slouching*, 99. The phrase "hip Salvation Army" was newspaper columnist Ralph Gleason's. Although Peter Coyote felt the phrase obscured the Diggers' true radicalism, Peter Berg thinks Gleason was trying to take the heat off the Diggers by mak-

ing them seem like selfless do-gooders: interview with Peter Berg. Doubtless, some Diggers were more scrupulous than others.

17. My account of the Free Store is drawn from my interview with Peter Berg; Coyote's account in Graham and Greenfield, *Bill Graham Presents*, 184; and Emmett Grogan's *Ringolevio*. According to Grogan, "only a fraction of the goods used and accepted were secondhand and they were made available and displayed to affect a Salvation-Goodwill-salvage cover to conceal the fact that the rest of the stuff was new and fresh and had been stolen." *Ringolevio*, 249.

18. Author's interview with Bob Seidemann.

19. Author's interview with Richard Hundgen.

20. Coyote, *Sleeping*, 138–39.

21. Author's interview with Jim Haynie.

22. Quoted in Nicholas von Hoffman, *We Are the People Our Parents Warned Us Against* (Chicago: Quadrangle, 1968), 131.

23. The phrase "civilian living" is Digger Emmett Grogan's, who is quoted in Coyote, *Sleeping*, 66.

24. Nat Hentoff, "We Look at Our Parents and . . ." *New York Times Magazine*, Apr. 21, 1968: 19.

25. Wolfe, *Electric Kool Aid*, 36.

26. Perry, *Haight-Ashbury*, 7.

27. Wolfe, *Electric Kool Aid*, 159.

28. Graham and Greenfield, *Bill Graham Presents*, 295.

29. Wolfe, *Electric Kool Aid*, 40.

30. Ray Gosling quoted in Andrew Ross, *No Respect: Intellectuals and Popular Culture* (New York: Routledge, 1989), 148.

31. Graham and Greenfield, *Bill Graham Presents*, 216.

32. Clinton Heylin, *Bob Dylan: Behind the Shades* (New York: Summit, 1991), 102.

33. David Crosby and Carl Gottlieb, *Long Time Gone: The Autobiography of David Crosby* (New York: Dell, 1988), 92.

34. Ibid., 83.

35. Ibid., 93.

36. McGuinn says that Dylan first heard their version in Los Angeles, not New York. Robert Shelton, *No Direction Home: The Life and Music of Bob Dylan* (New York: Penguin, 1986), 309.

37. Bob Spitz, *Dylan: A Biography* (New York: Macmillan, 1989), 210.

38. Eric Von Schmidt and Jim Rooney, *Baby Let Me Follow You Down: The Illustrated Story of the Cambridge Folk Years* (Amherst, Mass.: University of Massachusetts Press, second edition, 1994), 240.

39. Fred Goodman, *The Mansion on the Hill* (New York: Times Books, 1997), 9. My account of Newport '65 is drawn from Goodman and from Shelton, *No Direction Home*; Heylin, *Bob Dylan*; Michael Bloomfield's account in Ed Ward, *Michael Bloomfield: The Rise and Fall of an American Guitar Hero* (New York: Cherry Lane Books, 1983); and my interview with Peter Yarrow. For a behind-the-scenes account from the festival's production manager, see John Boyd's letter to the editor in the *New York Observer*, May 11, 1998. Although the *Observer* identifies him as "John" Boyd, the production manager at Newport was Joe Boyd. See Goodman, *Mansion*, 8.

40. Spitz, *Dylan*, 299.

41. Heylin, *Bob Dylan*, 147.

42. Author's interview with Bill Belmont.

43. Wolfe, *Electric Kool Aid*, 95.

44. Ibid., 210.

45. Author's interview with Chet Helms.

46. Author's interview with George Hunter.

47. Author's interview with Bob Cohen. The three-story Victorian with ten one- and two-bedroom apartments at 2111 Pine Street was home to everyone from Ronny Davis of the Mime Troupe to Janis Joplin. It wasn't located in the Haight, though it was close by.

48. The only political group considered part of the San Francisco rock scene—Country Joe and the Fish—was a Berkeley band.

49. Author's interview with Dave Getz.

50. Wolfe, *Electric Kool Aid*, 8. On the Bay Area's avant-garde, see Richard Cándida Smith, *Utopia and Dissent: Art, Poetry, and Politics in California* (Berkeley, Calif.: University of California Press, 1995). On the San Francisco Mime Troupe, see Graham and Greenfield, *Bill Graham Presents*; R. G. Davis, *The San Francisco Mime Troupe* (Palo Alto, Calif.: Ramparts, 1975).

51. Perry, *Haight-Ashbury*, 67.

52. Author's interview with Alton Kelley.

53. Author's interview with Peter Berg.

54. Gitlin, *The Sixties*, 223.

55. Grogan, *Ringolevio*, 238.

56. Author's interview with Milan Melvin.

57. Author's interview with Bob Simmons.

58. Michael Fallon, "A New Paradise for Beatniks," *San Francisco Examiner*, September 5, 1965. The article was the first in a series on the Haight. In the underground press "beatnik" continued to be used, too. For example, in early 1967, before the Summer of Love made "hippie" a household term, New York's *East Village Other* published "What Is a Beatnik?" in which sixth graders in a Lower East Side public school responded to said question. The article was reprinted in the *Austin Rag* 1, 20 (March 27, 1967): 8.

59. Crosby and Gottlieb, *Long Time Gone*, 69.

60. Hunter S. Thompson, "The 'Hashbury' Is the Capital of the Hippies, *New York Times Magazine*, May 14, 1967: 29.

61. Graham and Greenfield, *Bill Graham Presents*, 195.

62. Author's interview with Bob Seidemann.

63. In the spring of 1967, Ed Denson, who managed the Berkeley band Country Joe and the Fish, groused, "I get tired of hearing about what beautiful people we all are": Thompson, "Capital of the Hippies," 121.

64. Susan Gordon Lydon, *Take the Long Way Home: Memoirs of a Survivor* (New York: HarperCollins, 1993), 74.

65. On November 12, 1966, over a thousand young people gathered on the Sunset Strip in Hollywood to protest police enforcement of a 10 p.m. curfew in that area, where the counterculture of L.A. had taken root. The Strip was the scene of a series of demonstrations over the next month and the situation remained tumultuous through February 1967. Buffalo Springfield was a Los Angeles band whose guitarist, Stephen Stills, was inspired by the Strip riots to write "For What It's Worth."

66. Author's interview with Joshua White.

67. Darby Slick, *Don't You Want Somebody to Love: Reflections on the San Francisco Sound* (Berkeley, Calif.: SLG Books, 1991), 44.

68. By this point, Kerouac was leading a settled, suburban life and he felt alienated from his Beat compatriots, or those who were seduced by the sixties. He even referred to his friend Allen Ginsberg as a "hairy loss."

Steven Watson, *Birth of the Beat Generation: Visionaries, Rebels, and Hipsters, 1944–1960* (New York: Pantheon, 1995), 297.

69. Author's interview with Diane Di Prima.

70. Wolfe, *Electric Kool Aid*, 90.

71. Philip Ennis, *The Seventh Stream: The Emergence of Rocknroll in American Popular Music* (Hanover, N.H.: Wesleyan University Press, 1992), 334.

72. Wolfe, *Electric Kool Aid*, 23.

73. According to Peter Berg, the Diggers explained to Panther leader Bobby Seale that the box of fish was a gift from them. When he asked what kind of fish it was and was told it was sole, he said the fish was too weird looking to be sole. In the end, he accepted their gift, though he said the Party would verify the fish was truly sole. Peter Coyote writes that the Panthers sought the Diggers' help in starting a newspaper. Coyote says the Communication Company, the public information arm of the Diggers, printed the first and possibly second issue of the Panther paper. The Panthers, to the best of my knowledge, have never written of these encounters.

74. Author's interview with Bob Seidemann. Interviews with Peggy Caserta, Carl Gottlieb, Dave Getz, and Richard Hundgen corroborated his view.

75. Hinckle, "Social History of the Hippies," in Howard, *Sixties*, 225.

76. Quoted in Gitlin, *The Sixties*, 228.

77. Jack Kerouac, "The Origins of the Beat Generation," *Playboy*, June 1959: 32. For an interesting account of the Beats, see the interview with Neal Cassady's widow, Carolyn Cassady, in Gina Berriault, "Neal's Ashes," *Rolling Stone*, October 12, 1972: 32. Cassady maintains that all the men "enamored of the Neal myth . . . never knew and don't know how miserable these men were, they think they were having marvelous times—joy, joy, joy—and they weren't at all." See also Carolyn Cassady, *Off the Road* (New York: William Morrow, 1990); Hettie Jones, *How I Became Hettie Jones* (New York: Penguin, 1990); and the chapter on the Beats in Barbara Ehrenreich, *The Hearts of Men* (New York: Anchor, 1983).

78. Author's interview with Bob Seidemann. Rifkin's parents had been involved with the old left.

79. Ibid.

80. Coyote, *Sleeping*, 288–89.

81. Didion, *Slouching*, 113.
82. Author's interview with Travis Rivers.
83. Author's interview with Carl Gottlieb.
84. Author's interview with Bob Seidemann.
85. My account of the Red Dog Saloon is drawn from: Travus T. Hipp, "Legend of the Red Dog Saloon," *Edging West*, June/July 1995, 20; Mike Sion, "Capturing the Life and Times of the Red Dog Saloon," *Reno Gazette-Journal*, March 17, 1994, 1E; Charles Perry, *Haight-Ashbury*; Joel Selvin, *Summer of Love*; interviews with Bob Cohen, George Hunter, and Alton Kelley.
86. The Charlatans really were the original San Francisco band. However, the band's founder, George Hunter, was an artist, not a musician. When the group started out most of its members could barely play their instruments and they were surpassed very quickly by groups with better musicians.
87. Author's interview with Bob Cohen.
88. Author's interview with Jim Haynie.
89. Perry, *Haight-Ashbury*, 29.
90. Ibid., 30.
91. Author's interview with Alton Kelley.
92. Selvin, *Summer of Love*, 28.
93. Slick, *Somebody to Love*, 56.
94. Perry, *Haight-Ashbury*, 31.
95. John Glatt, *Rage and Roll: Bill Graham and the Selling of Rock* (New York: Carol Publishing Group, 1993), 31. The story is considerably more complicated, and bears mentioning. While the Family Dog was still in business it offered its services to Bill Graham. Luria Castell and Alton Kelley offered to help Graham organize the Mime Troupe benefit in exchange for a plug for the Family Dog on the poster advertising the event. In the course of conversation, Castell and Kelley told Graham about the Family Dog's plans to hold dances in the old Fillmore Auditorium, which could be rented for just sixty dollars a night. A well-known R&B venue, the Fillmore had fallen on hard times. Graham was noncommittal about their offer of help, but before Castell and Kelley secured the Fillmore, Graham had signed a four-year lease on the theater. Kelley claims Graham's actions "blew us right out of the water and

out of business. We didn't know any other halls we could rent in San Francisco for that price." They held their last dance on February 4, 1966. Castell then sold the name "Family Dog" to Chet Helms.

96. Graham and Greenfield, *Bill Graham Presents*, 123.

97. Helms had bought the name "Family Dog" from Luria Castell and after a short-lived and ill-starred partnership with Graham, opened up the Avalon Ballroom.

98. Author's interview with Peter Albin.

99. Steve Hochman, "Steve Miller," *Rolling Stone*, September 2, 1993: 22. Miller fronted a popular San Francisco band, The Steve Miller Blues Band, which played the electric ballrooms, but Miller was at odds with the prevailing ethos that favored improvisation and experimentation over tight arrangements and skillful playing.

100. When the Jefferson Airplane first started performing, they were the most polished band in the Bay Area, so much so that some San Francisco rockers felt they belonged in Los Angeles. Tellingly, the Airplane turned determinedly anticommercial after the success of their hit LP *Surrealistic Pillow*.

101. Author's interview with Sam Andrew.

102. Author's interview with Jim Haynie.

103. Author's interview with Bill Belmont.

104. Author's interview with Joshua White.

105. Allen Katzman, ed., *Our Time: Interviews from the East Village Other* (New York: Dial Press, 1972), 208.

106. Graham and Greenfield, *Bill Graham Presents*, 168.

107. Ibid., 176.

108. Ibid. Redding's manager Phil Walden, the speaker here, was describing the experience of Redding and other "black guys from the South" who hadn't spent any time around hippies.

109. L.A. record producer Lou Adler and John Phillips of the Mamas and the Papas organized the event. For a full account of the festival's origins, see *Scars of Sweet Paradise*, 162–63.

110. Goodman, *Mansion*, 52.

111. Robert Christgau, *Any Old Way You Choose It: Rock and Other Pop Music, 1967–1973* (Baltimore: Penguin, 1973), 121.

112. Goodman, *Mansion*, xi.

113. Author's interview with Todd Schiffman, February 1996.

114. Frank Barsalona quoted in Glatt, *Rage and Roll*, 98.

115. Christgau, *Any Old Way*, 52.

116. Heimel, *If You Can't Live Without Me, Why Aren't You Dead Yet?* (New York: HarperCollins, 1992), 187.

117. See Goodman for an example of this analysis. For an even more damning understanding of the counterculture, see Thomas Frank, *The Conquest of Cool* (Chicago, University of Chicago Press, 1997). Frank argues that the counterculture was actually the invention of hip capitalists.

118. Richard Goldstein, *Goldstein's Greatest Hits* (Englewood Cliffs, N.J.: Prentice-Hall, 1970), 119.

119. Heimel, *If You Can't Live Without Me*, 188.

120. Graham and Greenfield, *Bill Graham Presents*, 166.

121. David Dalton, *Piece of My Heart: A Portrait of Janis Joplin*, rev. ed. (New York: Da Capo, 1991), 164.

122. Lydon, *Take the Long Way Home*, 94.

123. Author's interview with Linda Gravenites.

124. Author's interview with Bob Seidemann.

125. On "life" drugs versus "death" drugs: Two influential articles about the Haight—Hunter Thompson's *New York Times* essay and Warren Hinckle's article in *Ramparts*—claimed hippies made a different distinction: between "head" drugs and "body" drugs. Both writers categorize speed as a "head" drug, as opposed to a bad "body" drug. See Hunter Thompson, "Capital of the Hippies," 122 and Hinckle, "Social History of the Hippies," in Howard, *Sixties*, 217. However, Chet Helms maintains that both Thompson and Hinckle were outsiders, whose knowledge of the scene was superficial. Speed, Helms insists, was not regarded as a good drug in Haight-Ashbury.

126. Perry, *Haight-Ashbury*, 293.

127. Ibid.

128. Hinckle in Howard, *Sixties*, 213.

129. Certainly some people within the counterculture were made uneasy by the Angels. Like his friend Janis Joplin, artist Jack Jackson was a transplanted Texan. "Janis and others thought that the Angels were part of

the whole crowd, but they weren't," says Jackson. "They had a lot of hair, but they were the type of people we left Texas to get away from." Author's interview with Jack Jackson.

130. Hinckle, in Howard, *Sixties*, 232.
131. Interview with Michael McClure conducted by Richard Ogar in 1968–1969, Manuscript Collection, Bancroft Library, University of California, Berkeley.
132. Coyote still holds to this position.
133. Author's interview with Bob Brown.
134. Author's interview with Bruce Barthol.
135. Jeff Jassen, "What Price Love?" *Berkeley Barb* 4, 18, issue 90 (May 5–11, 1967): 5.
136. Perry, *Haight-Ashbury*, 171.
137. Graham and Greenfield, *Bill Graham Presents*, 190. Bob Seidemann shot a Summer of Love photo essay in which he recorded young people making their journey up Haight Street. "You don't see any hippies. You see people looking for hippies," he says. As the newcomers traveled up the street they'd stop in boutiques so they could "get their act together." They'd buy an earring, then a groovy T-shirt, followed by a hip pair of bell-bottoms. Author's interview with Seidemann.
138. Davis, *San Francisco Mime Troupe*, 80.
139. Graham and Greenfield, *Bill Graham Presents*, 207.
140. Don McNeil, *Moving Through Here* (New York: Knopf, 1970), 136.
141. Ed Sanders, *The Family* (New York: Avon Books, 1972), 40.
142. Heimel, *If You Can't Live Without Me*, 187.
143. Author's interview with Bob Seidemann.
144. Perry, *Haight-Ashbury*, 422.
145. Selvin, *Summer of Love*, 131.
146. Author's interview with Raechel Donahue.
147. Perry, *Haight-Ashbury*, 243.
148. Gitlin, *The Sixties*, 235.
149. Christgau, *Any Old Way*, 254.
150. Digger Emmett Grogan dubbed it the "First Annual Charlie Manson Death Festival" days before the concert took place. Graham and Greenfield, *Bill Graham Presents*, 294.

151. Author's interview with Joshua White.

152. Abe Peck, *Uncovering the Sixties: The Life and Times of the Underground Press* (New York: Pantheon, 1985), 226.

153. Coyote, *Sleeping*, 66.

154. Brightman, *Sweet Chaos*, 127.

155. Ibid., 226.

156. Even citizen-initiated recycling programs, which grew out of the counterculture's concern with the environment, have made millions for waste management companies.

157. Simon Frith, "Rock and the Politics of Memory," in Sohnya Sayres, Anders Stephanson, Stanley Aronowitz, Fredric Jameson, eds., *The '60s Without Apology* (Minneapolis: University of Minnesota Press, 1988), 61. In the end, however, Frith concludes that sixties rock was, like all pop, primarily a "music of transitory private pleasures" rather than revolutionary. See page 68.

158. Author's interview with Judy Goldhaft.

159. Ellen Willis, "On the Barricades," a review of *The Sixties* by Arthur Marwick, *New York Times Book Review*, November 8, 1998: 16.

160. SDSers, for example, were often slow to experiment with drugs. Todd Gitlin says there was "nothing hippie dippie" about SDS's old guard. He doubts anyone in this group, of which he was a part, had even sampled LSD by 1967. Most, he reports, were "leery even of marijuana." Gitlin, *The Sixties*, 225.

161. Author's interview with Bob Seidemann.

162. Mario Savio, "An End to History," reprinted in Alexander Bloom and Wini Breines, eds. *Takin' It to the Streets* (New York: Oxford, 1995), 111.

163. Author's interview with Carl Gottlieb. Gottlieb is quoting a friend here.

164. The phrase "superhypermost" was Janis Joplin's.

165. Peter Coyote quoted in Graham and Greenfield, *Bill Graham Presents*, 197.

166. Slick, *Somebody to Love*, 63.

167. Philip K. Dick, *A Scanner Darkly* (New York: Vintage, 1991), 259.

168. Brightman, *Sweet Chaos*, 288.

169. Author's interview with Carl Gottlieb.

Chapter 2. The Ike Age: Rethinking the 1950s

1. Ed Ward, Geoffrey Stokes, and Ken Tucker, *Rock of Ages* (New York: Simon & Schuster, 1986), 107.

2. *Albuquerque Journal*, September 19, 1998.

3. ABC was so confident of the public's undying interest in the sixties that during sweeps week in February 1998 the network broadcast a thoroughly predictable miniseries that focused on the generation gap that tore apart two families—one white and one black. The network's gamble paid off with high ratings.

4. Patricia Cohen, "New Slant on the 60s: The Past Made New," *New York Times*, June 13, 1998: A13. Two years before the *Times* piece, *Lingua Franca* published a essay on the reported generational divide among historians of the sixties. In the essay, historian Thomas Sugrue is quoted saying that he sees a "bunch of commonalities" between "the land of *Leave It to Beaver*" and the sixties. See Rick Perlstein, "Who Owns the Sixties," *Lingua Franca*, May/June 1996: 37. The first scholar I know of to challenge the idea of fundamental discontinuity between the fifties and the sixties is Joshua Freeman. Freeman didn't challenge the caricatured view of the fifties; rather he argued that historians had overlooked the significance of conservatism in the sixties. At its peak in the mid-1960s, the John Birch Society had an estimated 70,000 to 100,000 members—almost exactly, he notes, the estimated membership of SDS at the height of its popularity. See Joshua Freeman, "Putting Conservatism Back into the 1960s," in "Teaching the Sixties: A Symposium," *Radical History Review* 44 (1989): 93–107.

5. Ibid., 13.

6. David Frum, *How We Got Here: The 70s—The Decade that Brought You Modern Life—For Better or Worse* (New York: Basic Books, 2000).

7. Blake and Cmeil are doing an anthology on the seventies.

8. David Halberstam, *The Fifties* (New York: Fawcett, 1993).

9. Aldon Morris, *The Origins of the Civil Rights Movement: Black Communities Organizing for Change* (New York: The Free Press, 1984), 51.

10. John D'Emilio, *Sexual Politics, Sexual Communities: The Making of the Homosexual Minority in the United States, 1940–1970* (Chicago: University of Chicago Press, 1983), 240.

11. Maurice Isserman, *If I Had a Hammer . . .: The Death of the Old Left and the Birth of the New Left* (New York: Basic Books, 1987), xiii.

12. Todd Gitlin, *The Sixties: Years of Hope, Days of Rage* (New York: Bantam, 1987), 110.

13. Isserman, *If I Had a Hammer*, 209.

14. Alan Wald, *The New York Intellectuals: The Rise and Decline of the Anti-Stalinist Left from the 1930s to the 1980s* (Chapel Hill, N.C.: University of North Carolina Press, 1987), 6.

15. Leila Rupp and Verta Rupp, *Survival in the Doldrums: The American Women's Rights Movement, 1945 to the 1960s* (New York: Oxford, 1987).

16. Amy Swerdlow, *Women Strike for Peace: Traditional Motherhood and Radical Politics in the 1960s* (Chicago: University of Chicago, 1993).

17. Joanne Meyerowitz, ed., *Not June Cleaver: Women and Gender in Postwar America, 1945–1960* (Philadelphia: Temple University Press, 1994), 4.

18. Ibid., 2.

19. Ibid., 220.

20. Sally Belfrage, *Un-American Activities: A Memoir of the Fifties* (New York: Harper Collins, 1994), 146.

21. Ibid., 85.

22. Ibid., 119.

23. Ibid., 128.

24. Ibid., 119.

25. Hettie Jones, *How I Became Hettie Jones* (New York: Penguin, 1990), 10.

26. Ibid., 45.

27. Ibid., 65.

28. Elaine Tyler May, *Homeward Bound: American Families in the Cold War* (New York: Basic Books, 1988).

29. Sara Evans, *Born for Liberty* (New York: Free Press, 1989), 230.

30. Thomas Sugrue, *The Origins of the Urban Crisis* (Princeton: Princeton University Press, 1996).

31. George Lipsitz, "Against the Wind," in Lipsitz, *Time Passages* (Minneapolis: University of Minnesota Press, 1990), 123. Lipsitz's examples include performers such as Janis Joplin, and while his hypothesis is arresting, one wonders to what extent white kids were really seduced by the "democratic and egalitarian propensities" of early rock 'n' roll (p. 100). That said, Lipsitz's incisive work is nonetheless a crucial

corrective to the pessimistic view of rock 'n' roll as hopelessly co-opted or fundamentally conservative.

32.   See Gitlin, *The Sixties*, chapter one.

33.   Wini Breines, *Young, White and Miserable: Growing Up Female in the Fifties* (Boston: Beacon, 1992), 23.

34.   Henry Louis Gates, *Colored People: A Memoir* (New York: Vintage, 1995), 25.

35.   "Telling a Mean Story: Amber Hollibaugh Interviews Dorothy Allison," *Women's Review of Books*, July 1992: 17.

36.   See George Lipsitz, *A Life in the Struggle: Ivory Perry and the Culture of Opposition* (Philadelphia: Temple University Press, 1988).

37.   Gitlin, *The Sixties*, 136.

38.   Quoted in Michael Schumacher, *Dharma Lion* (New York: St. Martin's Press, 1992), 532.

Chapter 3. "We Gotta Get Out of This Place": Notes Toward a Remapping of the Sixties

Acknowledgments: I presented different versions of this chapter at the October 1990 American Studies convention and the March 1991 conference on Contemporary Social Movements and Cultural Politics at the University of California, Santa Cruz. Many people helped me rethink and sharpen the arguments here, including the *Socialist Review* staff and Barbara Epstein in particular. Martha Vicinus encouraged me to think bigger. Connie Samaras, Paula Rabinowitz, Howard Brick, Becky Conekin, Laura Downs, Karen Merrill, and Peg Lourie provided thoughtful criticisms. In the end, of course, the essay's shortcomings should be laid at my doorstep. Finally, thanks to Jello Biafra, whose recent cover of the Animals' hit put the tune in my mind and in the title.

1.   See Vincent Harding, "It's Not Enough to Honor King; We Have to Continue His Human Mission," *Ann Arbor* (Michigan) *News*, January 18, 1988.

2.   Citizenship, principled protest, and rock 'n' roll genius are formulated as male in *JFK, Born on the Fourth of July*, and *The Doors* respectively. In *JFK*, for instance, citizenship is constructed as masculine both in

the closing courtroom scene where District Attorney Jim Garrison addresses his final remarks to his son, and in several scenes between Garrison and his son (played by Oliver Stone's son). Garrison's daughter is either absent or marginal to these scenes. The major female character, Garrison's wife, is depicted as aggressively antipolitical. Her interest is in her family, certainly not in her husband's apparently selfless and heroic struggle for truth and justice. In this film the public and private, formulated as masculine and feminine respectively, are opposed. One wonders if Stone's fascination with Kennedy and Garrison might stem in part from the antidomestic masculinity they seemed to embody.

3. For a discussion of Stone's engagement with the sixties, see Stephen Talbot, "'60s Something," *Mother Jones* 16, 2 (March–April 1991).

4. See, for example, James Miller, *Democracy Is in the Streets: From Port Huron to the Siege of Chicago* (New York: Simon & Schuster, 1987); Tom Hayden, *Reunion: A Memoir* (New York: Random House, 1988); Todd Gitlin, *The Sixties: Years of Hope, Days of Rage* (New York: Bantam, 1987); David Caute, *The Year of the Barricades: A Journey Through 1968* (New York: Harper & Row, 1988); Nancy Zaroulis and Gerald Sullivan, *Who Spoke Up? American Protest Against the War in Vietnam* (Garden City, N.Y.: Doubleday, 1984); Joan and Robert Morrison, *From Camelot to Kent State* (New York: Times Books, 1987); Abe Peck, *Uncovering the Sixties: The Life and Times of the Underground Press* (New York: Pantheon, 1985). The problem is not that most of these writers don't mention the women's liberation movement but that it is peripheral in their accounts. However, Zaroulis and Sullivan did manage to write a whole book on the antiwar movement without once mentioning women's liberation and its antiwar efforts. Worst of all is David Caute's five-hundred-page opus, which devotes less than five pages to women's liberation. Miller only alludes to the coming women's movement, but this exclusion is somewhat more excusable since his study ends with the Chicago Democratic Convention in August 1968. However, he, as well as the others listed above, could have explored the gendered politics of the New Left. *The Sixties Papers: Documents of a Rebellious Decade*, edited by Judith and Stewart Albert (New York: Praeger, 1984), includes a section on the women's liberation movement. But the authors devote just five pages to

it in their fifty-five page introductory essay. *The '60s Without Apology*, edited by Sohnya Sayres, Anders Stephanson, Stanley Aronowitz, and Frederic Jameson (Minneapolis: University of Minnesota Press, 1984), is a collection of essays that, largely through the inclusion of Ellen Willis's important essay "Radical Feminism and Feminist Radicalism," makes some attempt to integrate women's liberation into its constructions of the sixties. The one book-length study of the sixties that does integrate the women's movement (both the liberal branch epitomized by NOW and the more radical women's liberation movement) is Stewart Burn's synthetic account, *Social Movements of the 1960s: Searching for Democracy* (Boston: Twayne, 1990).

5.   Ellen DuBois, "Women Suffrage and the Left: An International Socialist Perspective," *New Left Review* 186 (March–April 1991).

6.   Both the women's liberation movement and the New Left were overwhelmingly white. However, some have argued that by the late sixties feminist struggles were being waged within, for instance, the black freedom movement. According to this argument, historians who have defined the women's liberation movement as an autonomous movement primarily concerned with ending male dominance have erased the emergent black feminist struggle that was embedded within the black movement (Barbara Omolade, panel remarks at the roundtable discussion of my book *Daring to Be Bad*, Berkshire conference on the history of women, June 1990). Tracye Matthews, a graduate student in the history department at the University of Michigan, is working on women in the Black Panther Party. Her research should tell us more about this.

7.   Mary King, *Freedom Song: A Personal Story of the 1960s Civil Rights Movement* (New York: Morrow, 1987); Angela Davis, *Angela Davis: An Autobiography* (New York: Random House, 1974); Jane Alpert, *Growing Up Underground* (New York: Morrow, 1981). One could add to this list Joan Baez, *And a Voice to Sing With* (New York: NAL, 1987). But Baez was a celebrity more outside than inside the Movement.

8.   James Forman, *The Making of Black Revolutionaries* (New York: MacMillan, 1972); Cleveland Sellers with Robert Terrell, *The River of No Return: The Autobiography of a Black Militant and the Life and Death of SNCC* (New York: William Morrow, 1973); Anne Moody, *Coming of*

Age in Mississippi (New York: Dell, 1971). However, this situation appears to be changing with the publication of two important Black Panther memoirs: Elaine Brown, *A Taste of Power: A Black Woman's Story* (New York: Pantheon, 1992) and David Hilliard and Lewis Cole, *This Side of Glory: The Autobiography of David Hilliard and the Story of the Black Panther Party* (Boston: Little Brown, 1993).

9.   Carlos Muñoz, *Youth, Identity, Power: The Chicano Movement* (New York: Verso, 1989). Of course, Muñoz's book is problematic in the way it universalizes male experience. Vicki Ruiz discusses Muñoz's inattention to Chicanas in her review of his book in the *American Historical Review* (December 1991), 1638.

10.   Solely in order to minimize confusion about which movement I am referring to, I will capitalize "Movement" when discussing the overlapping movements of the sixties (black freedom, student, antiwar, and New Left) and will use the lower-cased "movement" when discussing the women's liberation movement.

11.   Despite their similar treatments of women's liberation, these are very different books. Hayden wrote his book as a memoir; Gitlin acknowledges the autobiographical basis of his book but presents his work as a more general history of the sixties. Gitlin's decision to write a history makes his book more useful than Hayden's, but more problematic as well because his experiences and feelings so inform his construction of the period.

12.   Gitlin, *The Sixties*, 374, 375.

13.   Hayden, *Reunion*, 419.

14.   Hayden, like Gitlin, contrasts male and female experience in the movement at this time, noting that the women's consciousness-raising groups were "rather exhilarating, while the men went to morbid meetings" (*Reunion*, 421).

15.   Gitlin, *The Sixties*, 427.

16.   For a further elaboration of this idea see my book *Daring to Be Bad: Radical Feminism in America, 1967–1975* (Minneapolis: University of Minnesota Press, 1989), esp. 23–49 and 114–37.

17.   Winifred Breines, "Whose New Left?" *Journal of American History*, 75, 22 (September 1988).

18.   Richard Flacks has critiqued the idea that the New Left "project" died in the late sixties. He points to the vitality of grassroots, collective experiments into the seventies. See his useful article "What Happened to the New Left?" *Socialist Review* 19, 1 (January–March 1989).

19.   This is not to say that for either the New Left or the black freedom struggle the late sixties marked a time of unequivocal success. Indeed, many would argue that the organized black movement faltered when the struggle moved North. And SNCC fell apart long before SDS. But I would argue that any comprehensive history of the black freedom struggle would have to grapple with the significance of both black power and the Black Panther Party, which attempted to address both class and racial issues.

20.   Quoted in Paula Rabinowitz, *Labor and Desire: Women's Revolutionary Fiction in Depression America* (Chapel Hill: University of North Carolina Press, 1991), 4.

21.   In this groundbreaking article Epstein did problematize New Left men's masculinity. She maintained that both New Left men and women were ambivalent about commitment in their personal relationships. However, she suggested that women's ambivalence arose from their dissatisfaction with the quality of their relationships, while men were more apt to reject or at least feel ambivalent about the very idea of commitment. Epstein hypothesized that men's more global rejection of commitment might have stemmed from their memories of the "trapped quality of their fathers' lives." Epstein, "Family Politics and the New Left: Learning from Our Own Experience," *Socialist Review* 63–64 (May–August 1982), 153–54. On the relative status of women in the old left and the new, see Ellen Kay Trimberger, "Women in the Old and New Left: The Evolution of a Politics of Personal Life," *Feminist Studies* 5, 3 (Fall 1979); and Barbara Epstein (going by the name Easton then), "Women and the Left," *New American Movement* (Summer 1975).

22.   See Wini Breines, "The 1950s: Gender and Some Social Science," *Sociological Inquiry* 56, 1 (Winter 1986).

23.   See Rabinowitz, *Labor and Desire*, 37.

24.   Mills's *White Collar: The American Middle Classes* (New York: Oxford University Press, 1953) opens with a quote from Charles Peguy: "No one

could suspect that times were coming . . . when the man who did not gamble would lose all the time, even more surely than he who gambled."

25. Gitlin gets at this point, but without exploring gender, when he remarks, "Mills was a hero in student radical circles for his books, of course, but it was no small part of the persona for which he was cherished that he was a motorcycle-riding, cabin-building Texan, cultivating the image of a gunslinging homesteader of the old frontier" (*The Sixties*, 34).

26. Maurice Isserman, *If I Had a Hammer . . .: The Death of the Old Left and the Birth of the New Left* (New York: Basic Books, 1987), 116–23.

27. Gitlin, *The Sixties*, 108.

28. Hayden, *Reunion*, 80.

29. Of course, they didn't identify with male homosexuals, who also occupied the margins of American society. Just as their attitudes toward women mirrored those of the dominant culture, so did their attitudes toward homosexuality. Over the course of the period intolerance seems to have increased as many white new leftists equated militance with machismo and liberalism with wimpiness. See ex-SDS leader Gregory Calvert's review of Wini Breines's *Community and Organization in the New Left, 1962–1968* in *Telos* (Winter 1982–1983).

30. Gitlin, *The Sixties*, 38.

31. Gitlin, quoted in Sara Evans, *Personal Politics: The Roots of Women's Liberation in the Civil Rights Movement and the New Left* (New York: Vintage, 1980), 128.

32. Davis quoted in Evans, *Personal Politics*, 151.

33. Max quoted in Evans, *Personal Politics*, 149.

34. Evans notes that by the second year of ERAP many New Left men were engaged in the business of sexual conquest (*Personal Politics*, 152).

35. Interestingly, feminist accounts tend to be much less critical of the black freedom movement. It could be, as Sara Evans suggests, that white women found the black freedom movement more hospitable than the New Left, which was such an intellectual proving ground. But even if this is true, and I am not yet convinced it is (there were, after all, female intellectuals in the New Left and intellectual discussions in SNCC), I think feminists' more charitable account of the black freedom movement stems from a feeling of affinity with the philosophy of

black power and a desire to achieve legitimacy within the New Left through solidarity with that struggle. I have often thought that white women liberationists' erroneous attribution of the first memo on sexism in the Movement to an African-American woman, Ruby Doris Smith Robinson, reflected in part their desire for an easy cross-racial sisterhood, as well as for political legitimacy, because black women were at least understood as oppressed, if not usually as women.

36. Morgan, "Rites of Passage," a 1975 article reprinted in her *Going Too Far* (New York: Vintage, 1978), 10.

37. Dworkin, "Why So-Called Radical Men Love and Need Pornography," in her *Letters from a War Zone* (New York: Dutton, 1989), 217. See Dworkin on the New Left in *Right-Wing Women* (New York: Perigree, 1983). She contends that before the revival of feminism, New Left men "fought for and argued for and even organized for and even provided political and economic resources for abortion rights for women" (95). They did so because "access to safe abortion made more women willing to be fucked more often by more men" (129). Dworkin claims these same men deserted abortion rights when feminists redefined the issue as one of women's control of their bodies. This is pure fiction: The New Left never mobilized in support of abortion rights in the days before feminism. See Suzanne Staggenborg, *The Pro-Choice Movement* (New York: Oxford University Press, 1991).

38. This was a slogan of the antidraft movement and it was, ironically, coined by folksinger and antiwar activist Joan Baez. See her memoir *And a Voice to Sing With*, 152.

39. Gitlin, *The Sixties*, 108. Hayden's wording differs a bit, but he too notes this remark (*Reunion*, 107).

40. Ellen Willis, "Radical Feminism and Feminist Radicalism," in Sohnya Sayres et al., eds., *The '60s Without Apology*; Elinor Langer, "Notes for Next Time: A Memoir of the 1960s," *Working Papers for a New Society* 1, 3 (Fall 1973); Kathie Sarachild, "The Civil Rights Movement: Lessons for Women's Liberation" (unpublished 1983 speech delivered at the University of Massachusetts).

41. This genre of rancorous recollections was very much encouraged by the mid-seventies ascendance of cultural feminism. Briefly, cultural feminism is an antileft strain of feminism that reformulated the central task

of feminism as the construction of a women's culture where female values would be nurtured and celebrated. The reasons for cultural feminism's ascendance within the movement are too complicated to discuss here, but it was related to the political circumstances of the mid-seventies—the political impasse feminists found themselves in, what Robin Morgan called the "futilitarian" politics of radical feminism, and, perhaps most crucially, the movement's fragmentation along lines of class, sexual preference, and race. Cultural feminism with its universalizing discourse of "sisterhood" and its concern with achieving tangible change in the form of a women's culture had extraordinary appeal. Those who tried to raise the issue of the differences between women were denounced as dupes of the male left, which, it was argued, was out to derail feminism. Cultural feminists had a certain stake in presenting the New Left as intrinsically and chronically sexist.

42. See Echols, *Daring to Be Bad,* especially chapter 2.

43. See Echols, *Daring to Be Bad,* chapters 1–3.

44. The idea that radicalism involved fighting one's own oppression had only recently found acceptance in the white left, largely as a result of the black movement's expulsion of whites, and French theorists' invention of the "new working class"—an idea with complicated repercussions in the white left. The early New Left generally cast African Americans and the poor in the role of revolutionary agents of change. See Stanley Aronowitz's immensely instructive article "When the New Left Was New" in Sayres, et al., *The '6os Without Apology,* 35.

45. Mary King, who with Casey Hayden was among the first to challenge Movement sexism, writes in *Freedom Song* that both she and Hayden were drawn to Beauvoir's writings in part because her female characters were not defined by men.

46. Rosenfelt and Stacey, "Second Thoughts on the Second Wave," *Feminist Studies* 13, 2 (Summer 1987): 351.

47. Elsa Barkley Brown, "Polyrhythms and Improvisation: Lessons for Women's History," *History Workshop Journal* 31 (Spring 1991).

48. According to Leila Rupp and Verta Taylor, resource mobilization theory, in contrast to earlier scholarship on social change movements, stresses the importance of resources—expertise, money, publicity, and the support of influential groups and individuals not involved in the

movement—to a movement's success. Leila Rupp and Verta Taylor, *Survival in the Doldrums: The American Women's Rights Movement, 1945 to the 1960s* (New York: Oxford University Press, 1987). Aldon Morris, *The Origins of the Civil Rights Movement: Black Communities Organizing for Change* (New York: Free Press, 1984).

49. George Lipsitz, *A Life in the Struggle: Ivory Perry and the Culture of Opposition* (Philadelphia: Temple University Press, 1988; rev. ed. 1995), 47.

50. See, in particular, Barbara Ehrenreich, *The Hearts of Men: American Dreams and the Flight from Commitment* (Garden City, N.Y.: Anchor, 1983).

51. See Robert Draper, *Rolling Stone Magazine: The Uncensored History* (New York: Bantam, 1990), 61.

52. For the racial dimension of the attack on rock 'n' roll see Linda Martin and Kerry Segrave, *Anti-Rock: The Opposition to Rock 'n' Roll* (Hamden, Conn.: Archon Books, 1988).

53. The term "hillbilly cat" was slang for "white Negro." See Greil Marcus, *Mystery Train: Images of America in Rock 'n' Roll Music* (New York: Dutton, 1982), 181. Marcus's work was perhaps the first to grasp the full significance of Elvis's transgression of America's racial boundaries. See also George Lipsitz's inspired article "Land of a Thousand Dances: Youth, Minorities and the Rise of Rock and Roll," in Lary May, ed., *Recasting America: Culture and Politics in the Age of the Cold War* (Chicago: University of Chicago Press, 1985).

54. Eldridge Cleaver, *Soul On Ice* (New York: Dell, 1968), 197. Andrew Ross discusses Cleaver's observation in *No Respect: Intellectuals and Popular Culture* (New York: Routledge, 1989), 65–101.

55. Tom Holt, "Notes for a Paper: Reflections on Race-Making and Racist Practice: Toward a Working Hypothesis" (paper presented to the Committee for the Study of Social Transformation, University of Michigan, Spring 1991).

Chapter 4. "Nothing Distant About It": Women's Liberation and Sixties Radicalism

1. See Carol Hanisch, "A Critique of the Miss America Protest," in Shulamith Firestone and Anne Koedt, eds., *Notes from the Second Year:*

Women's Liberation, (New York: Radical Feminism, 1970), 87, and Judith Duffet, "Atlantic City Is a Town with Class—They Raise Your Morals While They Judge Your Ass," *The Voice of the Women's Liberation Movement* 1, 3 (October 1968). The protesters also criticized the pageant's narrow formulation of beauty, especially its racist equation of beauty with whiteness. They emphasized that in its forty-seven-year history, the pageant had never crowned a black woman Miss America. That weekend the first Black Miss America Pageant was held in Atlantic City.

2. See Lindsy Van Gelder, "Bra Burners Plan Protest," *New York Post,* September 4, 1968, which appeared three days before the protest. The *New York Times* article by Charlotte Curtis quoted Robin Morgan as having said about the mayor of Atlantic City: "He was worried about our burning things. He said the boardwalk had already been burned out once this year. We told him we wouldn't do anything dangerous—just a symbolic bra-burning." Curtis, "Miss America Pageant Is Picketed by 100 Women," *New York Times,* September 8, 1968.

3. See Jack Gould's column in the *New York Times,* September 9, 1968.

4. The Yippies were a small group of leftists who, in contrast to most of the Left, had enthusiastically embraced the growing counterculture. For a fascinating account of the 1968 convention, see David Farber, *Chicago '68* (Chicago: University of Chicago Press, 1988).

5. Curtis, "Miss America Pageant."

6. For the sake of convenience, I will use the term *Movement* to describe the overlapping protest movements of the sixties—the black freedom movement, the student movement, the antiwar movement, and the more self-consciously political New Left. I will refer to the women's liberation movement as the *movement;* here I use the lower case simply to avoid confusion.

7. Snitow, interview with author, New York City, June 14, 1984. Here one can get a sense of the disjuncture in experiences between white and black women; presumably, black women had not felt the same sense of distance about their civil rights activism.

8. Robin Morgan, *Going Too Far: The Personal Chronicle of a Feminist* (New York: Random House, 1978).

9. Yet virtually all of the recently published books on the sixties either slight or ignore the protest. This omission is emblematic of a larger

problem, the failure of authors to integrate women's liberation into their reconstruction of that period. Indeed, most of these books have replicated the position of women in the larger, male-dominated protest Movement—that is, the women's liberation movement is relegated to the margins of the narrative. Such marginalization has been exacerbated as well by the many feminist recollections of the sixties that demonize the Movement and present women's liberation as its antithesis. Sixties books that textually subordinate the women's liberation movement include James Miller, *Democracy Is in the Streets: From Port Huron to the Siege of Chicago* (New York: Simon & Schuster, 1987); Tom Hayden, *Reunion: A Memoir* (New York: Random House, 1988); Todd Gitlin, *The Sixties: Years of Hope, Days of Rage* (New York: Bantam, 1987); and Nancy Zaroulis and Gerald Sullivan, *Who Spoke Up?: American Protest Against the War in Vietnam*. A notable exception is Stewart Burns, *Social Movements of the 1960s: Searching for Democracy* (Boston: Twayne, 1990).

10.   Sara Evans, *Personal Politics: The Roots of Women's Liberation in the Civil Rights Movement and the New Left* (New York: Vintage Books, 1979).

11.   Sara Evans has argued that in their attempt to combine work inside and outside the family, educated, middle-class, married white women of the 1950s were following the path pioneered by black women. See Evans, *Born for Liberty: A History of Women in America* (New York: Free Press, 1989), 253–54. As Jacqueline Jones and others have demonstrated, black women have a "long history of combining paid labor with domestic obligations." According to Jones, in 1950 one-third of all married black women were in the labor force, compared to one-quarter of all married women in the general population. One study cited by Jones "concluded that black mothers of school-aged children were more likely to work than their white counterparts, though part-time positions in the declining field of domestic service inhibited growth in their rates of labor force participation." Jones, *Labor of Love, Labor of Sorrow: Black Women, Work, and the Family, from Slavery to the Present* (New York: Vintage Books, 1986), 269.

12.   Alice Kessler-Harris, *Out to Work: A History of Wage-Earning Women in the United States* (New York: Oxford University Press, 1982), 302.

13.   Evans, *Born for Liberty*, 252.

14. Jane De Hart-Mathews, "The New Feminism and the Dynamics of Social Change," in Linda Kerber and Jane De Hart-Mathews, eds., *Women's America: Refocusing the Past,* 2d ed., (New York: Oxford University Press, 1987), 445.

15. I think that this was an experience specific to white women. The problem of diffidence seems to have been, if not unique to white women, then especially acute for them. This is not to say that issues of gender were unimportant to black women activists in the sixties, but that gender seemed less primary and pressing an issue than race. However, much more research is needed in this area. It could be that the black women's noninvolvement in women's liberation had as much, if not more, to do with the movement's racism than with any prioritizing of race.

16. Carl Oglesby, "Trapped in a System," reprinted as "Liberalism and the Corporate State," in *The New Radicals: A Report with Documents,* edited by Paul Jacobs and Saul Landau (New York: Vintage Books, 1966), 266. For a useful discussion of the New Left's relationship to liberalism, see Gitlin, *The Sixties,* 127–92.

17. See Howard Brick, "Inventing Post-Industrial Society: Liberal and Radical Social Theory in the 1960s" (paper delivered at the 1990 American Studies Association Conference). In September 1963 the electoral politics faction of SDS had even succeeded in getting the group to adopt the slogan, "Part of the Way with LBJ." Johnson's official campaign slogan was "All the Way with LBJ." See Gitlin, *The Sixties,* 180.

18. Gregory Calvert, interview in *The Movement* 3, 2 (1967): 6.

19. Andrew Kopkind, "Looking Backward: The Sixties and the Movement," *Ramparts* 11, 8 (February 1973): 32.

20. That evening seven million people watched Johnson's speech to Congress announcing voting rights legislation. According to C. T. Vivian, "a tear ran down" Martin Luther King's cheek as Johnson finished his speech. Juan Williams, *Eyes on the Prize: America's Civil Rights Years, 1954–1965* (New York: Penguin, 1988), 278.

21. Elinor Langer discusses the ways in which Marcuse's notion of repressive tolerance was used by the Movement. See her wonderful essay, "Notes for Next Time," *Working Papers for a New Society* 1, 3 (Fall 1973): 48–83.

22. Ellen Kay Trimberger, "Women in the Old and New Left: The Evolution of a Politics of Personal Life," *Feminist Studies* 5, 3 (Fall 1979): 442.

23. Potter quoted from Miller, *Democracy Is in the Streets*, 196.

24. Miller quoted from Gitlin, *The Sixties*, 9. Although the broad outlines of Miller's argument are correct, some recent scholarship on 1930s radicalism suggests that it was considerably more varied and less narrowly economistic than has been previously acknowledged. For example, recent books by Paula Rabinowitz and Robin Kelley demonstrate that some radicals in this period understood the salience of such categories as gender and race. See Paula Rabinowitz, *Labor and Desire: Women's Revolutionary Fiction in Depression America* (Chapel Hill: University of North Carolina Press, 1991); Robin Kelley, *Hammer and Hoe: Alabama Communists during the Great Depression* (Chapel Hill: University of North Carolina Press, 1990).

25. Shulamith Firestone, *The Dialectic of Sex: The Case for Feminist Revolution*, rev. ed. (New York: Bantam Books, 1971), 10–11.

26. Robin Morgan, in Morgan, ed., *Sisterhood Is Powerful* (New York: Vintage Books, 1970), xxii.

27. Firestone, *The Dialectic of Sex*, 33. For a very useful history of women's rights activism (as opposed to women's liberation) in the postwar years, see Cynthia Harrison, *On Account of Sex: The Politics of Women's Issues, 1945–1968* (Berkeley: University of California Press, 1988).

28. T. Grace Atkinson, *Amazon Odyssey* (New York: Link Books, 1974), 10. In contrast to other founders of early radical feminist groups, Atkinson came to radicalism through her involvement in the New York City chapter of NOW, admittedly the most radical of all NOW chapters. Atkinson made this remark in October 1968 after having failed badly in her attempt to radically democratize the New York chapter of NOW. Upon losing the vote she immediately resigned her position as the chapter's president and went on to establish The Feminists, a radical feminist group.

29. Firestone, *The Dialectic of Sex*, 12.

30. Betty Friedan, *It Changed My Life: Writings on the Women's Movement* (New York: Random House, 1976), 153. Friedan was antagonistic to radical feminism from the beginning and rarely missed an opportuni-

ty to denounce the man-hating and sex warfare that she claimed it advocated. Her declamations against "sexual politics" began at least as early as January 1969.

31. Due to limitations of space and the focus of this essay, I do not discuss the many differences among woman's liberationists, most crucially the conflicts between "radical feminists" and "politicos" over the relationship between the women's liberation movement and the larger Movement and the role of capitalism in maintaining women's oppression. This is taken up at length in Alice Echols, *Daring to Be Bad: Radical Feminism in America, 1967–1975* (Minneapolis: University of Minnesota Press, 1989).

32. Firestone, *The Dialectic of Sex*, 1. It is the opening line of her book.

33. Adrienne Rich quoted from Hester Eisenstein, *Contemporary Feminist Thought* (Boston: G. K. Hall, 1983), 5.

34. Ellen Willis, "Sequel: Letter to a Critic," in *Notes from the Second Year*, edited by Firestone and Koedt, 57.

35. See Ann Snitow, "Gender Diary," *Dissent* (Spring 1989): 205–24; Carole Vance, "Social Construction Theory: Problems in the History of Sexuality," in *Homosexuality, Which Homosexuality?*, edited by Anja van Kooten Niekark and Theo van der Maer (Amsterdam: An Dekken/Schorer, 1989).

36. Ellen Willis discusses the centrality of abortion to the women's liberation movement in the foreword to *Daring to Be Bad*. For the young, mostly white middle-class women who were attracted to women's liberation, the issue was forced reproduction. But for women of color, the issue was as often forced sterilization, and women's liberationists would tackle that issue as well.

37. Stanley Aronowitz, "When the New Left Was New," in *The 60s Without Apology*, edited by Sohnya Sayres, Anders Stephanson, Stanley Aronowitz, and Fredric Jameson (Minneapolis: University of Minnesota Press, 1984), 32.

38. C. Wright Mills, quoted from Miller, *Democracy Is in the Streets*, 86.

39. The phrase is from SDS's founding statement, "The Port Huron Statement," which is reprinted in full as an appendix to Miller's book, *Democracy Is in the Streets*, 333. For instance, Irving Howe, an influential figure in the old left who attended a couple of SDS meetings, called

them "interminable and structureless sessions." Howe, "The Decade That Failed," *New York Times Magazine*, 19 September 1982: 78.

40. The statement appeared in a pamphlet produced by the Economic Research and Action Project of SDS. Miller quotes it in *Democracy Is in the Streets*, 215.

41. Gregory Calvert, "Participatory Democracy, Collective Leadership, and Political Responsibility," *New Left Notes* 2, 45 (December 18, 1967): 1.

42. See Breines's summary of prefigurative politics in Wini Breines, *Community and Organization in the New Left, 1962–1968* (New York: Praeger, 1982), 1–8.

43. Staughton Lynd, "The Movement: A New Beginning," *Liberation* 14, 2 (May 1969).

44. Pat Hansen and Ken McEldowney, "A Statement of Values," *New Left Notes* 1, 42 (November 1966): 5.

45. Tom Hayden, "Democracy Is . . . in the Streets," *Rat* 1, 15 (August 23–September 5, 1968): 5.

46. The Atlanta Project's position paper has been reprinted as "SNCC Speaks for Itself," in *The Sixties Papers: Documents of a Rebellious Decade*, edited by Judith Clavir Albert and Stewart Albert (New York: Praeger, 1984), 122. However, the title assigned it by the Alberts is misleading because at the time it was written in the spring of 1966, it did not reflect majority opinion in SNCC.

47. Rosalind Petchesky, *Abortion and Woman's Choice: The State, Sexuality, and Reproductive Freedom* (New York: Longman Press, 1984), 128.

48. Michelle Kort, "Sisterhood Is Profitable," *Mother Jones*, July 1983, 44.

49. Amiri Imanu Baraka, "A Black Value System," *The Black Scholar*, November 1969.

50. Jennifer Woodul, "What's This About Feminist Businesses?" *off our backs (oob)* 6, 4 (June 1976): 24–26.

51. Robin Morgan, "Rights of Passage," *Ms.*, September 1975, 99.

52. For a fascinating case study of this as it relates to women's music, see Arlene Stein, "Androgyny Goes Pop," *Out/Look* 3, 3 (Spring 1991): 26–33.

53. Kort, "Sisterhood Is Profitable," 44.

54. Stein, "Androgyny Goes Pop," 30.

55. Adrienne Rich, "Living the Revolution," *Women's Review of Books* 3, 12 (September 1986): 1, 3–4.

56. Quoted from Jane Mansbridge, *Why We Lost the ERA* (Chicago: University of Chicago Press, 1986), 266.

57. "Women's Liberation Testimony," *oob* 1, 5 (May 1970): 7.

58. Firestone, *The Dialectic of Sex*, 206.

59. Steve Halliwell, "Personal Liberation and Social Change," in *New Left Notes* (quotation); Rennie Davis and Staughton Lynd, "On NCNP," *New Left Notes* 2, 30 (September 4, 1967): 1.

60. See Charlotte Bunch, "The Reform Tool Kit," *Quest* 1, 1 (Summer 1974).

61. Frances Chapman, interview with author, New York City, May 30, 1984. Here Chapman was speaking of the radical feminist wing of the women's liberation movement, but it applies as well to women's liberation activists.

62. For more on the prefigurative, personal politics of the sixties, see Breines, *Community and Organization in the New Left*; Miller, *Democracy Is in the Streets*; and Aronowitz, "When the New Left Was New."

63. Quoted from Miller, *Democracy Is in the Streets*, 374.

64. Although individual social critics such as C. Wright Mills influenced the thinking of new leftists, the noncommunist left of the 1950s and early 1960s remained economistic and anticommunist. Indeed, the fact that the board of the League for Industrial Democracy—the parent organization of SDS in SDS's early years—ignored the values section of the Port Huron Statement suggests the disjuncture between the old leftists and the new. For another view, stressing the continuities between the old left and the new, see Maurice Isserman, *If I Had a Hammer . . .: The Death of the Old Left and the Birth of the New Left* (New York: Basic Books, 1987).

65. See Judith Newton, "Historicisms New and Old: 'Charles Dickens' Meets Marxism, Feminism, and West Coast Foucault," *Feminist Studies* 16, 3 (Fall 1990): 464. In their assumption that power has a source and that it emanates from patriarchy, women's liberationists part company with Foucauldian approaches that reject large-scale paradigms of domination.

66. Carmichael quoted from Clayborne Carson, *In Struggle: SNCC and the Black Awakening of the 1960s* (Cambridge, Mass.: Harvard University Press, 1981), 282.

67. Firestone and Koedt, "Editorial," in *Notes from the Second Year*, edited by Firestone and Koedt.

68. However, the reclamation of blackness was often articulated in a sexist fashion, as in Stokely Carmichael's 1968 declaration, "Every Negro is a potential black man." See Carmichael, "A Declaration of War," in *The New Left: A Documentary History*, edited by Teodori Massimo (Indianapolis: Bobbs-Merrill, 1969), 277.

69. Aronowitz, "When the New Left Was New," 18.

70. Richard Flacks, "Some Problems, Issues, Proposals," in *The New Radicals*, edited by Jacobs and Landau, 168. This was a working paper intended for the June 1965 convention of SDS.

71. Excerpts from Jerry Rubin's book, *Do It*, appeared in *Rat* 2, 26 (January 26–February 9, 1970).

72. "The Feminists: A Political Organization to Annihilate Sex Roles," in *Notes from the Second Year*, edited by Firestone and Koedt, 117.

73. Ehrenreich quoted from Carol Ann Douglas, "Second Sex 30 Years Later," *oob* 9, 11 (December 1979): 26.

74. The term *identity politics* was, I think, first used by black and Chicana feminists. See Diana Fuss, *Essentially Speaking: Feminism, Nature, and Difference* (New York: Routledge, 1989), 99.

75. Jeffrey Weeks locates the origins of identity politics in the post-1968 political flux. He argues that "identity politics can be seen as part of the unfinished business of the 1960s, challenging traditionalist hierarchies of power and the old, all-encompassing social and political identities associated, for example, with class and occupation." Perhaps Weeks situates this in the post-1968 period because class held greater significance for many British new leftists than it did for their American counterparts. Weeks, "Sexuality and (Post) Modernity" (unpublished paper).

76. Nancy Cott, *The Grounding of Modern Feminism* (New Haven: Yale University Press, 1987), 5.

77. Amy Kesselman, interview with author, New York City, May 2, 1984.

78. "The New York Consciousness Awakening Women's Liberation Group" (a handout from the Lake Villa Conference of November 1968).

79. Kathie Sarachild, "Consciousness-Raising: A Radical Weapon," in *Feminist Revolution*, edited by Redstockings (New Paltz, N.Y.: Redstockings, 1975), 132.

80. Betty Friedan, *It Changed My Life* (New York: Norton, 1985), 101.
81. Audre Lorde, *Zami: A New Spelling of My Name* (Freedom, Calif.: Crossing Press, 1982), 226.
82. Lorraine Kenney, "Traveling Theory: The Cultural Politics of Race and Representation: An Interview with Kobena Mercer," *Afterimage*, September 1990, 9.
83. Mercer makes this point as well in Kenney, "Traveling Theory," 9.

Chapter 5. The Dworkinization of Catharine MacKinnon

1. Catharine MacKinnon, "Feminism, Marxism, Method, and the State: An Agenda for Theory," *Signs* 7, 3 (Spring 1982).
2. Ibid., 541.
3. Catharine MacKinnon, *Only Words* (Cambridge, Mass.: Harvard University Press, 1993), 3.
4. Ibid., 113, fn. 1.
5. Martha Weinman Lear, "The Second Feminist Wave," *New York Times Magazine*, March 10, 1968.
6. Ti-Grace Atkinson, *Amazon Odyssey* (New York: Links, 1974), 103–4.
7. MacKinnon, *Only Words*, 533.
8. Ibid., 531.
9. Ibid., 316.
10. Catharine MacKinnon, *Feminism Unmodified: Discourses on Life and Law* (Cambridge, Mass.: Harvard University Press, 1987), 218.
11. Catharine MacKinnon, "Does Sexuality Have a History?" in Domna Stanton, ed., *Discourses of Sexuality: From Aristotle to AIDS* (Ann Arbor: University of Michigan Press, 1994).
12. Catharine MacKinnon, "The Male Ideology of Privacy: A Feminist Perspective on the Right to Abortion," in *Radical America* 17, 4 (July-August 1983): 30.
13. "Roundtable: Doubting Thomas," *Tikkun* 6, 5 (September-October 1991): 24.
14. MacKinnon, *Feminism Unmodified*, 219.
15. Ibid., 218.

16. Barbara Ehrenreich, "Life Without Father: Reconsidering Socialist-Feminist Theory," *Socialist Review* 73 (January–February 1984): 52.

17. MacKinnon, *Only Words*, 19.

18. Ibid., 21.

19. Ibid., 16. In this passage, MacKinnon's understanding of male sexuality seems to verge on biologistic. Yet, in contrast to many antiporn feminists, MacKinnon has always favored social constructionist explanations of gender and sexuality. For example, she has argued against difference feminism on the grounds that it enshrines as "women's values" those "differences that have been created in women under conditions of male domination." See the *Tikkun* roundtable, 29.

20. Ibid., 71–72.

21. Ibid., 108.

22. Ibid., 106.

23. Ibid., 107.

Chapter 6. "Totally Ready to Go": Shulamith Firestone and *The Dialectic of Sex*

1. Shulamith Firestone, *The Dialectic of Sex: The Case for Feminist Revolution* (New York: Quill, 1993), 45.

2. Unfortunately, it looks as though the book may be out of print, but used copies can be found.

3. Firestone, *Dialectic of Sex*, 19–20.

4. Ibid., 44, 188.

5. Ibid., 197–8.

6. Ann Snitow, "A Gender Diary," in Marianne Hirsch and Evelyn Fox Keller, eds., *Conflicts in Feminism* (New York: Routledge, 1990), 34.

7. Firestone, *Dialectic of Sex*, 89.

Chapter 7. The Taming of the Id: Feminist Sexual Politics, 1968–1983

Acknowledgments: Many people have made constructive criticisms of this piece. I would especially like to thank Kate Ellis, Constance Samaras, Sandra Silberstein, Bette Skandalis, Ann Snitow, Carole S. Vance, and Ellen Willis.

1. Bonnie Kreps "Radical Feminism 1," in Anne Koedt, Ellen Levine, and Anita Rapone, eds., *Radical Feminism* (New York: Times Books, 1973), 239; Janice Raymond, *The Transsexual Empire* (Boston: Beacon, 1979), 114.

2. Adrienne Rich, Susan Griffin, and Mary Daly are the best known proponents of this view. The belief that women's more extensive experience with nurturance inclines them toward peace and ecology is widespread among cultural feminists. See *off our backs (oob)*, January 1981, on the Women's Pentagon Action, and Ynestra King, "Feminism and the Revolt of Nature," *Heresies* #13, for an introduction to ecofeminism. For more sophisticated versions of this argument, see Jean Bethke Elshtain, "Women, War and Feminism," *The Nation*, June 14, 1980, and Sara Ruddick, "Maternal Thinking," *Feminist Studies* 6, 2 (Summer 1980).

3. The *reconstituted* Redstockings first termed this theoretical tendency "cultural feminism" in their 1975 publication *Feminist Revolution* (reissued by Random House in 1978). Although their critique did identify some of the problems with cultural feminism, it was seriously marred by paranoia and homophobia. More recently, Ellen Willis has analyzed cultural feminism especially as it informs the antipornography movement and ecofeminism. See her fine collection of essays, *Beginning to See the Light* (New York: Knopf, 1981) and "Betty Friedan's 'Second Stage': A Step Backward," *The Nation*, November 14, 1981. Major cultural feminist texts include: Adrienne Rich, *Of Woman Born* (New York: Norton, 1976); Mary Daly, *Gyn-Ecology* (Boston: Beacon, 1978); Raymond, *Transsexual Empire*; Kathleen Barry, *Female Sexual Slavery* (Englewood Cliffs, N.J.: Prentice Hall, 1979); Susan Griffin, *Woman and Nature: The Roaring Inside Her* (New York: Harper & Row, 1978). The now defunct Los Angeles-based magazine *Chrysalis* also served as a major outlet for cultural feminist work from its founding by Susan Rennie and Kirsten Grimstad in 1977. The best single radical feminist anthology is Koedt, Levine, Rapone, eds., *Radical Feminism*. Also see Shulamith Firestone, *The Dialectic of Sex* (New York: Morrow, 1970).

4. Ann Rosalind Jones, "Writing the Body: Toward an Understanding of *L'Ecriture Feminine*," *Feminist Studies* 7, 2 (Summer 1981): 255.

5. Raymond, *Transsexual Empire*, 114.

6. Anne Koedt, "Lesbianism and Feminism," in Koedt, Levine, Rapone, eds., *Radical Feminism*, 249.

7. Susan Brownmiller, *Against Our Will* (New York: Simon & Schuster, 1975), 16; Daly, *Gyn-Ecology*, 360. For an especially incisive analysis of Gilder, see Michael Walzer, "Gilderism," *New York Review of Books*, April 2, 1981: 3.

8. Mary Daly, quoted in *oob*, May 1979; Sally Gearhart, "The Future—If There Is One—Is Female," in Pam McAllister, ed., *Reweaving the Web* (Philadelphia: New Society, 1982), 271.

9. Firestone's *Dialectic of Sex* illustrates the problem with the radical feminist view of female biology.

10. Jane Alpert, "Mother-Right," *Ms.*, August 1973; and Rich, *Of Woman Born*, 39.

11. Gearhart, in McAllister, ed., *Reweaving the Web*, 271.

12. Robin Morgan, *Going Too Far* (New York: Random House, 1978), 164.

13. Daly, *Gyn-Ecology*, 12.

14. Ibid., 239.

15. Firestone, *Dialectic of Sex*, 12.

16. Personal communication from Ellen Willis, 1980. For the cultural feminist view of the left, see Kathy Barry, "Did I Ever Really Have A Chance? Patriarchal Judgement of Patricia Hearst," *Chrysalis I*, 1977; Morgan, *Going Too Far*; Rich, *Of Woman Born*, 285; Alpert, "Mother-Right,"; Kathleen Barry, " 'Sadomasochism': The New Blacklash to Feminism," *Trivia*, Fall 1982.

17. Barbara Deming, "To Fear Jane Alpert Is to Fear Ourselves," *oob*, May–June 1975.

18. Rennie and Grimstad of *Chrysalis* were instrumental in establishing the Circle of Support. It is worth noting that upon Alpert's surrender her lawyer stressed her "renunciation of radical activities and her conversion to the feminist movement." This prompted *oob* reporter Madeleine Janover to ask, "What does this mean for radical feminism?" See *oob*, December 1974: 5.

19. See Jennifer Woodul, "What's This About Feminist Businesses?" *oob*, June 1976.

20. It was this view which informed the ill-fated and short-lived Feminist Economic Network (FEN) founded in Detroit in 1975 and dissolved less than one year later. FEN was the brainchild of the Oakland Feminist Women's Health Center, the Detroit Feminist Federal Credit Union, and Diana Press. For detailed accounts see: Belita Cowan and Cheryl Peck, "The Controversy at FEN," *Her-Self*, May 1976; Jackie St. Joan, "Feminist Economic Seeds Split," in *Big Mama Rag* 4, 1; Martha Shelley, "What is FEN?" circulated by author; Janis Kelly et. al., "Money on the Line," in *oob*, March 1976; Alice Echols, "Cultural Feminism: Feminist Capitalism and the Anti-Pornography Movement," *Social Text*, 7 (Spring–Summer 1983). See Kathy Barry's apologia for FEN in *oob*, January 1977. This piece was originally submitted to the Bay Area feminist newspaper *Plexus*. However, Barry admitted to reporter Nancy Stockwell of *Plexus* that the article was a collaborative effort involving three of the major principals in FEN—Laura Brown, Joanne Parrent, and Barbara Hoke. Barry reasoned that an exoneration of FEN would be better received were it to "come from a community source" rather than from those responsible for its creation. *Plexus* refused to publish the article. See Shelley, "What is FEN?"

21. Barry (Brown, Parrent, Hoke),*oob* January 1977.

22. Barry, " 'Sadomasochism': The New Backlash to Feminism," *Trivia* 1 (Fall 1982): 83–84. Incredibly, Barry argues " 'lesbian sadomasochism' is the latest, and so far the most effective leftist strategy for isolating radical feminism, invalidating it, and attempting to annihilate it" (p. 89).

23. Their faith in women's moral superiority and commonality of interests allows them to assume that feminism can be reconciled with capitalism, sexual repression, and possibly biological determinism. Cultural feminism can easily degenerate into the view so cynically articulated by feminist entrepreneur Laura Brown that "feminism is anything we say it is." Quoted in Cowan and Peck, "Controversy at FEN."

24. Ti-Grace Atkinson, "Lesbianism and Feminism," *Amazon Odyssey* (New York: Links, 1974), 86.

25. Abby Rockefeller, "Sex: The Basis of Sexism," *No More Fun and Games: A Journal of Female Liberation* 6 (May 1973): 31.

26. Anne Koedt, "Lesbianism and Feminism," in Koedt, Levine, Rapone, eds., *Radical Feminism*, 250.

27. See "The Feminists: A Political Organization to Annihilate Sex Roles," in ibid., 374.

28. Rita Mae Brown, "The Shape of Things to Come," *Plain Brown Rapper* (Baltimore: Diana, 1976), 114. In a recent interview, Rita Mae Brown remarked, "Out of that outburst [of anger at homophobia within the women's movement] on my part developed the whole ideology of the lesbian as the ultimate feminist and superior human being which I would like to say, many years later, is pure horseshit." Chris Bearchell, "Interview with Rita Mae Brown," *The Body Politic* 95 (July–August 1983): 36.

29. See Brown, ibid.; Charlotte Bunch and Nancy Myron, eds., *Lesbianism and the Women's Movement* (Baltimore: Diana, 1975); Martha Shelley, "Notes of a Radical Lesbian," in Robin Morgan, ed., *Sisterhood Is Powerful*, (New York: Random House, 1970), 309.

30. Koedt, "Lesbianism and Feminism," 255.

31. Susan Chute, "Backroom with the Feminist Heroes: Conference for Women Against Pornography," *Sinister Wisdom*, Fall 1980, 2.

32. Firestone, *Dialectic of Sex*, 209.

33. Karen Lindsey, "Thoughts on Promiscuity," *The Second Wave* 1, 3 (1971): 3.

34. Muriel Dimen, "Variety is the Spice of Life," *Heresies* #12, (1981), 70.

35. Karen Durbin, "Can a Feminist Love the World's Greatest Rock and Roll Band?" *Ms.*, October 1974, 26.

36. Dana Densmore, "On Celibacy," Leslie Tanner, ed., *Voices from Women's Liberation* (New York: New American Library, 1970), 264. Although Atkinson's antisex perspective anticipated and contributed to the development of cultural feminism, she should be recognized for her incisive and prescient analysis of certain aspects of cultural feminism, or what she termed "female nationalism." See Judy Antonelli, "Atkinson Re-Evaluates Feminism," *oob* 5, 5 (May–June 1975): 19 for a regrettably hostile account of Atkinson's gloomy assessment of feminism.

37. Abby Rockefeller, "Sex: The Basis of Sexism," 25.

38. Roni and Vickie Leonard, "NOW Sexuality Conference," *oob* 4, 11 (November 1974): 3.

39. Deirdre English, Amber Hollibaugh, and Gayle Rubin, "Talking Sex: A Conversation on Sexuality and Feminism," *Socialist Review* 58 (July–August 1981): 44.

40. Andrea Dworkin, *Right-Wing Women* (New York: Perigree, 1983), 237.

41. This slogan originated with Robin Morgan's 1974 article, "Theory and Practice: Pornography and Rape," reprinted in *Going Too Far.*

42. The earliest discussion of "integrity" is probably in Janice Raymond, "The Illusion of Androgyny," *Quest* 2, 1 (Summer 1975). See Rich's critique of "male-identified" dualism in *Of Woman Born*, 56–83; Susan Griffin, *Pornography and Silence* (New York: Harper & Row, 1981). For a pithy critique of Griffin's analysis of dualism, see Robert Christgau's review in *Village Voice*, July 15, 1981: 26, 29).

43. Julia Penelope, "And Now For the Hard Questions," *Sinister Wisdom* (1980), 103. Cultural feminists use a double standard when analyzing fantasy—women's masochistic fantasies reflect their socialization, while men's sadistic fantasies reveal their fundamentally murderous nature. Interestingly, in *Homosexuality in Perspective* (Boston: Little, Brown, 1979) Masters and Johnson report that in their heterosexual sample men's second most frequently reported fantasy entailed forced sex. However, they reported fantasies of being forced to have sex slightly more frequently than fantasies of forcing another. See pp. 188–89.

44. Morgan, *Going Too Far*, 171.

45. Ibid., 181.

46. For the radical feminist view, see Firestone, *Dialectic of Sex.*

47. Andrea Dworkin, "Why So-Called Radical Men Love and Need Pornography," in Laura Lederer, ed., *Take Back the Night: Women on Pornography* (New York: William Morrow, 1980), 152.

48. Adrienne Rich, "Compulsory Heterosexuality and Lesbian Existence" in Catharine R. Stimpson and Ethel Spector Person, eds., *Women: Sex and Sexuality* (Chicago: University of Chicago Press, 1980), 73. Rich praises Catharine MacKinnon, author of *Sexual Harassment of Working Women*, for criticizing Susan Brownmiller's "unexamined premise that 'rape is violence, intercourse is sexuality,'" or, in other words, for differentiating between rape and intercourse.

49. The movement luminaries interviewed in the antipornography documentary *Not A Love Story* avoided their usual polemics against male

sexuality and heterosexuality and instead displayed a newly discovered concern for the ways in which pornography victimizes men. Of course, a humanist facade is not only more compatible with the movement's stated aim of eliminating pornography, but more likely to elicit support and sympathetic coverage. For a review of *Not a Love Story*, see B. Ruby Rich, "Anti-Porn: Soft Issue, Hard World," *Village Voice*, July 30, 1982.

50. Rich, "Compulsory Heterosexuality and Lesbian Existence," in Stimpson and Person, *Women: Sex and Sexuality*, 81.

51. Ethel Person, "Sexuality as the Mainstay of Identity: Psychoanalytic Perspectives," in ibid., 57.

52. See Larry Bush and Richard Goldstein, "The Anti-Gay Backlash," *Village Voice*, April 8, 1981; Deirdre English, "The War Against Choice," *Mother Jones*, February/March 1981.

53. Ann Snitow, "The Front-Line: Notes on Sex in Novels by Women, 1969–1979," in Stimpson and Person, *Women: Sex and Sexuality*, 165.

54. Rich, "Compulsory Heterosexuality and Lesbian Existence," in ibid., 79.

55. Raymond, *Transsexual Empire*, 104.

56. Raymond worries that male-to-female lesbian-feminist transsexuals might be used to transform "lesbian-feminist space [into a] harem." See ibid., 104–13. Daly is quoted on p. 104.

57. Dworkin, "Pornography and Grief," in Lederer, *Take Back the Night*, 289; Rich, "Compulsory Heterosexuality and Lesbian Existence," in Stimpson and Person, *Women: Sex and Sexuality*, 80; Jill Clark, "Interview with Robin Morgan," *Gay Community News*, January 20, 1979.

58. *Heresies* #12 (1981) published both the NOW resolution and two separate letters of protest, pp. 92–93; Scott Tucker, "The Counter-Revolution," *Gay Community News*, February 21, 1981.

59. Some gay men, like lesbian cultural feminists, are committed to maximizing gender differences—a course likely to have calamitous consequences for the already fractured "gay movement." For an introduction to this masculinist ethic, see John Preston, "Goodbye Sally Gearhart: Gay Men and Feminists Have Reached a Fork in the Road," *Christopher Street* 59; Eric Rofes, "The Revolution of the Clones / Talking with John Preston," *Gay Community News*, March 27, 1982: 8.

60. Rich, "Compulsory Heterosexuality and Lesbian Existence," in Stimpson and Person, *Women: Sex and Sexuality*, 81.

61. Daly, *Gyn-Ecology*, 373.

62. Quoted in Richard Goldstein, "I Left My Scalp in San Francisco," *Village Voice*, October 1, 1979.

63. Rich, "Compulsory Heterosexuality and Lesbian Existence," in Stimpson and Person, *Women: Sex and Sexuality*, 72.

64. Raymond, *The Transsexual Empire*, 113.

65. Quoted in Goldstein, "I Left My Scalp in San Francisco."

66. Brown, *Plain Brown Rapper*, 112.

67. Barry, " 'Sadomasochism': The New Backlash to Feminism," 82; Rich, "Compulsory Heterosexuality," 72; Penelope, "And Now for the Hard Questions," 103; Daly, *Gyn-Ecology*, 20.

68. Morgan, *Going Too Far*, 168.

69. See Ellen DuBois and Linda Gordon, "Seeking Ecstasy on the Battlefield: Danger and Pleasure in Nineteenth-Century Feminist Sexual Thought," in Carole Vance, ed., *Pleasure and Danger: Exploring Female Sexuality*, 31–49.

70. Barry, *Female Sexual Slavery*, 228.

71. Ibid., 211.

72. Person, in Stimpson and Person, *Women: Sex and Sexuality*, 50–51; Irene Diamond, "Pornography and Repression," in Lederer, *Take Back the Night*, 202; Florence Rush, *The Best Kept Secret* (Englewood Cliffs, N.J.: Prentice Hall, 1980), 190–91.

73. See Willis, *Beginning to See the Light* for a good analysis of the relationship between feminism and individualism.

74. Morgan, *Going Too Far*, 16.

75. Barry, *Female Sexual Slavery*, 227.

76. Diana Russell and Laura Lederer, "Questions We Get Asked Most Often," in Lederer, *Take Back the Night*, 29.

77. Willis, *Beginning to See the Light*, 225.

78. Judith Bat-Ada, "Playboy Isn't Playing," in Lederer, *Take Back the Night*, 132.

79. The parallel development within the left is the pro-family ideology promoted by cultural conservatives like Christopher Lasch, Michael Lerner, and Tom Hayden. See Michael Lerner, "Recapturing the Family Issue,"

The Nation, February 2, 1982, and Barbara Ehrenreich's response, "Family Feud on the Left," *The Nation*, March 13, 1982.

80. Barry, *Female Sexual Slavery*, 103. For an elaboration of this point, see Paula Webster, "Pornography and Pleasure," *Heresies* #12 (1981): 50.

81. See Carole S. Vance, conference concept paper, "Towards a Politics of Sexuality," in Vance, ed., *Pleasure and Danger*, 443–46.

82. For a discussion of cultural feminism's idealization of the mother-daughter bond, see Echols, "Cultural Feminism: Feminist Capitalism and the Anti-Pornography Movement," 39. For another view of the mother-daughter problematic, see Susan Contratto and Nancy Chodorow, "The Fantasy of the Perfect Mother," in Barrie Thorne, ed., *Rethinking the Family: Some Feminist Questions* (New York: Longman, 1982).

83. Some s/m lesbian-feminists suggest that s/m sex is more egalitarian and less solipsistic than "vanilla" sex. Like lesbian chauvinism of the early 1970s, s/m chauvinism is an understandable response to the near-unanimous vilification of s/m within the feminist community. Fortunately, it is hard to imagine that s/m will be venerated as *the* feminist sexuality, because, unlike lesbianism, it so fundamentally contradicts movement orthodoxy. However, the distinction between personal preference and prescriptivism is often confounded in a movement such as ours which requires that we justify our sexual impulses in political terms and which encourages us to generalize and theorize from our own experience. For example, at a recent Boston forum on s/m a woman in the audience—not a practitioner of s/m—suggested that "s/m may be the *only* way to lessen power imbalances that are rooted in our culture." (reporter's italics). Jil Clark, "Lesbian S/M Forum," *Gay Community News* 10, 50 (July 9, 1983): 6. By contrast, Pat Califia maintains that s/m is neither intrinsically feminist nor antifeminist. See Pat Califia, "The Advisor," *Advocate* 375 (October 13, 1983): 38.

Chapter 8. Queer Like Us?

Acknowledgments: Lois Banner, Jennifer Terry, Alice Wexler, and Gilda Zwerman helped me sharpen the arguments in this chapter.

1. Jonathan Ned Katz, *Gay American History: Lesbians and Gay Men in the U.S.A.* (New York: Avon Books, 1976).

2. Carroll Smith-Rosenberg, "The Female World of Love and Ritual: Relations Between Women in Nineteenth-Century America," *Signs* 1, 1 (Autumn 1975).

3. Ibid., 8. Christine Stansell, "Revisiting the Angel in the House: Revisions of Victorian Womanhood," *New England Quarterly* (September 1987): 471.

4. Smith-Rosenberg, "The Female World": 9.

5. My first substantial paper as a graduate student was a critique of Smith-Rosenberg's essay. My adviser encouraged me to submit it to *The Radical History Review*. After months of silence—my essay provoked intense debate, I was told—the *RHR* collective offered to publish an "*extremely* condensed" and substantially revised version, a "research note." I had known that my essay suffered from a reliance on secondary sources and was highly speculative, so I wasn't surprised by the response. However, I was taken aback by the readers' reports, one of which claimed that my paper read as though it were written by someone who was both "antifeminist" and "antilesbian." As corrective medicine, the reviewer prescribed Blanche Wiesen Cook's "Female Support Networks and Political Activism: Lillian Wald, Crystal Eastman, and Emma Goldman" in *Chrysalis* 3 (Autumn 1977). I did revise the paper, but I did not resubmit it to *RHR*. It was published subsequently as "The Demise of Female Intimacy in the Twentieth Century," *Michigan Occasional Papers in Women's Studies* 6 (Fall 1978).

6. Blanche Wiesen Cook, "The Historical Denial of Lesbianism," *Radical History Review* 20 (Spring/Summer 1979): 64.

7. Ibid.

8. Ibid.

9. Adrienne Rich, "Compulsory Heterosexuality and Lesbian Existence," in Catherine R. Stimpson and Ethel Spector Person, eds., *Women: Sex and Sexuality* (Chicago: University of Chicago Press, 1980), 89.

10. Lillian Faderman, *Surpassing the Love of Men* (New York: Morrow, 1981), 20. Faderman did modify her argument somewhat in *Odd Girls and Twilight Lovers: A History of Lesbian Life in Twentieth Century America* (New York: Penguin, 1992).

11. Leila Rupp paved the way for a more nuanced approach in the early '80s with her gentle rebuke to Blanche Cook and Adrienne Rich. Rupp warned historians against using expansive definitions of lesbianism that deny the reality of women's historical experience. Rupp argued that historians should "distinguish between women who identify as lesbians and/or are part of a lesbian culture, where one exists, and a broader category of women-committed women who would not identify as lesbians but whose primary commitment, in emotional and practical terms, was to other women." See Leila Rupp, " 'Imagine My Surprise': Women's Relationships in Mid-Twentieth Century America," *Frontiers, A Journal of Women's Studies* 5, 3 (Fall 1980). It was reprinted in Martin Duberman, Martha Vicinus, and George Chauncey, Jr., eds., *Hidden from History: Reclaiming the Gay and Lesbian Past* (New York: New American Library, 1989), where the quote mentioned above appears on p. 408.

12. Another reason that feminists were better able to address butch-femme was that at about the same time feminists of color such as Audre Lorde, Cherrie Moraga, and Baraba Smith were challenging feminists to deal with differences between women, rather than generalize from the experiences of white middle-class women.

13. Madeline Davis and Elizabeth Kennedy, "Oral History and the Study of Sexuality in the Lesbian Community: Buffalo, New York, 1940–1960," *Feminist Studies* 12, 1 (Spring 1986).

14. Esther Newton, "The Mythic Mannish Lesbian: Radclyffe Hall and the New Woman," *Signs* 9, 4 (Summer 1984).

15. Jennifer Terry, "Theorizing Deviant Historiography," *differences* 3 (Summer 1991).

16. George Chauncey, "Christian Brotherhood or Sexual Perversion? Homosexual Identities and the Construction of Sexual Boundaries in the World War I Era," *Journal of Social History* 19 (1985).

17. Lisa Duggan, "The Trials of Alice Mitchell: Sensationalism, Sexology, and the Lesbian Subject in Turn-of-the-Century America," *Signs* 18, 4 (Summer 1991): 793.

18. George Chauncey, *Gay New York* (New York: Basic Books, 1994); Elizabeth Kennedy and Madeline Davis, *Boots of Leather, Slippers of Gold* (New York: Routledge, 1993).

19. C. Vann Woodward, *The Strange Career of Jim Crow*, rev. ed. (New York: Oxford University Press, 1966), 65.

20. Ibid., 44 and 34.

21. I characterize it as largely defunct because Tomás Almaguer has shown that the active-passive model still exists among Chicano men. See "Chicano Men: A Cartography of Homosexual Identity and Behavior," in *differences* 3 (Summer 1991).

22. In making the case for tolerance, Chauncey does rely quite a bit on the testimony of middle-class men who fetishized working-class men, possibly not the most reliable sources.

23. See Lizabeth Cohen's review of Chauncey's book in *The Journal of American History* 83, 2 (September 1997): 685–87.

24. Kennedy and Davis, *Boots of Leather, Slippers of Gold*, 23.

25. Ibid., 370. For another discussion of butch, see Leslie Feinberg's novel *Stone Butch Blues* (Ithaca, N.Y.: Firebird Press, 1993).

26. Ibid., 322.

27. Ibid., 226.

28. Kennedy and Davis do make an effort to compare the experiences of lesbians and gay men and conclude that lesbians, like gay men, were "explicitly interested in exploring sexuality." However, gay men "have institutionalized enjoying sex for sex's sake, while lesbians have not." They also note that gay men have a "highly developed tradition of camp, whereas lesbians don't." See Kennedy and Davis, 382–83.

29. Chauncey, *Gay New York*, 27.

30. Adrienne Rich, "Compulsory Heterosexuality," 80.

31. Martin Duberman, et. al., *Hidden from History*, 6. In the eighties, gay and lesbian historians found themselves embroiled in what rapidly became a very tiresome debate about the relative merits of social construction theory, which holds that sexuality is historically and socially constructed, versus essentialism, which views sexuality as an intrinsic and essential quality that exists outside of culture and history. What made this a peculiar debate was that virtually all gay and lesbian historians identified themselves as social constructionists. Even Yale historian John Boswell, whose 1980 book *Christianity, Social Tolerance, and Homosexuality* was criticized as essentialist, identified with social constructionism. It was the larger culture (and often our students) that

defended essentialism. With the ascension inside the academy of queer theory, which proposes a radically denaturalized vision of sexuality, this debate has largely fizzled out, though many gay students and activists continue to favor essentialist, even biological, understandings of homosexuality. This anthology features Boswell's essentialist argument and David Halperin's critique.

32. Martin Duberman, *Stonewall* (New York: Dutton, 1993) and Esther Newton, *Cherry Grove, Fire Island* (Boston: Beacon, 1993).

33. Duberman, *Stonewall*, xv.

34. Esther Newton, *Cherry Grove, Fire Island*, 85.

35. Esther Newton explores the way that drag queens bear the stigmata of homosexuality in *Mother Camp: Female Impersonation in America* (Chicago: University of Chicago Press, 1979), 103–5.

36. Chauncey, *Gay New York*, 17.

37. See, for example, Alice Echols, *Scars of Sweet Paradise: The Life and Times of Janis Joplin* (New York: Metropolitan Books, 1999). I also presented a paper, "Thousands of Cats and Hundreds of Chicks," about Joplin's sexuality at a Fall 1995 conference sponsored by CLAGS, the Center for Lesbian and Gay Studies at City University of New York. It appears in this volume as "Thousands of Guys and a Few Hundred Women."

38. For an interesting critique of lesbian-feminism's requirement of exclusive lesbianism, see Jan Clausen, "My Interesting Condition," *Out/Look*, Winter 1990: 13.

39. At the time that these books appeared, queer theory was still pretty much confined to literature departments. However, the dissatisfaction with identity politics and cautious middle-of-the-road activism that fueled queer theory and its activist cousin, the flash-in-the-pan Queer Nation, were widely felt, I think, especially inside the academy.

40. Michael Warner, ed., *Fear of a Queer Planet: Queer Politics and Social Theory* (Minneapolis: University of Minnesota Press, 1993), xxvi.

41. Foucault quoted in Germaine Greer, *The Whole Woman* (New York: Knopf, 1999), 250. For other examples of queer theory's anti-identitarian stance see Warner, ibid., and Caleb Crain, "Pleasure Principles," in *Lingua Franca*, October 1997: 31.

42. Kennedy has criticized their approach in her insightful essay, "Telling

Tales: Oral History and the Construction of Pre-Stonewall Lesbian Identity," in *Radical History Review* 62 (Spring 1995): 74.

43. Warner, *Fear of a Queer Planet*, xxv.

44. Warner, quoted in Crain, "Pleasure Principles," 31.

45. Chauncey, *Gay New York*, 6–7.

46. Donna Penn raises this concern, too, in "Queer: Theorizing Politics and History," in *Radical History Review* 62 (Spring 1995): 33.

47. For tomboyish girls—and, of course, not all tomboys grow up to be lesbians—alienation may occur later in adolescence.

48. In certain ways, Gayle Rubin's wonderfully provocative essay "Thinking Sex: Notes for a Radical Theory of the Politics of Sexuality" prefigured queer theory's privileging of perversion. Rubin's essay appeared in Carole Vance, ed., *Pleasure and Danger: The Politics of Sexuality* (Boston: Routledge and Kegan Paul, 1984), 267–319.

49. Martha Umphrey, "The Trouble with Harry Thaw," in *Radical History Review* 62 (Spring 1995): 19.

50. A number of lesbian scholars have argued that queer is as universalizing a discourse as the older formulation "lesbian and gay." See Sue-Ellen Case, "The Apparitional Community," in *American Quarterly* 48, 1 (March 1996): 163; Teresa de Lauretis, "Film and the Invisible," in Bad-Object Choices, eds., *How Do I Look: Queer Film and Video* (Seattle: Bay Press, 1991); Donna Penn, "Queer: Theorizing Politics and History," 39.

51. Umphrey, "The Trouble with Harry Thaw," 20.

52. Penn raises this as well in "Queer: Theorizing Politics and History."

53. Eve Kosovsky Sedgwick, *Between Men: English Literature and Male Homosexual Desire* (New York: Columbia University Press, 1985), 2. This is admittedly an older book, but she has yet to focus on lesbian desire.

54. Teresa de Lauretis, "Film and the Invisible," 273.

55. Penn, "Queer: Theorizing Politics and History," 39. At a CLAGS Conference in 1995 Kennedy was criticized for having not considered that the butches in *Boots of Leather* were really transgendered. Being butch apparently wasn't queer enough for her critic.

56. Crain, "Pleasure Principles," 28.

57. My account is drawn from ibid., 33.

Chapter 9. "Thousands of Men and a Few Hundred Women": Janis Joplin, Sexual Ambiguity, and Bohemia

1. Author's interview with Richard Hundgen.

2. Ellis Amburn, *Pearl: The Obsessions and Passions of Janis Joplin* (New York: Warner, 1992), 104.

3. John Gill, *Queer Noises* (Minneapolis: University of Minnesota Press, 1995), 96.

4. Peggy Caserta (as told to Dan Knapp), *Going Down with Janis* (Secaucus: Lyle Stuart, 1973), 7.

5. Jill Johnston's 1971 *Village Voice* column was reprinted in her wonderfully mischievous brief for lesbianism, *Lesbian Nation* (New York: Simon & Schuster, 1973), 231. Her claim was then reported in "Random Notes," *Rolling Stone*'s gossip column, on January 20, 1972. However, Johnston's allegation received very little play in the press.

6. Marjorie Garber, *Vice Versa: Bisexuality and the Eroticism of Everyday Life* (New York: Simon & Schuster, 1995), 142.

7. The only time I ever saw Joplin make a move that might be interpreted as less than heterosexual was during a concert in Germany when she brought a woman up onstage to dance. However, she immediately brought other audience members up onstage, too. See the video *Janis: The Way She Was*.

8. "Melissa Etheridge on Janis Joplin," *Rolling Stone*, February 23, 1995: 50.

9. Charles Perry, *The Haight-Ashbury: A History* (Random House, 1984), 82; interview with Peter Berg.

10. Author's interview with Dave Getz, June 23, 1995.

11. Author's interview with Peggy Caserta, February 13, 1997.

12. Author's interview with Diane Di Prima.

13. Maria Damon, "Victors of Catastrophe: Beat Occlusions," in Lisa Phillips, ed., *Beat Culture and the New America, 1950–1965* (New York: Whitney Museum of Art, 1996), 144.

14. Carl Solomon, *Emergency Messages: An Autobiographical Miscellany* (New York: Paragon, 1989), 13.

15. I use the terms Beat and beatnik somewhat interchangeably because Joplin and her friends appear not to have made a distinction.

16. Author's interview with Linda Gottfried Waldron.

17. Myra Friedman, *Buried Alive: The Biography of Janis Joplin* (New York: Harmony, 1992), xxiv.

18. Edmund White, "Gender Uncertainties," *New Yorker*, July 17, 1995, 81. One might also explore the effects of gay liberation on transvestites like Sylvia Rivera, who was one of the drag queens who started the ruckus at the Stonewall Inn that June night in 1969. To gay activists, Rivera and other drag queens often seemed a throwback to an earlier model of male homosexuality, one rooted in effeminacy, and as a result Rivera and other transvestites were sometimes shunned by the fledgling gay movement.

19. Gore Vidal put forward this view, and though he wasn't a Beat, his position shares quite a lot with the beatnik skepticism of sexual labeling. See Henry Abelove, "The Queering of Lesbian/Gay History," in *Radical History Review* 62 (Spring 1995): 56, fn. 11.

20. Foucault quoted in Germaine Greer, *The Whole Woman* (New York: Knopf, 1999), 250.

21. Martin Duberman, *Stonewall* (New York: Dutton, 1993), 209.

Chapter 10. Gender Disobedience, Academia, and Popular Culture

1. Esther Newton, *Mother Camp: Female Impersonators in America* (Chicago: University of Chicago Press, rev. ed., 1979).

2. Janice Raymond, *The Transsexual Empire: The Making of the She-Male* (Boston: Beacon, 1979).

3. Judith Butler, *Gender Trouble: Feminism and the Subversion of Identity* (New York: Routledge, 1990).

4. "The Body You Want: Liz Kotz Interviews Judith Butler," *Artforum*, September 1992: 84.

5. Sandy Stone, "The Empire Strikes Back: A Posttranssexual Manifesto," in *Body Guards: The Cultural Politics of Gender Ambiguity* (New York: Routledge, 1991).

6. Kate Bornstein, *Gender Outlaw: On Men, Women and the Rest of Us* (New York: Routledge, 1994).

7. Marjorie Garber, *Vested Interests: Cross-Dressing and Cultural Anxiety* (New York: HarperCollins, 1993).

8.   Charles Murray and Richard Herrnstein, *The Bell Curve: Intelligence and Class Structure in American Life* (New York: Free Press, 1996).

Chapter 11. "Shaky Ground": Popular Music in the Disco Years

1.   Bill Graham and Robert Greenfield, *Bill Graham Presents: My Life Inside Rock and Out* (New York: Doubleday, 1992), 287.
2.   Along with the originator of funk, James Brown, Sly moved R&B into funk, the percussive, polyrhythmic dance music that '80s and '90s rappers have so relentlessly plundered. But Brown went deep—"knee deep"—into the groove, while Sly's funk was more hook-driven and experimental, with its psychedelic guitars and freaky horns.
3.   Ed Ward, Geoffrey Stokes, Ken Tucker, *Rock of Ages: The Rolling Stone History of Rock & Roll* (New York: Rolling Stone Press, 1986), 427. In writing about Sly Stone, I have also relied upon Greil Marcus's wonderful essay about his music in *Mystery Train: Images of America in Rock 'n' Roll Music*, rev. ed. (New York: Dutton, 1982).
4.   Sixties soul artists generally didn't record songs that were openly political.
5.   Ward, Stokes, Tucker, eds., *Rock of Ages*, 534. Shortly before he died, Hendrix, who in 1967 had bragged that he wasn't "going in for any of this 'Midnight Hour' kick," was even toying with the idea of forming an R&B band. Harry Shapiro and Caesar Glebeek, *Jimi Hendrix Electric Gypsy* (New York: St. Martin's Press, 1990), 156. Hendrix's interest in forming an R&B group can be found in Charles Shaar Murray's brilliant book, *Crosstown Traffic: Jimi Hendrix and the Post-War Rock 'n' Roll Revolution* (New York: St. Martin's Press, 1989), 180.
6.   According to Steve Perry, from 1955 to 1958 "the roster of rock 'n' roll'ers was more racially equal than at any time before or since. See Perry, "Ain't No Mountain High Enough: The Politics of Crossover," in Simon Frith, ed., *Facing the Music* (New York: Pantheon, 1988), 67. George Lipsitz contends that the percentage of best-selling records by black artists increased from 3 in 1954 to 29 in 1957. After 1959, the percentage by black artists declined every year. See Lipsitz, *Time Passages* (Minneapolis: University of Minnesota Press, 1990), 126.

7.   One Stones fan, angry about rock journalist Ken Tucker's criticisms of the crowd, wrote the critic an anonymous letter that read, "Us W.A.S.P. rock 'n' rollers pay to see white performers and not niggers, faggots, or tawdry critics like yourself." Quoted in Greil Marcus, *Ranters and Crowd Pleasers: Punk in Pop Music, 1977–1992* (New York: Doubleday), 206. In hiring black musicians to open for them the Stones were paying homage to the R&B and blues musicians who had so inspired them.

8.   My account of the disco wars draws on a number of articles. I am especially indebted to two brilliant essays: Andrew Kopkind, "The Dialectics of Disco," *Village Voice*, August 12, 1979 and Tom Smucker, "Disco," in Jim Miller, ed., *The Rolling Stone Illustrated History of Rock & Roll*, rev. ed. (New York: Random House, 1980). Also very useful are: Walter Hughes, "Feeling Mighty Real: Disco as Discourse and Discipline," *Village Voice Rock & Roll Quarterly*, Summer 1993; Frank Rose, "Discophobia," *Village Voice*, November 12, 1979; Jefferson Morley, "Three Cheers for Disco," *The Reader: Los Angeles's Free Weekly*, February 3, 1989; Peter Braunstein, "The Last Days of Gay Disco," *Village Voice*, June 30, 1998; Carolyn Krasnow, "Fear and Loathing in the '70s: Race, Sexuality, and Disco" in *Stanford Humanities Review* 3, 2: 37–45.

9.   Smucker, "Disco," 427. Jackson's *Thriller* was released in 1983.

10.   Mikal Gilmore, "Disco!" *Rolling Stone*, April 19, 1979: 54.

11.   Stephen Holden, "The Evolution of a Dance Craze," *Rolling Stone*, April 19, 1979: 30.

12.   Andrew Kopkind, "Dialectics of Disco," 11.

13.   Jon Pareles, "Disco Lives! Actually It Never Died, *New York Times*, October 17, 1999, section 2: 40.

14.   Bob Cannon, "Disco's 'Fever' Pitch," *Entertainment Weekly*, January 22, 1993.

15.   The *Rolling Stone* Interview with Madonna, *Rolling Stone*, September 10, 1987: 88.

16.   John Payne, "His Way," *L.A. Weekly*, August 8–14, 1997: 44.

17.   Jon Pareles, "Disco Lives!" 1. Pareles wrote this piece because the staged version of *Saturday Night Fever* was opening on Broadway.

18.   Rob Kenner, "That Ol' Black Magic," *Vibe*, September 1999: 188.

19.   Nelson George, *The Death of Rhythm and Blues* (New York: Plume, 1989), 181.

20. Lester Bangs, *Psychotic Reactions and Carburetor Dung* (New York: Knopf, 1981), 277.

21. Robert Draper, *Rolling Stone Magazine: The Uncensored History* (New York: Doubleday, 1990), 270.

22. Morley, "Three Cheers for Disco," 7.

23. Peter Herbst, quoted in Draper, 270.

24. Some writers differentiate between R&B and soul music, but I use the terms interchangeably in this essay.

25. The Editors of Rolling Stone, *The Rolling Stone Interviews: The 1980s* (New York: St. Martin's Press/Rolling Stone Press, 1989), 348.

26. Ward, Stokes, Tucker, eds., *Rock of Ages*, 378.

27. KMPX included in its public service announcements meetings of SNCC and the Black Panthers' breakfast program. White support for the Panthers was such that even Bill Graham reluctantly held benefits for them.

28. It's no accident that the ballrooms featured the same musicians that free-form radio played. Graham's booking practices at the Fillmore had been the model for KMPX's eclectic programming.

29. Ward, Stokes, Tucker, eds., *Rock of Ages*, 484.

30. Marcus, *Ranters and Crowd Pleasers*, 202.

31. As Ed Ward writes, "Funkadelic finds itself a rock band with no rock audience to speak of." See Ward, "The U.S. Funk Mob: 'We Can Be As Bad As We Need To Be,'" *Village Voice*, July 25, 1977: 39.

32. Letter to the Editor, *Rolling Stone*, May 9, 1974: 16.

33. There are important exceptions, including Dave Marsh, Robert Christgau, Greil Marcus, Tom Smucker, Russell Gersten, and Vince Aletti.

34. David Morse quoted in Iian Chambers, *Urban Rhythms* (New York: Macmillan, 1985), 117.

35. Gleason quoted in Murray, *Crosstown Traffic*, 79.

36. Jon Landau, who went on to become Bruce Springsteen's manager, was by far the worst in this regard.

37. Although Motown was taken to task for sounding too "white" and Stax celebrated for its "blackness," the musicians, songwriters, and producers at Motown were almost uniformly black whereas the creative nucleus at Stax was integrated. Steve Perry writes perceptively about

the racial politics of popular music—and Stax's interracialism—in his "Ain't No Mountain High Enough" in Frith, *Facing the Music*, 51–87.

38. Simon Frith, *Sound Effects* (New York: Pantheon, 1981), 22; Jon Landau, "Rock 1970," *Rolling Stone*, December 2, 1970: 43.

39. "Soul '67," *Rolling Stone*, February 24, 1968: 18. Writers like Landau didn't share Ralph Gleason's enthusiasm for acid rock, but they often did share his disdain for black music's commercialism.

40. Jon Landau, "Otis Redding," in Miller, ed., *Rolling Stone Illustrated History*, 212.

41. Ibid., 210.

42. Norman Mailer's 1957 essay "The White Negro" is reprinted in Judith and Stewart Albert, *The Sixties Papers* (New York: Praeger, 1984), 97.

43. Arnold Shaw, *Honkers and Shouters: The Golden Years of Rhythm and Blues* (New York: Macmillan, 1978), 524. See also James Miller, *Flowers in the Dustbin: The Rise of Rock 'n' Roll, 1947–1977* (New York: Simon & Schuster, 1999), 47–52. Miller calls Atlantic Records' R&B "white Negro music," though he doesn't use the term disparagingly. However, it's not clear from Miller's narrative if Ahmet Ertegun, the founder of the company, was consciously gearing the music toward young white listeners. On the one hand, Miller quotes Ertegun claiming that he tried to get Ruth Brown, who went on to become Atlantic's first big star, to sing more like a "real" Negro and less like Doris Day. On the other hand, he also says that he and his partners "discovered that white kids started buying these records because the real blues were too hard for them to swallow." What is clear from Ertegun's comments is that Atlantic was aware of its white fans and that the company did walk a tightrope of sorts as it tried to appeal to both black and white listeners.

44. Gerald Early, "One Nation Under a Groove," *The New Republic*, July 15 & 22, 1991: 38. However, as Suzanne Smith points out, Gordy also established a distinct label, the Soul label, for music like Junior Walker and the All-Stars' "Shotgun," that was more geared to the black market. As Smith points out, "Shotgun's" success on the pop charts revealed how "dubious these racial music categories were." See Smith, *Dancing in the Street* (Cambridge, Mass.: Harvard University Press, 1999), 164.

45. Peter Guralnick, *Sweet Soul Music, Rhythm and Blues and the Southern Dream of Freedom* (New York: Harper and Row, 1986), 250.

46. There were, however, some people at Stax, like producer/songwriter Isaac Hayes, who thought Motown's music was whiter. Hayes objected to Motown's enormous whomp of a backbeat, which had once prompted Beatle John Lennon to ask one of the Four Tops if their drummer beat on a "bloody tree" to "get that backbeat." Hayes said, "Now it was the standard joke with blacks, that whites could *not*, cannot clap on a backbeat. You know—ain't got the rhythm? What Motown did was very smart. They beat the kids over the head with it. That wasn't soulful to us down at Stax, but baby, it *sold*." Gerri Hirshey, *Nowhere to Run: The Story of Soul Music* (New York: Penguin, 1985), 184.

47. Ertegun quoted in Miller, ed., *Rolling Stone Illustrated History*, 50, 52.

48. Ed Ward, "In the Beginning of the Blues, There Was a Violin," *New York Times*, October 17, 1999, section 2: 37.

49. Stanley Crouch, *Notes of a Hanging Judge: Essays and Reviews, 1979–1989*, (New York: Oxford, 1990), 101.

50. Francis Davis, *The History of the Blues* (New York: Hyperion, 1995), 69.

51. Ibid, 68.

52. Sam Cooke's record producers tell of the time they asked Cooke to do another take of a song in which he'd sung "ax" rather than "ask." On the fourth take he complied, but not before he laughed and said, "Hey, man, you're taking my heritage." Hirshey, *Nowhere to Run*, 111.

53. For example, when the Supremes met the Beatles, the Brits iced them out. Mary Wilson says they were dismayed because they'd shown up "perfectly poised," in "elegant" day dresses and fur coats. Years later, George Harrison revealed to Wilson the reason for their coolness. "We expected soulful, hip girls. We couldn't believe that three black girls from Detroit could be that square!" Ibid., 178.

54. See Murray, *Crosstown Traffic*, 90. Wonder's version of the Dylan song went to #1 on the R&B charts and #9 on the pop charts.

55. Hirshey, *Nowhere to Run*, 171.

56. Ellison quoted in Perry, "Ain't No Mountain High Enough," 86. Ellison was criticizing black nationalists, and in particular Leroi Jones, but the same assumptions held sway among any number of white rock critics.

57. Mary Wilson recalls the time one British critic scolded the Supremes, "Get back to church, baby!": Mary Wilson, *Dreamgirl: My Life as a Supreme* (New York: St. Martin's Press, 1986), 210–11. Martha Reeves of Martha and the Vandellas was an exception; she sang in her father's church, but she also trained in classical music at her high school. The Detroit schools had an exceptionally strong music program. Gerald Early, "One Nation Under a Groove," 37.

58. Wilson, *Dreamgirl*, 211.

59. Ibid., 210–11.

60. O'Connell Driscoll, "Stevie Wonder in New York," in Jann Wenner, ed., *Twenty Years of Rolling Stone* (New York: Straight Arrow Press, 1987), 254.

61. Hirshey, *Nowhere to Run*, 334. Redding and Cropper knew what they needed to make a pop hit because the song that had helped Otis first cross over, 1965's "Loving You Too Long," was, in Cropper's words, "real slick R and B . . . real crafted stuff."

62. Russell Gersten, "Aretha Franklin," in Miller, ed, *Rolling Stone Illustrated History*, 252. For those unfamiliar with Aretha Franklin's career, it's important to know that her first label, Columbia Records, tried to make her over into a pop singer. Although she had several Top 10 R&B hits in the early sixties, her career didn't take off until she switched labels and began recording straight-ahead soul music on Atlantic Records.

63. Guralnick, *Sweet Soul Music*, 338. White R&B songwriter Jerry Leiber was blunter, blaming Aretha's new sound on her desire for "upward mobility."

64. Beginning in 1968, Gamble and Huff jump-started Butler's sagging career with a series of Top 20 hits and the aptly titled album, *The Ice Man Cometh*.

65. MFSB was an acronym for Mother, Father, Sister, Brother.

66. Like Motown's Berry Gordy, Kenneth Gamble and Leon Huff had no qualms about making crossover music, but Gamble was a black nationalist who tried to put a "message in the music," specifically that African Americans needed to build strong male-headed families. However, he never let his family values get in the way of selling records, preferring for the most part to limit his preaching to his

albums' liner notes. "Assimilation worked for a black nationalist capitalist who could write hit songs," was critic Nelson George's cynical
observation: *Death of Rhythm and Blues*, 146.

67. Hirshey, *Nowhere to Run*, 349–50.

68. Ibid., 351–52. Sam Cooke was the logical referent, a man who made
    music that crossed the color line, but who was no Uncle Tom. At a time
    when even most white musicians were routinely exploited by lousy
    contracts, Cooke was fully in control of his business, owning his own
    record label, music publishing, and management companies.

69. Monk quoted in Andrew Ross, *No Respect: Intellectuals and Popular Cul-
    ture* (New York: Routledge, 1989), 68.

70. "Lady Soul: Singing It Like It Is," *Time*, June 28, 1968: 62.

71. Frith, *Sound Effects*, 21.

72. Ibid., 22.

73. For some musicians the ability to make music that spoke to conditions
    in the black community or reflected racial pride was, of course, exhil-
    arating. You can hear it in Curtis Mayfield's "We're a Winner," James
    Brown's "Say It Loud, I'm Black and I'm Proud," Marvin Gaye's
    "What's Going On," Aretha's cover of Nina Simone's "Young, Gifted
    and Black," and Stevie Wonder's "Living for the City," to name a few.

74. R&B musicians had not been expected to be "political" in the halcyon
    years of the civil rights movement. Indeed, the strong-arming of artists
    was a sign of the black movement's growing wobbliness, not its strength.
    By the time the Black Panthers started leaning on Jimi Hendrix and Sly
    Stone, most of the group's leaders were either in jail or in exile.

75. Hirshey, *Nowhere to Run*, 191.

76. This was an especially vexed issue at Motown, which sold 70 percent of
    its records to whites. The company established a label that released
    some of Martin Luther King's speeches, but avoided cutting message
    music until 1970. However, Gordy and some of his stars appeared at
    Dr. King's funeral in 1968. And by mid-1969, the Supremes were be-
    ginning to "go black power," as *Rolling Stone* put it, by wearing
    "African" clothes. See *Rolling Stone*, June 4, 1969: 25. The report was
    sarcastic, calling the move "very daring stuff."

77. Brown's difficulty in penetrating the pop charts also reflected the in-
    creasingly funky groove music he was making.

78. Marcus, *Mystery Train*, 83. Both Greil Marcus's essay on Sly Stone in *Mystery Train* and Dave Marsh's article on early '70s R&B in his collected essays, *Fortunate Son* (New York: Random House, 1985) are excellent.

79. The Family Stone included two of Sly's siblings.

80. See Timothy Crouse, "The Struggle for Sly's Soul at the Garden," in Wenner, ed., *Twenty Years of Rolling Stone* (New York: Straight Arrow Publishers, 1987), 135–44. The interview was originally published in November 1971.

81. "Slit-eyed pessimism" was critic Ken Tucker's assessment. "Despairing, courageous, and very hard to take," wrote Robert Christgau. Greil Marcus found its unflinching exploration of "the state of the nation, Sly's career, his audience, black music, black politics and a white world" groundbreaking.

82. Critic Vince Aletti attributed *Riot*'s commercial success to its dance tracks, and Marsh agreed.

83. Marsh, *Fortunate Son*, 271.

84. Ward, Stokes and Tucker, *Rock of Ages*, 498. The writer is Tucker.

85. Sly's voice would be endlessly imitated by funk groups from the Gap Band to the Ohio Players.

86. In 1979, Epic Records disco-ized Sly's hits on the album *Ten Years Too Soon*, but it fell flat.

87. Marcus, *Mystery Train*, 95.

88. There was no comparable movement in white rock or pop, although there were isolated songs such as Don McLean's 1972 hit, "American Pie," which was ostensibly about the deaths of Buddy Holly, Richie Valens, the Big Bopper, and Janis Joplin but nonetheless captured some of the wistfulness felt by whites who'd had higher hopes for rock 'n' roll, the Movement, or themselves.

89. Marsh, *Fortunate Son*, 274.

90. Sly was rumored to have had an affair with Doris Day; he was friends with her son, Terry Melcher.

91. Marsh, *Fortunate Son*, 268.

92. Marcus, *Mystery Train*, 103.

93. Ibid., 107.

94. Ibid., 101.

95. In 1978, Nile Rodgers and Bernard Edwards, the cofounders of Chic,

wrote and produced the hit song "We Are Family" for Sister Sledge. He has spoken of this work as political in the documentary *Public Enemy*. Rodgers met Nelson Mandela years later at a dinner honoring the freed South African leader. According to Rodgers, Mandela told him that hearing "We Are Family," which apparently slipped past South African radio censors and was audible on a nearby radio, had helped him endure prison.

96. George, *Death of Rhythm and Blues*, 153.
97. Kopkind, "Dialectics of Disco," 13.
98. Paul Gilroy quoted in Robin Kelley, "Black Working-Class Opposition in the Jim Crow South," *The Journal of American History* 80, 1 (June 1993): 85.
99. Ironically, it was an electronics genius who worked for that bastion of family values Disneyland who put together the Ice Palace by taking "old stereo systems, and light bulbs and Christmas lights" so that for the first time the "music went with the lights." See Esther Newton, *Cherry Grove, Fire Island* (Boston: Beacon, 1993), 244.
100. Kopkind, "Dialectics of Disco," 11.
101. Richard Goldstein, Big Science," in Larry Gross and James D. Woods, eds., *The Columbia Reader on Lesbians and Gay Men in Media, Society, and Politics* (New York: Columbia University Press, 1999), 414.
102. Quoted in Kopkind, "Dialectics of Disco," 13. Women were not altogether outside of rock culture, of course. Lots of women loved rock 'n' roll, but they tended to be less narrow-minded than men, for whom rock could become a kind of fetish. Some women might also have been more open to disco because it encouraged greater contact with one's dance partner than did dancing to rock, which, as this speaker suggests, could become an exercise in solipsism.
103. Chambers, *Urban Rhythms*, 188.
104. Houston Baker, "Hybridity, the Rap Race, and Pedagogy for the 1990s," in Andrew Ross and Constance Penley, eds., *Technoculture* (Minneapolis: University of Minnesota Press, 1991), 198.
105. Andrew Holleran, *Dancer from the Dance* (New York: Bantam, 1979), 32.
106. Aletti quoted by Frank Broughton and Bill Brewster, who wrote the liner notes for the *Larry Levan Live at the Paradise Garage* CD, released 2000.

107. Hughes, "Feeling Mighty Real."

108. Ibid.

109. When Nile Rodgers of the disco group Chic pointed out that rock 'n' roll had once been trashed as "repetitious," his words fell on deaf ears. Rodgers quoted in *Rolling Stone*, April 19, 1979: 32.

110. Smucker, "Disco," 433. Smucker was actually much more openminded about disco than this one comment would suggest.

111. Walter Hughes makes this point, too.

112. Frank Owen, "Spirituality Having Flown," review of *Larry Levan Live at the Paradise Garage*, *Village Voice*, September 12, 2000: 137.

113. Hughes, "Feeling Mighty Real," 10.

114. Certainly lots of heterosexual men embraced the beat, but enough didn't to make Sandra Bernhard's evocation of a straight man's initial reaction to a gay disco especially resonant. See her film *Without You, I'm Nothing*.

115. Ward, Stokes, and Tucker, eds., *Rock of Ages*, 524.

116. White quoted in Vince Aletti, "Lost in Music: The Dancing Machine: An Oral History," *Village Voice Rock & Roll Quarterly*, Summer 1993: 15.

117. Smucker, "Disco," 430.

118. Some rock critics looked to punk, which had appealed to the working class in Britain, as a subversive force in much the way that they believed sixties rock had been.

119. "A Lasting Impression: The *Rolling Stone* Interview with Curtis Mayfield," *Rolling Stone*, October 28, 1993: 66.

120. George, *Death of Rhythm and Blues*. In contrast to most rock critics, he liked early disco but believed that a whole host of people conspired to "defunk disco."

121. Ibid., 157–59.

122. He argued that they tried to "remove the modifying adjective 'black' from their lives." The music George deemed authentically "black" seemed to be music he happened to like. Thus, Michael Jackson's "Rock with You" has soul, according to the critic, but Stephanie Mills' "What You Gonna Do with My Loving?" is nothing more than "corporate black pop."

123. As evidence, George says that only one song that topped the black charts in 1983, Donna Summer's "She Works Hard for the Money,"

even made it into the pop Top 10. See ibid., 181. Yet according to the *Billboard* charts, a number of songs that topped the black charts, including Michael Jackson's "Billie Jean," Lionel Ritchie's "All Night Long (All Night)," and Marvin Gaye's "Sexual Healing" headed up the pop charts too.

124. Ward, Stokes, Tucker, eds., *Rock of Ages*, 594. This was originally reported in the December 1983 article in *Rolling Stone*. Prince's straight-ahead rock 'n' roll hit of 1982, "Little Red Corvette," was among the first videos by a black performer to land in MTV's rotation. By the time "Little Red Corvette" was released on *1999*, his fifth album, Prince was already a well established hitmaker. Jon Pareles and Patricia Romanowski, eds., *The Rolling Stone Encyclopedia of Rock & Roll* (New York: Rolling Stone Press, 1983), 444.

125. MTV's definition of rock was expansive enough to include white middle-aged comic Rodney Dangerfield's "Rappin' Rodney," but too narrow to accommodate Prince, or virtually any other black artist. Dance music wasn't regularly programmed on the station until American bands like the Talking Heads and British bands, in particular, started experimenting with it. Just as '50s and early '60s blues and R&B acquired cachet in the States through British Invasion bands like the Rolling Stones, '80s dance music gained legitimacy in the U.S. by way of Britain, with groups like the Eurythmics and Culture Club with Boy George. There were three ways to guarantee inclusion in MTV's rotation: "no black faces, pretty women, and athletic guitar solos": Ed Steinberg of the video club Rock America, quoted in Linda Martin & Kerry Segrave *Anti-Rock: The Opposition to Rock 'n' Roll* (Hamden, Conn.: Archon Books, 1988), 279.

126. Dave Marsh, "Freddie's Dead and Diana Ross Is Singing the Blues," in Marsh, *Fortunate Son*, 191. Ken Tucker says that Columbia was "rumored" to have threatened MTV. See Ward, Stokes, Tucker, eds., *Rock of Ages*, 595.

127. Prince was not only racially and sexually ambiguous, he was also unabashedly sexual, in contrast to Jackson. "No black performer since Little Richard," wrote George, "had toyed with the heterosexual sensibilities of black America so brazenly" (174). George found Michael Jackson's case especially unsettling because this "alarmingly unblack,

unmasculine figure" was the most popular black man in America. Nor was Jackson the only black star whose masculinity seemed somehow thwarted or underdeveloped. Other than Bill Cosby, white America's favorite black male TV stars in the '80s were Emmanuel Lewis and Gary Coleman, who were literally growth-impaired. Clearly Michael Jackson's appeal to white Americans had something to do with the fact that for a time he seemed sexually innocent, even neutered.

128. George, *Death of Rhythm and Blues*, 192. See Ernest Hardy, "Home of the Brave: Alone Together with P. M. Dawn," *L.A. Weekly*, December 25–31, 1998: 35, for an analysis of the way that rapper Prince Be's blackness and sexuality were called into question by other rappers.

129. Interestingly, Houston Baker cites Johnnie Taylor's "Disco Lady" as one of the first singles to be marketed for a white audience. Yet the musicians backing Taylor on "Disco Lady" were none other than the super funky players in Funkadelic. See Dave Marsh, ed., *For the Record: George Clinton and P-Funk: An Oral History* (New York: Avon, 1998), 93.

130. Baker, "Hybridity, the Rap Race, and Pedagogy," 198.

131. Dave Marsh makes a different, but related, argument in "Freddie's Dead and Diana Ross Is Singing the Blues." Marsh argues that disco's privileging of the beat over the performer "played into the hands of white racists (both those who hated the stuff, and used it to bait, and those who liked it, and used it to avoid a more direct confrontation)": *Fortunate Son*, 268.

132. There were female rappers from the beginning, as Tricia Rose has pointed out. However, the men were the first to record and were rap's first stars.

133. Touré, "In the End, Black Men Must Lead," *New York Times*, August 22, 1999, section 2: 1.

134. Also important was rapper Afrika Bambaataa who formed the Zulu Nation to encourage inner-city kids to compete with each other as rappers and dancers, in an effort to stop gang violence.

135. Vince Aletti, "Inside the Flavor Factory," *Village Voice Rock & Roll Quarterly*, Winter 1992: 18.

136. Run-D.M.C. not only had a penchant for including the word "rock" in lots of their songs' titles, they even featured a searing rock guitar on one cut from their first album.

137. On "It's Like That" Run raps of feeling so disillusioned, "I just go through life with my glasses blurred." "Wake Up" depicts a utopian world of love and brotherhood that's just a dream people need to rouse themselves from, a point underscored by the sound of someone snoring in the background.

138. The album was mistaken by most listeners for a frat party album rather than a send-up of one.

139. Nancy Hass, "A TV Generation Is Seeing Beyond the Color Line," *New York Times*, February 22, 1998: 38.

140. Jon Pareles, "Still Tough, Still Authentic. Still Relevant?" *New York Times*, November 14, 1999, arts section: 14. NWA's 1989 release, *Straight Outta Compton*, turned gangsta rap into a "full-fledged genre and growth industry." MTV's aggressive hyping of Snoop's 1993 release, *Doggystyle*, helped rap edge out rock 'n' roll in the hearts and minds of teenaged white boys.

141. Hass, "A TV Generation Is Seeing Beyond the Color Line," 38.

142. Neill Strauss, "A Land With Rhythm and Beats for All," *The New York Times*, August 22, 1999, arts section: 28. Tricia Rose argues, however, that it's possible that the percentage of white rap consumers is not as great as generally thought because the prevalence of bootleg street tapes and CDs in poor communities make it difficult to gauge sales to urban black and Latino buyers. See Rose, *Black Noise: Rap Music and Black Culture in Contemporary America* (Hanover, N.H.: Wesleyan University Press, 1994), 7.

143. Strauss, ibid., 28. As Strauss and others point out, for children of white boomers listening to rap also has been a way to rebel against their parents. Rap's popularity with young people has opened up a generation gap among both blacks and whites. Many older black Americans now tune into oldies R&B radio. Alienated from rap and heavy metal, some graying white boomers have found themselves turning the dial to oldies stations, too, or to country radio. In fact, one country music insider, Charlie Monk, claims that "the best thing that ever happened to country was rap." See Peter Applebome, "Country Graybeards Get the Boot," *New York Times*, August 21, 1994, section 2: 28. Of course, others have continued listening to classic rock or metal. Among some hardcore rockers, like Metallica's James Hetfield, there's a racist edge

to this shunning of rap. Asked his opinion of hip-hop music, he said, "Rap is just to me very annoying. . . . Just the fact that it's extra-black, too—blacks, y'know, we want everything, we deserve it, give it to us." "Rockbeat," *Village Voice*, June 2, 1992.

144. Anthony DeCurtis, "Their Way," *Rolling Stone*, May 19, 1994: 97.

145. Performance artist Danny Hoch has given us delicious send-ups of this world, most recently in the film *Whiteboys*. Norman Mailer found Hoch's whiteboys so uncannily like his '50s hipsters that he assumed the actor had read his 1957 essay. Yet Hoch's research took him no further than his own multiethnic Queens neighborhood.

146. Baby Gerry of Full Force Crew, which puts together much of the music in the world of teeny-bop pop. Kenner, "That Ol' Black Magic," 188.

147. N. R. Kleinfield, "Guarding the Borders of the Hip-Hop Nation," *New York Times*, July 6, 2000.

148. Danny Hoch, "Straining to Live Black," *New York Times*, October 10, 1999, section 2: 18.

149. Calvin Sims, "Gangster Rappers: The Lives, The Lyrics," *New York Times*, November 28, 1993, section 4: 3.

150. Quoted in ibid. Stanley Crouch is far more critical. "They are a bunch of opportunists who are appealing to an appetite that America has for vulgarity, violence and anarchy inside Afro America," he says.

151. For example, Chuck D. of Public Enemy grew up in a middle-class home in Long Island. See Rick Marin, "The Ice Man Cometh," *Spin*, May 1994: 62.

152. Richard Wright, review of Zora Neale Hurston's *Their Eyes Were Watching God*, *New Masses*, October 5, 1937.

153. Hughes quoted in Smith, *Dancing in the Street*, 172.

154. Robert Christgau, *Any Old Way You Choose It: Rock and Other Pop Music, 1967–1973* (Baltimore: Penguin, 1973), 31. At first, critic Richard Goldstein felt much the same way as Christgau about Hendrix. According to Charles Murray, some older black Americans considered Hendrix "a stoned clown acting like a nigger for the amusement of white folks." See Murray, *Crosstown Traffic*, 82.

155. Ibid., 84.

156. James Baldwin, "A Fly in the Buttermilk," in *Nobody Knows My Name* (New York: Dell, 1961), 172.

157. By the early nineties, rap had developed several different strands. Hammer and Sir-Mix-A-Lot made infectious pop rap and Levert put out R&B-flavored hip-hop. There was the edgy black nationalist rap of Public Enemy and KRS-One. De La Soul, the Jungle Brothers, Arrested Development, Digable Planet, and PM-Dawn were frequently lumped together as "alternative rap." Different though the "alt-rappers" were, they did share a desire to move beyond the macho posturing of much rap. And once Roxanne Shanté demanded equal time, women rappers, most notably Salt-n-Pepa, MC Lyte, Queen Latifah, and TLC, challenged the hip-hop patriarchy. See Rose, *Black Noise*, 154.

158. Recent CDs by TLC and Janet Jackson come to mind.

159. Here Rose is criticizing Nelson George, who has argued that rap's commercialization will bring about its "cultural emasculation." George has warned that rap's commercialization could cause its "cultural emasculation." As Tricia Rose points out, "For George, corporate meddling not only dilutes cultural forms, but also it reduces strapping, testosterone-packed men into women!" See Rose, *Black Noise*, 152.

160. Kevin Powell, "Enemy Territory," *Vibe* 2, 7 (September 1994): 64.

161. Neill Strauss makes a similar argument in "A Land With Rhythm and Beats for All."

Chapter 12. White Faces, Black Masks

1. Eric Lott, *Love and Theft: Blackface Minstrelsy and the American Working Class* (New York: Oxford University Press, 1993).

2. Greil Marcus, *Mystery Train: Images of America in Rock 'n' Roll Music* (New York: Dutton, rev. ed., 1982), 181, 198.

3. Nelson George, *The Death of Rhythm and Blues* (New York: Plume, 1988), 63.

4. Marcus, *Mystery Train*, 198.

5. George Lipsitz, *Time Passages* (Minneapolis: University of Minnesota Press, 1990), 120–30.

6. Johnny Otis, *Upside Your Head! Rhythm and Blues on Central Avenue* (Hanover, N.H.: Wesleyan University Press, 1993).

INDEX

Abortion. *See* Reproductive rights
Acid (LSD, lysergic acid diethylamide),
    19, 20, 23, 27, 34, 43
ACT (American Conservatory Theater),
    29
African Americans. *See* Blacks/African
    Americans
Afrika Bambaataa, 281*n*134
Aletti, Vince, 183
Allison, Dorothy, 59
Alpert, Jane, 111
Altamont rock festival, 44, 46
Amburn, Ellis, 146
Andrew, Sam, 38
The Animals, 25
Anna Halprin Dance Company, 28
Anticommunism, 50, 54, 55
Antipornography movement: attempts
    to silence critics, 113–14; Catharine
    MacKinnon's views, 97–102; as
    conflict within women's movement,
    100; cultural feminists as activists
    in, 123; demonization of maleness
    and heterosexuality, 123; dichoto-
    mizing male versus female sexuality,
    4–5; fantasy as dangerous, 119;
    insistence on incorrigibility of male
    sexuality, 126; as juggernaut, 95;
    mobilizing feminists, 116; pornog-
    raphy as responsible for male

domination, 101; pornography
    as symptom of patriarchal
    conditioning, 152; pornography
    victimizing men, 259–60*n*49; rift
    between academics and activists,
    4–6; women as sexually alienated,
    victims, and moral guardians, 126–
    27; women's sexual inhibition as
    confirmation of superiority, 110
Antiwar movement: demonstration
    at Oakland induction center, 36;
    ignored in some accounts of
    women's liberation movement,
    237–38*n*4
Aronowitz, Stanley, 90–91
Atkinson, Ti-Grace, 83, 99, 114–15,
    118, 248*n*28, 258*n*36
Atlanta Project, 86
Atlantic Records, 273*n*43
Avalon Ballroom, 27, 37

"Badness" versus good-girlism, 7, 8,
    103, 105, 107, 108, 183
Baker, Houston, 67, 183
Baker, Russell, 55
Ballard, Florence, 171
Bangs, Lester, 163
Baraka, Amiri (formerly LeRoi Jones),
    87
Barbiturates, 42

Du Bois, Ellen, 63
Du Bois Club, The, 28
Duggan, Lisa, 133
Durbin, Karen, 117
Dworkin, Andrea: bashing of, 6;
    critical of biological determinism
    of gender, 112; on male sexuality,
    120; on New Left men, 69; as
    proverbial wild-eyed radical, 97,
    98; on sex oppression of women,
    119
"The Dworkinization of Catharine
    MacKinnon," 91–102
Dylan, Bob, 24–27, 73, 198, 212, 218–19

Egan, Jennifer,, 223n2
Ehrenreich, Barbara, 91, 100
Ellison, Ralph, 171
Elshtain, Jean, 106
English, Deirdre, 118
Epstein, Barbara, 66
Equal Rights Amendment (ERA), 54, 88
ERAP (Economic Research and Action
    Projects) (SDS), 68
Ertegun, Ahmet, 169, 273n43
Essentialism, 265–66n31
Etheridge, Melissa, 147
Evans, Sara, 68, 69, 77, 78
Everly Brothers, 25

Faderman, Lillian, 132, 143
Family: feminism as reaction to
    subjugation in, 104; as final outpost
    of compassion and nurturance, 106;
    radical feminism's attacks on,
    105–6; as source of women's
    oppression, 119; versus individ-
    ualism, 124; women's subordination
    in as "tapeworm of exploitation," 83
Family Dog, 35, 229–30n95
Feminism: boundary between good and

bad, 3; desire for connectedness
and intimacy versus desire for
freedom and autonomy, 221;
feeding feelings of sexual shame, 5;
in fifties, 56; granting too much
power to gender, 220; heterosexual,
as suspect, 116; as humorless and
uptight, 6; lesbianism and, 114;
link with sexual freedom, 95;
marriage augmenting men,
diminishing women, 57; notoriety
in, 6; as postfeminism, 99; racism
and "snow blindness" of, 108; rifts
in, 54–56; sexual repression versus
sexual liberation, 99; threatened by
antipornography movement, 95; as
unstylish, humorless, and prudish,
96; women as closer to nature, 110.
See also Cultural feminism; Radical
feminism
Feminist Economic Network (FEN),
257n3
Ferlinghetti, Lawrence, 26
Fifties, The: beginnings of civil rights
movement and antimaterialism, 52;
connection to sixties, 52; kids
rejecting segregated suburbs, 194
Fillmore Auditorium, 27
Fillmore district, 37, 42
Firestone, Shulamith: on child-care
centers, 88; *The Dialectic of Sex* and,
96, 103–8; on Marxist interpretation of women's oppression, 82;
on need for sexual revolution, 113,
117; on NOW's political stance, 83;
on value of women's movement, 90
First Amendment and antipornography
legislation, 101–2
Flack, Roberta, 172
Flacks, Richard, 91
Flower children, 30. *See also* Hippies

Folk music, 19, 23–24
Fonda, Peter, 213
Food co-ops, 48
Foucault, Michel, 90, 134, 140, 150
Franklin, Aretha, 172, 275n62
Freed, Alan, 58
Freedom Schools, 86
Freeman, Jo, 103
Freeman, Joshua, 234n4
Free Speech Movement (UC-Berkeley 1964), 27, 49, 155
Freud, Sigmund, 104, 108
Friedan, Betty, 83, 93, 106
Friedman, Myra, 149
Frith, Simon, 48
Frum, David, 52
Funk music, 205, 270n2

Gamble, Kenneth, 173, 275–76n66
Gangsta rap, 190
Garber, Marjorie, 146, 154
Garcia, Jerry, 23, 27, 31, 33
Gates, Henry Louis, 59, 191
Gaye, Marvin, 171, 176
Gay liberation movement: discos and bath houses as adhesive, 181–82; and "gay is good," 148–49; gay rights movement, 138, 139; as transformative, 150. *See also* Historiography of gays and lesbians; Homosexuality
Gay New York, 135, 136
Gearhart, Sally, 111, 112, 122
Gender: Beat versus hippie attitudes, 34–35; biological determinism of differences, 111–12; constructedness and "performativity," 153; and women's liberation movement, 84; music as refuge from conventions of, 219–21; and New Left, 66–69; refusal of difference by radical

feminism, 106–7; shifts in radical feminist thinking on, 109–10; supplanted by sexuality as domination/subordination for radical feminists, 99; women's liberation movement achieving fundamental realignment of roles, 94
"Gender Disobedience, Academia, and Popular Culture," 96
Gender Outlaw, 154
George, Nelson, 186, 187, 193–94, 205
Getz, Dave, 29, 148
Gilder, George, 111
Gill, John, 146
Ginsberg, Allen, 26, 36, 148, 150
Gitlin, Todd, 47, 53, 64–65, 67, 68, 233n160
Gleason, Ralph, 26, 29, 36, 168
Goldhaft, Judy, 48
Goldstein, Richard, 182
Goodman, Benny, 200
Gopnik, Adam, 157
Gordy, Berry, 169, 170–71, 275n66
Gottlieb, Carl, 30, 35, 50
Graham, Bill, 36, 39, 229–30n95
Grandmaster Flash and the Furious Five, 188
Grateful Dead, 18, 27, 32, 33, 39, 45
Gravenites, Linda, 42
Green, Al, 172–73
Greenwich Village, 57
Grogan, Emmett, 34, 43, 49, 223n2
Guerin, John, 216
Guralnick, Peter, 169
Guthrie, Arlo, 45

Haight-Ashbury: contrasted to North Beach and Beats, 148; drugs destabilizing, 42–43; as epicenter of hippie counterculture, 17; flooded

Hurston, Zora Neal, 191
Huxley, Aldous, 23
Hynde, Chrissie, 221
"Hype," 40

Ice Palace, 182
Identity politics, 12–13, 72, 91–94,
    252*n*74
"The Ike Age: Rethinking the 1950s,"
    12, 51–60
Integration, 59–60
Isserman, Maurice, 53, 54, 67

Jackson, Jack, 43
Jackson, Michael, 187, 280–81*n*127
Jagger, Mick, 146
Jefferson Airplane, 41
Johnston, Jill, 146
Jones, Hettie, 56, 57
Jones, LeRoi (Amiri Baraka), 57, 87
Joplin, Janis: closing rock's "girl gap,"
    11; moving away from Haight-
    Ashbury, 45; as original bad girl, 8;
    as part of Beat scene of North
    Beach, 148; as screwed-up hippie
    chick, poster child of sixties
    dysfunctionality, 8–9; seeing
    herself as cultural provocateur,
    41–42; subject of " 'Thousands of
    Men and Few Hundred Women',"
    96, 145–50; sexuality, 145–50; as
    symbol of seismic changes of
    sixties, 53, 145–50; as victim of drug
    overdose, 49; wanting "something
    now rather than a little of hardly
    anything over seventy years," 23

Kantner, Paul, 39
Katz, Jonathan Ned, 129
Kelley, Alton, 29, 36, 229–30*n*95
Kennedy, Elizabeth, 133, 136–38

Kerouac, Jack, 32–33, 227*n*68
Kerr, Clark, 19
Kesey, Ken, 17, 26, 27, 29, 43, 45, 49
Kessler-Harris, Alice, 78
Klein, Larry, 216
Koedt, Anne, 90, 115
Kopkind, Andrew, 80, 180–81, 182, 183
Kravitz, Lenny, 158
Kreps, Bonnie, 110

Labor. *See* Working class, labor,
    unionism
"Labor metaphysic," 70, 81, 91
Langer, Elinor, 70
Lauretis, Teresa de, 142
League for Industrial Democracy (LID),
    54, 251*n*64
Leary, Timothy, 27, 34, 46
Lennon, John, 213, 274*n*46
Lesbianism: attempts to redefine
    asexually, 131–32; butch-femme
    roles, 129–30, 132, 136–38, 139, 153;
    cultural stereotype, 2–3; disapproval
    of male homosexuality, 129;
    feminism and, 114; hairstyles, 3,
    137; as matter of political principle,
    129, 131; need to dissociate from
    male homosexuality, 122–23; in
    passionate romantic friendships of
    Victorian period, 130–31; power as
    sexy rather than oppressive, 132;
    separatism from men, 115; working-
    class, 133. *See also* Historiography of
    gays and lesbians; Homosexuality
Lesch, Phil, 24
Levan, Larry, 183
Levay, Simon, 154
Liberalism: black radicals rejecting,
    80; as both compromised and
    compromising, 81; corporate versus
    humanist, 80; grassroots rebellion

failure of current historiography to engender, 62–63; as gendered generational revolt, 72, 77; identifying with those on margins (such as black men), 67; and "labor metaphysic," 70, 81, 91; as problematized male masculinity, 240n21; roots in groups of Howe, Schachtman, and Muste, 53; SDS as leading group, 18; as willfully blind to sexism, 69, 70. *See also* Movement, The

Newport jazz festival (1965), 200

Newton, Esther, 133, 138, 139, 152

Newton, Huey, 49

Nichols, Pat "Sunshine," 30

1950s. *See* Fifties, The

1960s. *See* Sixties, The

Nomadism, 33

North Beach, 9, 19, 148

"Nothing Distant About It," 7, 15, 75–94

NOW (National Organization for Women), 82–83, 93, 121–22

Oakland induction center, antiwar demonstration, 36

Oglesby, Carl, 80

Old Left, 53–54, 81

Olivia Records, 87–88

Open Theater, 29

The Organization Man, 66–67

Ortner, Sherry, 105

Otis, Johnny, 194–95

Owens, Frank, 184

Pacifism, 55

Paglia, Camille, 6, 99

Paradise Garage, 183

Pareles, Jon, 162

Parks, Rosa, 53

Participatory democracy, 72, 85

Parties. *See* Dances/parties/party circuit

Pastorius, Jaco, 215

Patriarchy, 84

Penelope, Julia, 119

Penn, Donna, 143

Perry, Charles, 42–43, 223n2

Person, Ethel, 120

Philadelphia International Records (PIR), 173

Pine Street Group, 35

PIR (Philadelphia International Records), 173

"'Play That Funky Music': An Interview with Lenny Kravitz," 201–6

Politics: confused with culture, 157; as policing of attitudes through suppression of speech, 102; reformulated by Sixties radicals, 94; sixties radicals' profound impact on, 89–92

Pop music, 170

Postfeminism, 99

Postmodernism, 153, 155

Poststructuralism, 4, 153, 155

Potter, Paul, 81

Powell, Kevin, 191

Power, conceptualizations of, 90

Powers of Desire, 5, 6

Pranksters, 27, 32, 33, 49

Presley, Elvis, 73, 193–94, 244n53

Prince, 160, 280n124, 280n127

Promoters of music events, 37

Psychedelics, 23, 42

Public Enemy, 189, 192

Punk rock, 279n118

"Queer Like Us?," 96, 129–44

Queer theory and studies, 140–44, 265–66n31, 266n39, 267n50